What People Are Saying About Mary Jo Copeland...

"Mary Jo Copeland has devoted her life to caring for the homeless in Minnesota and has been a strong voice for those who too often are not heard...Mary Jo is a shining example of the strong tradition of service in our state, and I was proud to be at the President's ceremony today, [February 15, 2013] recognizing her tireless work."

— Amy Klobuchar, U.S. Senator from Minnesota

"I think of Mary Jo Copeland, whose ministry called Sharing and Caring Hands serves 1,000 meals a day in Minneapolis, Minnesota...Government cannot do this work. It can feed the body, but it cannot reach the soul. Yet government can take the side of these groups, helping the helper, encouraging the inspired."

— Then-Texas Governor George W. Bush

Acceptance speech for Presidential nomination

Republican National Convention 2000

"[Mary Jo Copeland] doesn't give her clients just a pat on the back or even a gentle caress on the cheek. She gets down on her knees and washes their feet."

— *People Magazine*

"Having known suffering and sorrow, Minneapolis's Mary Jo Copeland ministers selflessly to anyone in need or hurting."

— *Reader's Digest*

GREAT LOVE

The Mary Jo Copeland Story

Revised Edition

Michelle Peterson Hinck

Quixote Publications

Quixote Publications

490 Merrimak Drive

Berea, Ohio 44017-2241

ISBN 978-0-578-12170-3

Library of Congress Catalog Number 2002036775

Cover design: Susan Lee

Front cover photo: Cindy Kelsey

Back cover photos: The White House Photo Office

Author family photo

One hundred percent of the proceeds from the sale of this book will benefit Sharing and Caring Hands.

Acknowledgments

Thank you to Mary Jo Copeland, for living a life so worth writing about. Thank you for your friendship, love, and your incredible faith in me with this story. Thank you to Dick Copeland for your continued encouragement and working so hard on this with me. I have learned so much about life and love from the two of you — thank you.

Thank you to all of those who granted me interviews, research assistance, support, and other needed information: Mary Jo and Dick Copeland, Richard Davenport, June Blanski, Brian Philbrick, Janey, Bev Van Lith, Lou Gacek, Barb Copeland, Father Don Meisel, Steve Copeland, Jim Ramstad, Mike Copeland, Jeff Copeland, Joyce Krueger, Pinky, Emily Bastain, Al Davis, Al Gerszewski, Charlotte Feather, Robbie Wills, Little John, Tony Bouza, Mark Schindeldecker, Lorraine and Darla DeGidio, Barbara Carlson, Antonio, Brian Weeber, Pat White, Father Bernie Reiser, Darliss Wise, Roger Orr, Jack LaVigne, Jean Arends, Don Monroe, Archbishop Flynn, Kevin and Melisa Demers, Diamond, Amy and Shannen Brown. Also thanks to the Minnesota Historical Society and the Minneapolis and St. Paul public libraries. A million thanks to all of the volunteers, staff, donors, and clients at Sharing and Caring Hands for your encouragement, support, and enthusiasm for this project. Thank you to all the folks living in the former Copeland residences for allowing me to poke around your homes.

Thank you to Susan E. Peterson for your steady encouragement, wisdom, and careful eye. Thank you for contributing your editorial talents, time, connections, financial support, and love to this project. It would not have gone past chapter one without you.

Thank you to Patricia Mote, editor and consultant at Quixote Publications, and her editorial assistants, Chrissy Kadleck and Tammy Sanderell, and to Susan Lee, graphic designer, for the revised cover design. Quixote Publications ' editorial insight, artistic talent, and commitment brought the revised edition of this book to fruition.

Thank you to my incredible family and friends for your continued encouragement and support. Thank you to all the wonderful and inspiring ladies of the WOW group. Thank you to Paul Irmiter for donating your time and talents for publicity photography and videography. Thank you to Carolyn Will for your publicity and marketing assistance.

M.P.H.

Foreword

You are about to read the story of "Minnesota's Mother Teresa" —
Mary Jo Copeland. A story of heartache and hope. A story that
will bring tears and joy. A story that will inspire you to count
your blessings and reach out to people in need.

Above all, *Great Love* is a story about the power of love
personified by Mary Jo Copeland. Great love for God, her family
and friends. Great love for the people she serves every day —
people suffering the ravages of poverty, homelessness, addiction,
mental illness, and abuse. Great love for all the children with no
other place to go.

I will never forget that day in 1985 when I first saw Mary Jo
Copeland washing the bloody, blistered feet of a homeless, sick,
and broken man. Since that day, this totally selfless, caring, and
loving woman has been my friend and inspiration.

Working frequently with Mary Jo, as a volunteer at Sharing
and Caring Hands has been a true blessing as I've seen countless
lives transformed by her big portions of God's love. One thousand
hungry and homeless people fed, clothed, healed, and loved every
day by Mary Jo and her legions of dedicated volunteers.

We've prayed together, laughed together, and cried together.
And Mary Jo is the glue that brings us together.

All this without one penny of government assistance!

During his visit to Sharing and Caring Hands, President
George W. Bush was moved to say, "We need to replicate what
Mary Jo Copeland has done throughout the nation and around the
world."

Just as Mary Jo Copeland has touched the lives of hundreds of
thousands, so will all who read her amazing story be deeply
touched by the miracles of her great love.

Jim Ramstad
Former U.S. Congressman, Minnesota, 3rd District

Preface

It is very hard for me to share the painful parts of my life with the world. It was only my deep love of Jesus Christ and the Blessed Mother that carried me through those hard times, and I have shared my story in the hope that it will help others to overcome adversity in their own lives and enable them to rise above their problems to make a difference in the lives of others. The only way any of us can face life's difficulties is through the power, the peace, and the strength in prayer.

For nearly thirty years, I have had the honor of helping thousands of people each month with food, clothing, shelter and emergency needs. Sharing and Caring Hands has been blessed with the help of donors, beneficiaries and volunteers who have enabled this ministry to grow and help meet the ever-increasing needs of the poor, starting with a small storefront operation that now encompasses a multi-building, downtown Minneapolis campus. May God bless all of those who make Sharing and Caring Hands their outreach to fight poverty.

For just such a time as this, we are all put on this earth to listen to the voice of God and to do His holy will. My prayer is that as you are reading this book, you will hear the voice that I have heard — calling you to make a difference in the lives of others, one person at a time. To the world you may be one person, but to that person you may be the world. We must all pray, love, serve and forgive.

May God's grace guide you and bless you on your journey.

—Mary Jo Copeland

Brian

Homelessness, by textbook definition, is a temporary condition caused by financial hardship. But out on the streets, the explanation is often not that simple. More often than not, homelessness is endured by people who are victims of emotional tragedies that are embedded in their day-to-day lives, their self-esteem, the way they see others. The root of the problem is not homelessness; it is lovelessness. Too many people go through their lives without ever hearing "I love you," without ever receiving a hug or even acknowledgement from anyone.

Brian Philbrick was one of those people. He was belligerent, angry, dirty, drunk, and alone. It seemed impossible to help him. But Mary Jo Copeland knew that he needed much more than a free meal and used clothing. He ached for someone to understand who he was and what he'd been through. His life was just one of thousands that Mary Jo touched, but the change he went through with her, and she with him, was perhaps the most dramatic of all.

Brian was cursed with blond hair. If only he had been born with darker hair, like his siblings, maybe his father wouldn't have beat him every day. Maybe then he wouldn't have been a runaway at fourteen.

He had been gone about nine months before the cops caught him on the beach in Fort Lauderdale, Florida. A savvy cop recognized his Boston accent and after detaining him in a juvenile center for a couple of days, Brian showed up in the missing persons' records. He was on a plane home, or rather to the place where he grew up with his parents, three brothers, and a sister.

Brian's father was on his deathbed when he got there. He had been hit by a truck while Brian was gone. Brian stood beside his dying father in the hospital, searching for any shred of empathy for the man. He found none. The only images that swirled in his head were the beatings he and his mother endured. His security cop father came home every day, without taking the time to change out of his uniform, and beat Brian with his club. The boy had become so numb to the beatings that all he had left were images that triggered the fear and pain that never went away. For the rest of his life, Brian's reflex to seeing anyone in a police uniform was a wave of terror and pain.

Brian stood out from the other children in the Philbrick brood. Because his siblings all had dark hair, his father believed that his mother had been unfaithful since Brian was born blond. He thought Brian wasn't his, and he beat him for it every day. His older brother was taught to beat Brian too, and soon his father and brother were beating him together. Then they'd beat his mother. That was Brian's family— every single day.

By the mid-1980s, Brian had been traveling for eleven years on the rails from place to place with the other vagrants. Strapped down with his gear—his backpack, his bedroll—Brian wandered through towns looking for work, barely surviving. He learned to specialize in odd jobs, anything for a few dollars.

Cops greeted him at almost every train station, asking for his ID, wanting to know where he was from and where he was going. When they arrested him, the charge was trespassing on railroad property or stealing a ride—theft of transportation, they called it. "Vagrancy" was his favorite one. He liked making the cops try to explain to him how it could be illegal to be homeless.

Whenever he had enough money saved from working, it was time for him to hit the road again. His life was to be on the rails. He dedicated nearly half of his life to his travels, going coast to coast, hitting different states and collecting information about every little nook and cranny of the United States. Brian couldn't avoid collecting his fair share of heartache along the way either.

In Sacramento, Brian encountered a local news reporter who was writing a story about homeless people. The reporter was nosing around the train yard where Brian was hanging out. One day while Brian was curled up in the far, dark corner of an abandoned boxcar, he was jarred awake by the reporter and his young assistant. Lucky for the reporter that Brian wasn't sleeping with his gun loaded that day because he wasn't happy about waking up with bright lights and a camera in his face. He told the guy to get lost. When the reporter started explaining about the story he was doing about the homeless, Brian said, "You got the wrong guy, I ain't homeless. Leave me alone."

Brian wasn't so polite the second time they came around. "I told ya before, you're in the wrong spot. Turn that damn camera off me and get the hell outta here!" When they woke him up the third time, Brian had had it. The reporter just kept pushing him and pushing him, and Brian couldn't take it. He got up from his corner and started coming towards them, but they still kept filming. "I warned ya ta knock it off before. Ya don't just come up on a guy like that, ya idiot." They still kept filming. "I've had enough. That camera's mine now . . ." Brian grabbed the camera and smashed it.

The reporter started screaming, "That's a $3,000 camera!"

Before long the cops arrived. The reporter went on whining about the camera, saying that he was afraid for his life. Brian admitted to breaking the camera and told them the reporter deserved it. The reporter didn't like that. The cops didn't like it either, but Brian had long since grown out of the habit of taking whatever beating he got. So when the cops came toward him, Brian started swinging. All at once, it seemed as if the entire Sacramento police force was on him.

The next thing he knew he was being dragged into the jailhouse with blood coming out of everywhere. His nose was broken and bleeding, he was coughing blood from being clubbed so hard. Blood was coming out of his ears. Instead of a hospital, the cops took him to jail, put him in a cell, and let him bleed.

Brian was left in that cell for a week before he was brought to the courthouse. He remembers hearing the formalities read: "Next up is the case of the state of California vs. Brian Philbrick . . . " He thought that was impressive. He thought he must be some kind of celebrity or something now with the whole state of California against him.

Just then a man in the back of the courtroom stood up and interrupted the proceedings. A local lawyer named John McDonald was in the station the day they brought Brian in, and he had seen the shape he was in. He told the judge that he watched the officers drag Brian through the station by the back of his head, dripping blood everywhere. He testified that Brian was so beat up that he couldn't even hold his head up, and that while they were booking him, one of the officers continued to slap Brian's head around, saying, "Come on, boy, we gotta take your mug shot one way or the other." John McDonald told them everything.

Brian was released with all charges dropped. The arresting officers were reprimanded but not suspended. John McDonald took Brian to the doctor, got him some medication for the pain, and then offered him a job working as a groundskeeper at his house. John had a little brick cottage in back of his house with its own little kitchen and bedroom and bathroom where Brian could live as long as he kept the lawn mowed.

This was a good place for him to heal, and Brian stayed with John for more than a year, working on the yard and working on the garden. When the time came to leave, it was hard for Brian to say goodbye.

John had done so much for him, but he had to keep moving. His life was on the road. The trains were calling him.

Brian got a refillable prescription for Percodan from the doctor he saw in Sacramento. This way he could go to drugstores all over the country and have it refilled. Already addicted by the time he left John's cottage, things only got worse after he left. He grew more lonely and depressed as each day passed. The only bright point happened while he was traveling through Oregon and found a puppy with ears twice as big as his body. Brian thought he would be just the friend he needed, so he named him Rusty and took him on the road.

With his gun (which he always carried now), his dog, and the Percodan impairing his judgment, Brian decided to head to Boston and pay his big brother a visit. He tracked him down in a little town just outside of Boston, and it wasn't a very warm reunion. His brother tried to threaten him, just as he did when Brian was a kid, but the nine-year difference in their ages didn't matter anymore. Brian was just as big as his brother now, and angry as hell. Even with a snarling dog just a few feet away and the barrel of a shotgun inches from his face, Brian's brother kept saying he was gonna beat him.

"You ain't doin' nothin'. You ain't beatin' me today. You ain't puttin' your hands on me ever again."

He didn't pull the trigger. He wanted to, he really wanted to, but he backed off and left his brother there, trembling.

Brian and Rusty traveled around together for the next few years. Wherever they went, Rusty never left his side. One night in Idaho, a cop came up to where they were sleeping. Rusty shot up on all fours and started barking and growling—he hated cops as much as Brian did. Brian yelled out for the cop not to come any closer, but he kept coming. Brian yelled again for him to keep his distance, but he still kept coming. Rusty's growling grew quieter and more vicious, daring that cop to take one more step. He was luring him in.

By the time Brian grabbed for Rusty's collar, it was too late. In one calculated move, Rusty took a leap and landed with his jaws lodged around the cop's kneecap. The cop screamed and kicked Rusty in the ribs with his other foot, which only made the dog force his teeth further into his flesh. The cop screamed again and fired his gun. Rusty fell to the ground.

Brian stared at Rusty lying there, still on his leash. He was horrified. "I told you to back off," he said to the cop. "Why didn't you listen to me? You killed him!" He was crying. The cop just stood there, bleeding. "Why didn't you listen, you stupid moron! You killed my friend!" The cop arrested him.

After Rusty died, Brian wasn't working much anymore. He was drinking heavily and eating his Percodan like candy. He couldn't even keep track of where he was half the time. He never talked to anyone. He didn't make any friends. He floated around from place to place, angry as anything when he wasn't drunk and numb. He lived like that for years.

He woke up one day and realized he was back in northern Minnesota. Brian first heard about Mary Jo Copeland from some of the guys around town. He heard about all the things she was doing for people. One guy told him that she even brought him to the hospital one day because of an infection. But Brian didn't believe them. He was soured on everyone, including himself. "No one would do somethin' like that for guys like us. It ain't happenin', so just shut up about it." All he wanted to do was drink.

The more he heard about Mary Jo, the madder he got. He had been to just about every food shelf in the country, and he'd never once seen the kind of compassion they were talking about. They said she stood up for them against the county. They said she acted like their mom or something, which Brian knew was a load of crap. The best you could get in any place like that was a meal and maybe some dry goods if you were lucky. Everyone knew that.

Finally, so fed up with hearing about this do-gooder, he went to see for himself. He watched the entrance of Sharing and Caring Hands, Mary Jo's storefront operation, from across Glenwood Avenue for a long time before he went in. He found a chair in the back where he could sit and watch without any of the other jerks bugging him. He watched all of the people who came in and went out. He knew some of them, but he didn't talk to anyone. He just wanted to watch. A few days went by, and he had seen Mary Jo in there every day that week, all day long. She had seen him in there too; she kept saying hello and waving at him. He sat there thinking, *Well, would ya look at this. Look at this lady down here. All these people down here. This woman's down here hangin' out, talkin' with these old scummy bums all day. She's over there smilin' and wavin' at me like an idiot. What's the matter with her?*

A couple of weeks went by, and Mary Jo ventured back to talk to Brian. "Hi, I'm Mary Jo," she beamed. "What's your name?"

Well, he wasn't going to have anything to do with telling this woman his name. Forget that. The cops didn't even get his name, and he certainly wasn't going to give it to her. He didn't say anything to her. He turned his back and looked in the other direction until she walked away and left him alone. He sat there silently. *She wants to know my name. Whatever. I got enough problems, lady. I'm tryin' to get off these damn pills. I don't need some nutbar comin' round askin' what's my name. Who does she think she is?* He glanced up across the room, and Mary Jo smiled at him again. That made him so mad!

After a while, Brian began going back to Sharing and Caring Hands regularly. He was sitting by himself in the back one day, thinking about his life. He thought about his father and brother and how much he still hated them. He thought about those cops who nearly beat him to death. He thought about Rusty. Without realizing it, he began crying. Suddenly, Mary Jo was right next to him. He wanted to yell at her to leave him alone, but he just couldn't do it. He had been on his own for too long, in pain for too long, poor and hungry and unloved for far too long. He was cold and sick, and his feet were hurting so bad that he could barely walk. He didn't have the energy to hold up his wall anymore. He needed help. He needed someone to love him.

1

"Little John? Little John, come right away. It's time to do the feet," Mary Jo calls out over the intercom. She rushes down the hall and enters a waiting room filled with people, old and young, whose worn-down appearance reflects a lifetime of sadness. They all glance up as she enters, their eyes filling with hope. Most of them have never met Mary Jo Copeland before, but despite her warm smile, her five-foot-six-inch frame, and her loose curls pinned whimsically to the side by two barrettes, her imperious demeanor tells them that she's the one in charge here. She's the one they need to talk to.

There is a brief pause, just long enough for Mary Jo to take all of this in, and then the clamor starts: "Mary Jo, my car got towed yesterday, and I can't get it out until I pay insurance and tabs. I don't have the money for it, and I can't get to work." . . . "Mary Jo, this family has an apartment set up for next month, but they need a deposit." . . . "Mary Jo, the volunteers in the conference room want to meet with you." . . . "Mary Jo, the county will take the family of five, but they need a hotel for two nights" . . . "The toilet in 310 has backed up again."

Her cell phone rings. "Mary Jo speaking . . ."

It's a Monday.

Little John, a Romanian immigrant with a smile as wide as an open door, waits patiently nearby, carrying a laundry basket full of latex gloves, cuticle trimmers, antiseptic ointments, and paper towels—Mary Jo's tool kit for one of her most renowned acts of kindness: washing the feet of the poor. She makes her way through the waiting area, handling one emergency after the next, finally settling at the end of the hallway where a row of folks are relaxing with their feet soaking in tubs of warm soapy water. She tends to each of them individually, washing out the sores on their feet, asking their names and if there is anything she can do for them. Some of them are too tired and don't want to talk today. A man named Frank is so overwhelmed by his hardships and so stunned by the way Mary Jo reaches out to him that he cries. She hugs him and cries right along with him. "You've been having a hard time, I know," she says to him. "You're not alone, though. God is here, and I am here, and I'll help you." She puts her hand up to his cheek, wipes his tears. A smile comes to his face, and he nods.

She moves on to the next set of feet—a young single mother with four children in tow. She received her Section 8 papers approving her for housing assistance today, but her landlord has evicted her. She and her children have nowhere to go. The rent was paid the previous month, the woman explains, "but we're living with mice and roaches, crawling on my children at night, and the sink was broken and we always had to use the neighbor's washroom. I didn't pay the rent this month because of the conditions, and he gave me a UD." Mary Jo knows this situation well. An "unlawful detainer," otherwise known as an eviction notice, is the kiss of death for anyone trying to rent an apartment in this tight housing market.

"Emily!" Mary Jo calls over her shoulder before moving on to the next person. Emily Bastian, a volunteer in her seventh year with Sharing and Caring Hands and a college senior majoring in theology and social work, steps in to take the woman's information and admit her and her family into Mary's Place, Mary Jo's 500-bed temporary housing shelter. This is one family that is no longer homeless.

Mary Jo handles the next set of feet with extra tenderness. The man's left foot and ankle are nearly twice the size of his right. "What did the doctor say about this swelling?" she asks him. The man answers her indifferently. He couldn't get to a doctor. "That's just not right for a man not to know what's going on with his own feet," she says. "We've gotta get you in to see a nurse downstairs." Her cell phone rings—it's someone at Mary's Place. As she listens to the emergency on the phone, she finishes tending the swollen foot, beckons a volunteer to fetch a nurse, and hands the man some cash from her pocket. A woman a few seats down catches her eye. She's been waiting to talk to Mary Jo all afternoon and is worried that she won't have time to get to her. Mary Jo already knows what she needs. "Honey, I'm gonna help you," she calls over to the woman, interrupting the person on the other end of her phone, "and I've got something for your children here too. Come see me as soon as I'm done doing the meal, all right?"

She finishes her call, answers another, outfits all the clean feet with new socks and shoes, and passes out hugs, dollars, and coloring books to the children. After the waiting area has finally cleared out, one more man approaches. He doesn't have enough to pay his room rent. She considers him for a moment and then says, "You've been making some progress here, Al, but you still have a way to go. I'll pay half your rent for you." He nods and accepts her hug. "God bless you, Mary Jo," he tells her, "that really helps me." In the eyes of her beholders, she has performed about thirty miracles during the past half hour—a miracle every minute—and she still isn't done.

"Everyone line up for dinner, please," her voice booms over the intercom to the three to four hundred people in the dining room. "No line-butting, no pushing, no fighting. There's enough for everyone. Be quiet, be still, behave, or be gone. It's time to eat."

She greets the fifteen volunteer servers in the kitchen and thanks each of them for their devotion and hard work. For some of them, it's their first time serving a meal to the poor, and Mary Jo eases their apprehension about the people there. "God has provided this opportunity for us to fill our own need to share our hearts, and to understand that we are all connected to each other. Every one of us."

She enters the dining room and passes the same message to the assembly of poor:

"Okay, everyone, quiet down. First of all, I would like to give thanks to our volunteers today for coming in to serve all of you and for giving so generously of their love and their time. They care as God cares, and I care. I know that the pain you all have on these streets is not easy to bear, but you are not alone. God loves you, and I love you. Never forget that. I also want to remind you that we always need to do what is right and to love what is good. Remember that every day we live, every day we set out, there is a new gift for us. Yesterday is gone, and we don't know tomorrow. The only way we can get through today is by praying for it."

There is a shuffle among the crowd that signals a shift in focus. A woman moves her child from one hip to the other. A man removes a heavy pack from his shoulders, dropping it to the floor beside him. Everyone is listening to Mary Jo's words, but from the beaten down looks on their faces, many of them must wonder how all of this is supposed to apply to them. They appear to be consumed by their circumstances and poverty and more concerned about that than loving thy neighbor. Yes, it would be wonderful if everyone could just love each other and get along, but what about the wet cardboard they had to sleep on, the angry gang members next door, and the crying infant whose mother appears to be living on vodka alone? Mary Jo answers with her own experience:

"There is a lot of anger, a lot of hurt, a lot of addiction, a lot of abuse that's going on inside of everyone in this room and everyone we touch. And the only reason we are staying inside it is that we haven't done anything about it. We've got a lot of people hurting. I know that. I'm one of them. We all need to let it go and try to start doing some positive things. We can let it go through prayer. Prayer is what gives us the grace to go on with our lives, to forgive the people who have hurt you. I see so many times here, people carrying around nothing but what other people have done to them. I see over and over again, mothers coming to see me that have husbands that beat them senseless. I don't care what your situation is, there's *never* an excuse for a man to hit a woman, and there's never an excuse for a woman to take it. We all have the responsibility to take care of ourselves and take care of each other. We are all the same, every one of us."

Janey, a full-time volunteer standing nearby, has a tear welling in her eye. She has heard this speech a hundred times, but it rings truer for her every day. A few years back, she was one of the people standing in line for a meal. She had three children, no home, and had lived in a string of abusive relationships since high school. Just as nearly every person in the room, she never thought she would wind up there. She had been adopted into a loving home with plenty of money and had everything growing up, but after what she'd been through since then, she understood clearly that tragic circumstances can and *do* happen to anyone. She learned that, and the unconditional love it takes to get past it, from Mary Jo.

"My story is no different from anyone's in this room," Mary Jo goes on. "I grew up watching my dad beat up my mom every day, every time he had the chance to punch her. When you see that and you've lived with that, it's hard to get over the fear that comes with it. You can spend the rest of your life with that fear. No one has to come home to that, and no one has to live with it. We have to start being kind to one another. We have to build our generosities. We have to leave this world better than we found it. Every one of us has that responsibility. Every one of you can take your life in your hands and start over. Every one of you has the power to make some tough choices. God will help you make those choices. The very least you can do right now is something kind for someone else—a smile, a hug, or carry someone's bag if it's heavy. It will have a ripple effect on everyone you come in contact with, and it will leave the day better than when you woke up. We have to stop living our lives as one big complaint. There is a lot we all have to be grateful for. All of you have these volunteers who come to serve you, you have food to eat, air to breathe, and love to share. It is well within your power right now to have a smile on your face and warmth in your heart. Enjoy this meal, and enjoy each other."

Mary Jo finishes up with a prayer and then an energetic round of the sing-a-long, "If you're happy and you know it, clap your hands!" While she might not have the power to solve every problem, in these moments, she has succeeded in getting this group of tired, worn-out people to clap, sing, and smile graciously as they receive a hot, nutritious meal. They still have problems, but in that moment, they are loved. Mary Jo greets each person who comes through the line, hugs the children who approach her, hands out more bus tokens, and answers her ringing cell phone.

After spending only an hour with Mary Jo Copeland, you'll probably shake your head and wonder, How does she do this? Approaching sixty years old, she has more energy than any five people put together; you're exhausted from just watching her. When you consider the stamina it takes not only to tend individually to these hundreds of poor people all day, but also to head up the independently funded multimillion-dollar organization that houses, feeds, clothes, and protects them, it's clear that Mary Jo's got a secret.

Evidence of the generosity, independence, and devotional spirit that she displays today are found in her childhood, but she wasn't just born this way. Her strength comes from her incredible faith, but her ability to put that faith into action comes from the very circumstances that challenged it. Her secret, her central truth, is the greatest love of all. Her belief in the love of God and the Blessed Mother is the one thing that propelled her through her own days of despair, and all of her days of hope. This is what will see her through all adversities she has yet to face. Her story shows that there is nothing in this world we cannot overcome, nothing we cannot share, nothing we cannot have. Her life is one profound demonstration of how to love unconditionally, as God intended.

2

From her earliest memories, there were only two places that could bring peace to Mary Jo's life—church and the garden. When she was young, her grandmother brought her to church because it was "proper." Mary Jo loved going because it was the only place that made sense to her. She developed a bond there with God, and especially with the Blessed Mother, that would be the one constant source of nurture in her life. She spent most of the rest of her early childhood among the daffodils, lilies, and daises in her grandparents' backyard. The garden was magical for her. Mary Jo had no other children to play with and was allowed almost no social contact outside of her family. Since her hours in the garden were the only experience available to her, she formed a lifelong bond with nature.

Soon after she was born, Mary Jo and her mother moved in with her grandparents—her father's parents—in a spacious house in south Minneapolis. Her father, Woodrow A. Holtby, whom everyone called "Woody," was away fighting in World War II. His parents, Fred and Nellie Holtby, were well-to-do people with a strong desire to maintain a prosperous appearance. They weren't the richest of the rich, but they had very distinct attitudes about how people in their position ought to behave, and they carried themselves as such.

Mary Jo's mother, Gertrude Oelke, was a farmer's daughter from Blue Earth, Minnesota. Little is actually known about Gertrude's family or about what her relationship with Woody was like in the early days of their courtship. The subject was never talked about. There are no wedding pictures or other personal mementos, and it seems they had little in common. They are said to have met while working together in a hair salon. Woody and "Gert," as she was known, married in October 1941, at a time when many young people were hurrying to the altar before the men had to go off to war. Gert became pregnant with Mary Jo about a month before Woody reported for duty in the army, early in March 1942.

Although Woody had been exposed to varied cultural and economic privileges, he also had grown up as the only boy in a houseful of women. His father was a busy vice president of T. E. Ibberson, a Minnesota grain company, so Woody spent nearly all of his time with his sister, his mother, and her sisters. He went where they went, he did what they did, and he paid attention to whatever they told him. He was nicknamed Little Lord Fauntleroy as a young boy. He showed no interest in things such as politics, business, or higher education. Despite all of his advantages and the opportunities available to him, Woody chose to go to barber college after high school graduation.

Woody and Gert worked together in the salon at Thomas's department store in Minneapolis until Woody had to leave for the war. Gert continued working for a while but finished out her pregnancy back at home with her parents in Blue Earth. On October 23, 1942, just two days before Woody's and her one-year anniversary, Gert gave birth to a baby girl, Mary Joan Holtby.

Fred and Nellie regarded Gert as a small-town nobody, and they were less than confident in her ability to raise the baby properly. With Woody away at war, they were not going to let Gert take care of their grandchild on her own. They convinced Gert that it would be better to raise Mary Jo in the city and that she and the baby would be better off financially if they lived with them.

From the day they moved in, everyone but Gert was in charge of Mary Jo's upbringing. It became understood immediately that Gert was only residing in that house as a matter of obligation. Since she was the mother, they had to let her in, but she was ostracized at every opportunity. Perhaps the Holtbys did not deliberately set out to drive her away, but they certainly did not make it comfortable for her to be there. Gert was defenseless against all of them. They had blackballed her from the start, deeming her a second-class, unworthy farm girl who wouldn't amount to anything, which they reportedly told her on a regular basis. Before long, she discovered that the less time she spent at the Holtbys' house, the better it was for everybody. She went back to work as a hairdresser and filled the rest of her time at the bingo parlor with her friends. From those early years of her life, Mary Jo has almost no recollection of her mother.

It never seemed strange to Mary Jo that she didn't know her parents in those early years—she hadn't known anything different. She didn't know any other children or other families. She didn't experience any other mothers or fathers. She didn't know there was a war going on, which was why her father was absent. She didn't know that a bond between her and her mother was missing either. How could she? Mary Jo's entire world was secluded within the gates surrounding a beautiful garden and Fred and Nellie Holtby's grand home on Pillsbury Avenue. She grew up surrounded by the endless chatter of Nellie and her sisters, Mary Jo's great-aunts—Marie, Adelaide, and Babe. She wore dainty dresses that were tended and laundered by the housemaids, while she was taught in the tearoom to sip gently, not slurp. Her grandmother doted on her, read to her, sang to her, and bathed her in a magnificent tub with golden-clawed feet. Subjects unpleasant were simply not discussed in those days, not in Fred and Nellie's house. Everything there was lovely, all the time. Mary Jo did catch their usual derogatory gossip about her mother, but she did not form any real concept of her parents until much later.

The downside of her grandmother's pampering was that Mary Jo was almost completely isolated from other children. In part, Nellie just wanted to keep Mary Jo to herself, but there were no other children within Nellie's circle for Mary Jo to play with. Mary Jo spent day after day playing in the garden, kept company only by nature. She has one faint memory of a day spent playing with a neighbor girl, whose name she pronounced "Nay-nay." Mary Jo remembers spending the next several days after that with her tiny fingers hooked around the white picket fence that stretched behind the backyard, her little face peeking between two slats, watching the stillness and waiting for Nay-nay to return.

But Nellie didn't want her mixing with "those neighbor children." Mary Jo created her own little world for herself. Nature provided her amusements; the garden flowers became her best friends. She spent her days singing and talking to them while they swayed and danced in the breeze.

On many days at lunchtime, Mary Jo's grandmother would come out to collect her from the yard, followed by her sisters, the gossiping aunts. They were hardly ever separated, and they always kept young Mary Jo in tow.

On lovely and pleasant days, Nellie, the aunts, and Mary Jo would all dress up and go downtown to shop and lunch. As Mary Jo quickly understood, this was the life of a lady. She marveled at how, no matter which restaurant they went to, no matter what store they browsed, no matter whose neighbors they saw along the way, these ladies had enough talk in them to fill up every second of the day, without actually saying anything at all. This fascinated her for quite some time. Not only were they able to maintain a constantly flowing conversation about absolutely nothing, but also they had the ability to recount accurately the very same nothing in every restaurant, every store, and to every neighbor they met. Mary Jo thought they were amazing—Grandma Nellie, most of all.

Among their favorite restaurants were the Nankin, Harvey's, the

Hasty Tasty, and Murray's. Mary Jo's favorite was Ivy's, where they served olive nut sandwiches. Aside from the regular lunch gossip, the ladies would spend a considerable amount of time praising Mary Jo's remarkable talent for dance. At age four, Mary Jo was introduced to her first activity with other children: dance lessons at the McPhail Dance Studio. In the eyes of her family, she was going to be the next little Shirley Temple.

Mary Jo was always excited when the day for her dance recitals finally came. For her, being out on stage felt wonderful and natural. It was her first break from being told what to say, how to walk, how to sit, how to dress. When she was out on stage, no one told her any-thing—she just danced.

She remembers at one recital, while waiting on the side of the stage to go on, she was trying to be patient. She just wanted that other group of girls to finish up and get off the stage so it would be her turn. Finally, the music stopped, everyone applauded, and the group exited.

Mary Jo tapped around the stage that day like never before; her performance was remarkable. As the music ended, she made a curt-sey, then pranced gracefully off stage. She was so pleased with herself that she didn't even realize until later that she had danced with the wrong group.

That was the last time that Mary Jo would enjoy a carefree child-hood. Soon after the recital, word arrived that Woody had been wounded and was being honorably discharged from the war.

When Woody first arrived home, Mary Jo's life did not change very much. His presence in the house didn't seem to have anything to do with her. It was as if she was merely an observer to the changes in the household dynamics. Fred and Nellie and her aunts seemed pleased to have him home at first, but Mary Jo never understood why. As far as she could tell, he was just a big grouch. He was yelling all the time at what seemed like nothing at all. All he did all day was order everyone around. The only time he could manage to sit quietly was when Grandpa Fred was home.

Nellie told her it was best just to stay out of his way while he got used to being back home. So they did, except for Gert. Nellie also said it was time for Gert to start acting like a proper wife. She had to quit going to work at that beauty shop and quit going to that bingo parlor too, she said. She was needed at home.

If there had ever been any love between Gertrude and Woody Holtby, no one would know it now. Before Woody came home, Gert may not have been completely happy, but she was at least independent. If her husband's family wasn't going to accept her, she decided that she didn't have to put up with them either. She had spent her time doing her own thing, but now that was taken away from her too. The combination of Woody's erratic behavior and Gert's resentment of her situation eventually transformed that house into a tense volcano.

3

The tension at the Holtby residence continued to worsen, but Nellie at least did her best to keep Mary Jo out of the crossfire between her parents. Mary Jo was sent to kindergarten at Incarnation Catholic Church, where she had a very hard time adjusting. Outside of her dance lessons, she hadn't spent much time with anyone but her grandparents and aunts before; she didn't know how to interact with other children. She felt as isolated among the children at school as she did at home. It took a long time for her to feel comfortable being in school or to generate friendships.

Keeping Mary Jo out of the way at school during the day was beneficial, but no one was able to establish any kind of peace in that house in the evenings. Woody and Gert did manage to stop arguing long enough for Gert to get pregnant again. At this point, Mary Jo's grandfather declared that it was time for his son to get a job and raise his family elsewhere. He helped them financially to get a house, but beyond that, they were on their own.

Mary Jo was six years old when they moved. She never knew what went wrong or when. It was as if she went to sleep one night and accidentally woke up in someone else's life. She no longer had her cozy bedroom and magical garden to play in. She had to get herself up in the morning now, instead of being roused with a smile and hug from her grandmother. She would tiptoe through the house quietly, carefully sidestepping each creak in the floor, trying not to make any noise to set off her father. In the kitchen, her mother would be working frantically each morning over a frying pan while her father read the paper, waiting for his breakfast. Every morning it was the same thing. Gert would put his plate in front of him, he'd stare at it, maybe poke the eggs around with a fork a little, and then yell, "This is terrible! You can't even cook an egg! Do it over!"

Mary Jo knew he was going to be angry whether the eggs were cooked the way he wanted them or not. It had been the same thing at Grandma's, and a new house wasn't going to change that. But everyone continued to ignore his manic behavior. Mary Jo couldn't have grasped an understanding of his problem at her age. All she knew was that he was a mean man, whose anger was unpredictable and frequently, without reason, he would focus on her. His gaze would shift from the paper over to her, standing in the doorway: "What are you looking at? Why aren't you in school? Get out of here!"

As weeks went by, she tried to adjust, but she couldn't understand what was happening. She hardly knew these people. She was sure that there must have been some mistake; she didn't belong there. But every time she tried to go home to her grandmother's house after school, she was brought back. There was a vague explanation about "being together as a family now," or some such thing. A nice, neat family. That's what everyone wanted. She was too young to realize at the time, but what was really going on became clear much later. All of them, Mary Jo included, were being brushed aside by the Holtby family. Their precious son had returned from the war, damaged and too much for them to handle. Rather than taking that on, they tucked him and his pregnant wife and their daughter all into a little house in the corner of the city, away from all their pretty things, away from all their pleasant days, away from their good social standing.

———————————————————————

Several months after they moved, Gert delivered a baby boy. With a new baby in the house, once again the dynamics shifted. Since Nellie and the aunts had taken over Mary Jo's care in the beginning, Gert never had a chance to form any kind of bond with her. But now that the Holtby clan had become disenchanted with their family, Gert had this new baby all to herself. She named him John, after her father.

Mary Jo now was not only dislocated but also ignored. Gert spent every moment with the baby. Woody had very little to do with him, and Gert had very little to do with Mary Jo. That never changed. Mary Jo remembers her brother being there, but they never were with each other. They never played together. She was never offered a relationship with him. She was seven years old and, essentially, on her own.

Mary Jo started growing more and more fond of her time in school and in church. She attended Annunciation Grade School in Minneapolis, where she started learning about the life of Jesus. Compared to the dysfunction going on at home, being in school all day, listening to the nuns talk about this wonderful place called heaven, to her, that *was* heaven. She grew even closer to the Spirit of God and the Blessed Mother. The absence of love from her parents had left a hole that could only be filled by the Holy Spirit. She didn't find any other children who loved religion as much as she did though. They all thought she was weird. She still had a hard time making friends. Being so sheltered in her early years was really working against her now. She spent her school time listening quietly and observing her teachers and her classmates as well. She watched those children for years. She learned more about human behavior in grade school than a lot of people know as adults.

She continued to visit her grandparents' house after school whenever possible, but she had given up all hope of having them rescue her from her parents. They just didn't see things the same way she did. They knew about all the fighting that surrounded her, but they felt it wasn't their place to interfere. They wanted to believe it was all Gert's fault anyway; they would never talk against their Woody. When Mary Jo complained that Gert was spending all the time closed in her room with the baby and that she didn't have any clean clothes to wear to school anymore, they just treated it as fuel for their gossip pool. "Yes, that Gertrude has a lot of problems. She can't even do the laundry." Beyond that, they didn't want to talk about her or hear about her, especially not after Mary Jo started telling them about Gert's black eyes and bruises. That sort of thing just wasn't discussed. All Mary Jo wanted was for someone to hug her, someone to pay attention to her. She didn't have that anymore.

Woody got a job as a traveling jewelry salesman and was gone a lot of the time. Mary Jo was finally able to relax a little while he was gone, but things kept getting much worse when he wasn't. When he was home, fighting went on, and night after night it escalated to violence. He eventually wore Gert down, and she stopped fighting back. His abuse grew stronger than her will, and it stole any dignity she had. She began giving in to him constantly, trying to appease him. Mary Jo spent those nights alone in her room, curled up as tightly as possible, too scared even to get up to go to the bathroom. With every night that passed, she became more frightened and more isolated.

Since her grandparents weren't going to do anything about her situation, Mary Jo did what she could to make herself scarce around the house. Being alone so much of the time left room for her innovative spirit to flourish. Her fascination with nature was stronger than ever, and she started spending much of her time in her new backyard. She spent hours watching the bees hover, dip, and zoom off as they pollinated the flowers. She was curious about what kinds of lives they led when they left her yard—if they had mothers and fathers that were good to them, if they had friends they could go around with, if they knew that God was looking after them, and the Blessed Mother was there to nurture them. She wished there were some way she could get them to stay with her.

She remembers one day she saw a fat, black and yellow fuzzy bee hovering over the hollyhocks. It was the largest, most remarkable bee she'd ever seen. It didn't buzz like all the others, it just kind of floated from bloom to bloom. Mary Jo was sure that this must be the queen bee. She decided to follow it.

There was an empty lot next door that was covered with clovers and weedy dandelions. When Mary Jo followed the "queen," she discovered that this had to have been their jackpot. The bees didn't care as much about the dandelions, but there were hundreds of them swarming around the clovers. Mary Jo thought if she could only get some of those clovers in her own yard, the bees would probably never want to leave. She found an old jar, filled it up with clovers from the lot and then set it out near her garden.

Sure enough, the bees flew right in. She filled jar after jar with clovers and got jar after jar full of bees. She was even more thrilled when she saw that they started building hives there. She'd given them a home. Mary Jo had just put up her first shelter—and she never once got stung.

Her entrepreneurial roots sprouted early as well. Finding a new way to keep herself scarce from her parents, Mary Jo discovered a peaceful hideaway up in the attic. She found a stash of old costume jewelry and broken gems that her father had brought home. As she picked through the bags, she separated the broken stones from the good ones and glued and fastened them together to make bracelets, necklaces, and hair clips. Once she had a good selection, she decided she might as well try to make some money. She gathered all the jewelry and started going door-to-door selling them. Her neighbors answered their doors to this wide-eyed, curly-headed little sprite, offering her handmade creations for five cents apiece. Who could resist that? She sold every piece she made.

Over the next ten years, along with beekeeping and jewelry making,

Mary Jo joined the Girl Scouts, learned to ice skate, read Nancy Drew mysteries, and started a wonderful paper doll collection. She sold stamps, she sold candy, she sold magazines, she sold just about everything that was within her reach. In 1955 she sold more Girl Scout cookies than anyone in her troop. She did anything she could to avoid her parents. She didn't ask them for things or ask to do things because no matter what it was, she would be told "no." Whatever she asked her mother for, she would be told, "No, that isn't healthy." That was one of the first indications that her mother was losing control. Gert was being hit all the time now; the abuse had become just another part of their lives. There was always screaming and carrying on in the middle of the night. Woody would be beating Gert until two or three in the morning and then demand something to eat. And Gert would stand there, bleeding, cooking his eggs. "You can't cook anything! You're trying to poison me with that cooking. I'm going to Mother's!" Whenever Gert was around Woody, she couldn't function. She couldn't pay attention. One day at school, Mary Jo found that her mother had packed garbage in her lunch bag and not her lunch.

With her usual bruises and cuts, Gert stopped minding her appearance, rarely bothering with a shower or even a hairbrush. Mary Jo's hygiene went neglected as well with no clean clothes to wear and having to bathe in a tub that was never cleaned. Mary Jo had gone from living in her grandmother's consistently spotless, perfectly ordered home to this place where, even when Gert did make attempts to get things under control, the place was never clean underneath. She would start cleaning whenever Woody began to yell at her. Without paying attention to what she was doing, she would pick up a dirty rag and frantically wipe the counter. When the sink was full of dirty dishes, Gert would wipe them out, but all she was doing was moving the filth around. These conditions, along with the fact that Woody was likely to blow up at any moment, for any reason, were what kept Mary Jo from ever inviting anyone to her home. She knew that her situation was terribly wrong, and she did everything she could to stay away from there as much as possible.

When Mary Jo was at home, she'd go to her room as quickly as possible and stay there. There was inevitably a confrontation about one thing or another. According to her parents, nothing she did was right. She was yelled at for being late, whether she was or not. She was yelled at for not cleaning her room, when hers was the only clean room in the house. If they told her to stay home all day and sit in the corner, she'd get yelled at for doing that too. The abuse Mary Jo took was mostly verbal, but she was slapped a few times. Woody kicked her in the mouth once, although she can't remember why. She'd lie in her bed, crying and praying all night long.

Only when Woody went out of town was the house quiet. When he was home, Mary Jo would spend the whole time praying for him to leave. No one knows how he ever functioned on the road or how he ever sold anything to anyone. For that matter, Mary Jo doesn't know how she was able to get to school every day either, but school and the chapel were the only places where she found peace. She knew that her parents were wrong for the way they treated her and each other. She never accepted her situation as normal; she just prayed that she would be able to endure it. She made it through the nights with her bedroom door closed tightly, as well as her eyes and ears. The louder they yelled, the harder she'd pray . . . *You can't get anything right. You're stupid!* Hail Mary, full of grace . . . *You're worthless!* The Lord is with thee . . . *Stop upsetting your father! Get in your room!* Blessed art thou amongst women, and blessed is the fruit of thy womb Jesus . . . *You stupid, stupid girl! You'll never amount to anything!* Holy Mary, Mother of God . . . *Stop that crying! Nobody cares! You're nothing! Do you hear me? Nothing!* Pray for us sinners, now . . . and at the hour of our death. Amen.

Mary Jo reached a turning point in the spring of 1958. She was fifteen years old, and by then, the only constant she'd had in her life was prayer. It was the only thing that calmed her. It was the one thing in her life that felt right. She knew that her path was toward serving God; there was never a question for her about that. Right then it was only a matter of time. She had to finish high school before she could fulfill her dream of becoming a nun.

But everyone has a limit on the amount of pressure they can take, and she'd reached hers. Mary Jo was sick of tiptoeing around her parents. She was sick of that house, sick of the insanity, and sick of her isolation. Nothing there changed, no matter how hard she prayed for it, and one day the realization hit her that nothing was *ever* going to change. She was never going to make sense of her life this way. She'd been spending this whole time trying to be perfect, trying to do everything perfectly, yet there was no such thing. Perfect wasn't real. It wasn't even desirable.

One Friday, DeLaSalle High School invited her sophomore class at Holy Angels Academy to a dance, and Mary Jo decided that she was going to attend. No matter that her parents would never give permission for her to go. She was determined to go to this dance.

The night of the dance, Mary Jo came out of her bedroom and quietly closed the door behind her. She stepped down the hallway softly, but deliberately, the crinoline rustling under her skirt as she rushed toward the front door. With her hand already on the doorknob, she turned her head only slightly and said, "I'm going to a dance at school. I'll be home at eleven." She didn't wait for her father to start yelling and for her mother to forbid it. She walked out the door and then ran.

Mary Jo did not breathe easily until she had her seat on the bus and was on her way to the dance. No one had come after her. They weren't going to stop her. Although she was prepared for the inevitable war she would face with her parents, she would face that battlefield when she got home.

From the moment she stepped into the DeLaSalle gym-turned-ballroom that night, Mary Jo was enthralled. She sat at the edge of the action, not knowing what to do first. She didn't even mind that she was all by herself. She found a chair and bounced along with the music, watching all the others sock-hopping. She scanned the room slowly, trying to take in every movement, every color, shape, and sound. Everyone was having a wild time. Mary Jo was having serenity.

Suddenly, her eyes shifted across the room to where two boys were sitting together at a table, laughing. One of them looked very nice. He was well dressed and looked as if he was really having a good time. But it was the other one who caught her eye. He was broad-shouldered. She liked that. He was wearing a black and white plaid shirt and khaki pants. What color socks? White socks. His socks were white. She didn't know why this was important, only that she wanted to know every little thing about him. He had such a solid, protective frame and such kind eyes. She felt she had no choice. She had to meet him. Mary Jo didn't have a girlfriend she could send over to find out about him. No one had told her that the boys were supposed to be the ones doing the approaching. Before she knew how she got there, she was standing right in front of them.

"Uh . . . hello. Excuse me . . . Hi, I'm Mary. Aren't you . . . uh . . . " It suddenly occurred to her that she had absolutely no idea what she was doing or what to say. She quickly made up a name.

"Aren't you Tom Kelly?"

"No, I'm sorry. You've got the wrong person," he replied.

"Oh." Mary Jo had thought of something really spectacular to say right after that, but she couldn't remember what that was. His eyes were so enchanting.

"Uh . . . okay. I'm sorry," and she turned away. She felt her heart fall into her stomach.

Confused, he watched her as she walked away. "Ow!" He rubbed his arm where his buddy had just socked him. "What's the big idea?"

"Go ask her to dance, you idiot!"

"Huh? Oh, yeah! Hey! Hey, Mary, wait up."

Mary Jo danced with Dick Copeland that night. They danced together the whole night. Dick couldn't believe who he'd just met. She was so different from the other girls. She didn't act coy with him, she wasn't aloof, thinking he'd like it if she acted like she didn't care whether she was talking to him or to a brick wall. She looked him in the eye when she spoke and when she smiled. It was so rare, this quality about her. She was just—herself. Her presence was so strong. He felt a connection with her immediately. He'd never met anyone like her, and he knew he probably never would again. He wasn't taking any chances. At the end of the evening, he didn't bother with what was proper. "May I please have your phone number? I need to see you again as soon as possible."

Mary Jo had a smile on her face as she said her prayers that night. She thanked God for sending this boy into her life. She knew that God would forgive her too. It took about a year for her to realize that she didn't want to be a nun anymore. She wanted to marry Dick Copeland.

4

As with every intriguing love story, the beginning of Mary Jo's and Dick's romance was filled with many surprising discoveries. They had lived practically around the corner from each other for much of their lives. Without ever knowing each other, they had attended the same church. They had played at the same park.

From the start of their relationship, Mary Jo wanted so much for Dick to be her future. She clung to every second they spent together, enjoying everything she learned about his life and his family, desperate to postpone his discovery of hers. She thought when he found out about her unhappy family, he wouldn't be interested in her anymore. Why should he have to contend with her problems? He certainly had never had to deal with miseries like hers. He had a normal life with a normal family.

For most Minnesotans during the 1950s, the pace of life was structured and steady. Fathers went to work, mothers stayed home, and children were independent, for the most part. On Saturdays, Dick and his three brothers would get up, have breakfast as a family, go out and play all morning and not come back until they were hungry. After lunch they would go back out and not come home until they were hungry again. Most of the time they didn't even play together; they all had their own friends, their own bikes, their own games. Most fathers didn't go to their children's baseball games and other activities. Many worked on weekends to keep their families up with the Joneses. Dick really only saw his father at breakfast, dinner, church, and on vacations. His family wasn't struggling by any means; Dick's father was a well-paid production manager at the *Minneapolis Star* newspaper, a position he excelled in. Early baby boomers like Dick learned that important men were working men. That was the standard that their fathers set.

Dick's mother's life was prescribed by the times too. Mom ran the house, and she was always there. The structure was there. The supervision was there. Whatever the children did behind a closed door, their mother knew it as soon as they had done it. Mom knew everything, and whatever Mom knew, Dad knew. The reinforcement of responsibility was consistent. When Dick was growing up, there was no question about things such as getting his homework done. Going to school with unfinished homework was as unthinkable as going to school without any clothes on.

Dick's childhood seemed to be the very definition of normal, until he was eight years old. Just after he entered the second grade, he started having blackouts. He didn't completely pass out; he just dropped out every now and then. He'd go blank for a moment, not responsive to any stimulus at all. He could be sitting and talking, and then, strangely, he'd just freeze. When he was walking, he'd stop suddenly, or find himself walking around in a circle for a moment. None of the doctors he saw had ever seen anything like it. When these seizures started happening regularly throughout the day, his parents took him to the Mayo Clinic in Rochester, Minnesota. The specialists there were equally baffled. They were looking for a tumor or blood clot on his brain, but they repeatedly came back with nothing. They had no explanation. Dick spent a lot of the second grade in a fog of drugs, making him numb to much of what went on around him and impairing his enjoyment of life.

About a year later, Dick's father was discussing the problem with a friend of his, Dr. Axelrod, who posed a very peculiar question.

"Is Dick a big boy? For his age, is he big?"

"Well, yes. All of my boys are."

"Why don't you bring him over to see me? I think I may know what's going on here."

At last—someone who might know something. Finally, there might be some answers. The Copelands took Dick to see Dr. Axelrod first thing the next morning.

Dr. Axelrod looked as if he could have stepped out of a mad-scientist movie. He lived in a historic house made of thick old stone that looked like a castle. The doctor led them through a mahogany paneled hallway into the library where all but one wall was lined with books from floor to ceiling. Dr. Axelrod looked Dick over for a bit. Then he walked over and climbed up a sliding library ladder. He picked out a book and read for a while. Dick and his father waited silently as the doctor flipped through the pages, letting out an occasional "Mmhmm," "interesting," "ah-ha," and "I see." Dick thought Dr. Axelrod must be the smartest man in the whole universe. Dick's father thought he must be a lunatic.

"Well?" he said finally, "what's wrong with my boy?"

"Basically, his body has grown faster than his spinal cord," said the doctor. He explained that this had caused several pinched nerves in Dick's back that were interfering with the impulses to his brain. He experienced the periods of shutting down because his nervous system was literally shorting out.

He turned and replaced the book on the shelf. "Unfortunately, there is not a treatment available yet," Dr. Axelrod went on. The condition had first been reported in Swedish medical journals just a few years before. The good news, he said, was that the problem would take care of itself. Dick would grow out of it on his own.

Dick's parents took him back to the Mayo Clinic, and the doctors there could not absolutely confirm or refute any of this new information. The only thing they agreed on was that it was as good a diagnosis as they had. They took him off the drugs, and Dick coped with periodic blackouts until he was in the sixth grade. Then the problem disappeared.

Dick's condition did not change many things at home. He was treated the same. He was still independent; he kept up his paper route and other activities. Socially though, the entire dynamic with his friends had changed. Before Dick's blackout problems started, he had been the class clown and something of a bully but very popular. He was sent to the principal's office a lot, but he became popular there too. But now everyone was so careful around him; they were afraid of setting off a seizure or worried about what to do if one happened. Dick was now the one they all thought was weird, and his popularity became replaced by watching *The Lone Ranger* at Bobby Thompson's house. His family had the first television set on the block. Without realizing it, Dick became more and more detached. He had never felt particularly connected with any of his family members, and now he had withdrawn from his friends too. Even after his condition went away and he had control of his faculties, his independence and emotional isolation had already set in. He stayed that way for the most part, until the night that lovely young girl mistook him for Tom Kelly. Dick never felt bad about poor old Tom missing the dance that night.

Mary Jo did the best she could to concentrate on all the fun they had together, instead of dreading the price she would pay for it when she got home. The minutes she spent waiting for him to pick her up for their dates felt just like the hours she spent wondering if her mother would ever come home when she'd been gone to the bingo parlor all night. Mary Jo was always prepared for him not to show up but relieved and delighted every time she saw his car pull up. He couldn't believe how happy she always was to see him. He loved it. They had both been starving for the connection they found, and now they couldn't be together enough. Dick spent every moment he could with Mary Jo. He took her to the Lafayette Club for his graduation dance, they went roller skating, to movies, and took drives up to Taylor's Falls to picnic. Less isolated than he had been in his earlier years during his nervous system problems, Dick shared his high school friends with Mary Jo, hanging out at dance parties in their basements and playing records.

Although Mary Jo had grown more socially adjusted than when she was younger, she still had not felt a real closeness with friends. She was known at school for her deeply spiritual demeanor and no-nonsense views; she was the one everyone went to for advice. No one knew about all the trouble she had to dodge at home. As described in her high school yearbook, the only side of Mary Jo that people knew was that she was "a whirlwind." She got through her childhood and teenage years by staying on the go. She spent her time praying instead of feeling sorry for herself and her situation. Through prayer, she learned to focus on other things. The conditions at home did not change, but her ways of coping with them did.

Despite seeing her consistently projecting this positive side of her personality, Dick was realizing that there was something very un-settled about Mary Jo—but that only drew him closer.

Although her parents did not like Mary Jo spending time with Dick, she had Dick pick her up right from school nearly every day. That way her parents wouldn't have the opportunity to stop her from going out. When he dropped her off, she would never let him walk her up to the door. She didn't want him anywhere near all the filth and chaos inside. She'd smile and wave until he pulled away before she went in. She didn't want him to hear her father's yelling.

Before long, Dick learned what was really going on with Mary Jo at home. They had only known each other about a month when she finally told him about her parents. He didn't turn away as she feared he would; he held on to her. He said he wished there were some way he could take her away, take her out of there. It just wasn't right, her being treated that way. It wasn't right. It made him angry. You don't slap the face of an angel. You just don't. Didn't her parents know that?

No, they didn't know. Woody and Gert were too far gone down their own dismal path. Woody was demented, and Gert was afraid of him, and that's the way they lived.

As a teenager, Dick knew there wasn't a lot he could do about her situation. He wanted to give her everything she never had. He wasn't very close to his family either, but at least he had one. The first time Dick brought Mary Jo to his home, his mom was very nice and polite to her, as she was to everybody. She was proud of the house she ran and she showed it. When she attended church with her family, she marched them up to the front pew. Being seen as a prominent family at church was as important for her as going to church. She was very concerned about how they dressed and how they acted. She had a very strong sense of what her family's image should be, and for whatever reason, she decided from the start that Mary Jo did not fit that.

Any hopes that Dick had of sharing his family with Mary Jo went immediately out the window. They acted cordially toward her, but that was as far as they would ever go. It was very difficult at the time for Dick to understand why his parents opposed their relationship so much. In the beginning they had been aloof about the whole thing. They had never interfered in anything he did before, but now for some reason they really started causing problems. Their feeling was that Mary Jo had too many emotional needs and that Dick was too young to be spending so much time with one person. More than anything else though, the impression Dick's family had of Mary Jo was hurt by bad timing. It wouldn't have mattered who she was because there was a crisis that arose in his family, and they only saw her as an outsider who was in the way.

Dick's father suffered a brain aneurysm around that time, and he wasn't able to work with the same authority in his position. For a man whose self-image was grounded entirely in his work, this condition devastated him. When he left his job, the family still had money coming in from his investments and retirement plan, but he was lacking a purpose. He started drinking heavily. Until that time, his father had lived largely in his own world outside of the family. Now his entire world existed within the family. Everything was family. And Mary Jo was not family.

With both sets of parents against them, Mary Jo and Dick did what any teenagers might do: They rebelled. The more their parents tried to pull them away from each other, the closer they became. When both mothers got on the phone together and decided to start limiting their telephone privileges to ten minutes per call, Mary Jo and Dick stopped relying on the phone. Dick had his own car and a job, so there wasn't a lot his parents could do to stop him from doing what he wanted. Mary Jo was the one with all the pressures at home, but she had learned years before just to stay out of sight there. Now she had someone to stay out of sight with.

After more than a year, Dick's parents realized that this whole Mary Jo thing was more than just a phase. They decided something needed to be done. They knew she had a lot of problems, they knew that she didn't have a good background, and they wanted more than that for their son. Dick's father asked Mary Jo to meet him one day at Culbertson's Bar on Excelsior Boulevard to discuss this issue, just the two of them.

When she arrived, Mr. Copeland was already settled into a booth with a whiskey and a fat cigar. His demeanor was hard and unwelcoming as she sat down.

"I want you to leave my son alone," was the first thing he said.

She wanted to jump up and walk out, but her purpose that day was to try to make him see that she wasn't a bad person.

"I don't want to leave him. I love him," she said.

Dick's father explained to her that he understood that she had a lot of problems, and then he suggested that perhaps he could help her more than his son could. He offered to pay for her to go to a psychiatrist. That way, he explained, she could get the help she needed and stop clinging to Dick so desperately.

"I'm not going to any psychiatrist, and I'm not going to leave Dick. I told you, I love him."

"No, you don't," was his reply. "You're too young. And you're wrong for him. When I married his mother, I at least knew that she was a good, pure girl. She was a virgin."

A small part of Mary Jo wanted to laugh at this suggestion. Was he actually sitting across the table, accusing a devout Catholic girl of sinning with his son? That's not the part of her that reacted. The only thing Dick's father saw of Mary Jo after that was how much he had just hurt her. She began to cry. She managed the strength to get up from the table, and without a word, she left him with his whiskey.

Dick withdrew even further from his parents after that. When his parents realized that they were only pushing the two of them closer together and losing him in the process, they stopped trying to control the relationship. They never accepted Mary Jo, but from then on they tolerated her. For someone so in need of acceptance, Mary Jo was set back even further emotionally because of their treatment toward her. It was hard for Dick too—he wanted to give her the wonderful loving family that she had never had. As time went by though, it became more and more apparent that he didn't have a loving family either.

Mary Jo was being counseled by a priest named Father Leonard Dosh during this time. There have been many people who were important in Mary Jo's life, many of whom seemed to be attracted to the almost childlike spirit that she's retained. People were drawn to that, Father Leonard included. He became aware of her family situation and really felt compelled to help her. He knew she needed to get out of that house.

Father Leonard knew several foster families, and he knew the judge who assigned children into foster care. After all of the arrangements were set, Mary Jo and Father Leonard planned a day when both her parents would be away to pack her things and move her in with a family he knew, the Hamiltons. The Hamilton family had eight children and lived in a big house near the Lake of the Isles in south Minneapolis. Mary Jo was apprehensive about this upheaval, but she knew she had to go through with it. The day she went against her parents to move in with this strange new family, she knew it had to be done and she just did it. For someone who had been browbeaten for so long and had survived all the tempers, the prodding, the battering, the shaking, the yelling, she emerged with a strong sense of who she was and what was right for her. Even later in her life, she was never dissuaded by what was easy or what was popular.

Within hours of her arrival at the Hamiltons, Mary Jo called her father. He wanted her sent home immediately. As instructed by the judge, Mary Jo informed him that she was now a legal adult and had moved out of her own free will. Then her father said that her mother had been sent to the hospital with a heart attack, but he didn't say which hospital, only that Mary Jo had to come home immediately. There was no heart attack, of course. Mary Jo did not return home. She had contacted her parents to let them know she was all right, but now that she was eighteen, she was not obligated to have any further contact with them. It was done.

After the move, Father Leonard felt that he needed to continue to guide Mary Jo's life, including her relationship with Dick. Although he was glad that she had Dick for support, he thought that she was too young to be so connected to him. Father Leonard saw bigger things in store for her.

"You're in a transitional period right now," he said to her. Urging her patience, he told her that if she wanted to marry Dick someday, it should be a long way off. She needed room to grow and to move on, he said, because she'd been through so much.

Mary Jo was so grateful for everything Father Leonard had done for her, but she just didn't agree. She trusted her feelings for Dick, and especially at that time, she wasn't going to let someone else control her life. Not her parents, not Father Leonard, not anyone.

Her experience at the Hamiltons' wasn't the solution to all of her problems, but it was much better than home. Everyone was very nice to her, especially the eight children. But with Mary Jo coming out of such a dysfunctional family, she needed a lot of attention. It was safe for her there, but she never felt as though she belonged.

Mr. Hamilton made a special effort to be a father figure for her, but that was difficult too. Mary Jo was eighteen by then, and he was another who thought that she and Dick were spending too much time together. He was an artist with an adventurous spirit and was a proponent of encouraging young folks to go out and live their lives a bit before making a decision about who to live it with.

Despite all of the naysayers, Mary Jo and Dick continued their relationship. By that time, Dick was attending college at St. Thomas and working at the *Minneapolis Star*, and Mary Jo had taken a job as a nursing assistant at St. Mary's Hospital. Whenever they weren't working, they were together. Mary Jo's family was out of the loop now, but as the crisis in Dick's family worsened, they started giving more and more indications that they didn't want Mary Jo involved in family matters in any way. Dick's father declared, in his desperate depression, that it was time to "regroup the family." It was time to focus on what was important. During the holiday season, he wanted them all to be together. Dick insisted that they include Mary Jo.

On Christmas Day 1960, Dick invited Mary Jo for dinner with his family. Christmas dinner was usually at two in the afternoon, but since Mary Jo didn't get off from work until four, he asked if they would postpone it for a couple of hours. His mother refused. She said that dinner would be ready at two o'clock, and that's when they were eating. Dick had heard enough. His mind was made up.

"I want to share my Christmas dinner with Mary, and if you can't even wait for two hours, then I'll go somewhere else to eat with her," he told his mother.

He left the house and went for a drive until it was time to pick up Mary Jo from work. By the time he arrived at St. Mary's, there was a message for him at the nurses' station. The note said for him to come to Methodist Hospital right away.

Dick and Mary Jo arrived at the hospital to find his family gathered in grief and shock. Not long after Dick had left the house, his father went upstairs and shot himself. A doctor approached the group and explained that there was nothing they could do to save him. The damage was too severe. He was dead.

Dick's brothers were crying, but his mother just stood there, emotionless. She then walked over to Mary Jo and stared at her with steel eyes. "This was your fault," she said to her. Clouded with grief, Dick's mother had concluded that her husband had become too overwhelmed with his failure in bringing the family together, and Mary Jo was to blame for luring her son away.

Dick left the hospital with Mary Jo and headed back to his house. They saw a police car parked outside as they pulled into the driveway. Inside, Dick's mother was talking to the police, and his brothers were crying, still in shock. Nobody said a word to Dick. He went slowly upstairs. There was blood everywhere. His father's blood. All over the walls, covering the floor, everywhere.

Mary Jo tried to talk to Dick's younger brother. She began praying with him, trying to comfort him, but Dick's mother would have no part of that. She didn't want Mary Jo near any of them. She told Dick to take her home immediately.

Mary Jo grew more and more uncomfortable at the Hamiltons'. Mr. Hamilton began to put more pressure on her about spending less time with Dick. He was trying to consider Mary Jo the same as he would his own daughter, and he didn't think it was good for her. Yet, what they were doing wasn't any different from other young people at that time. They spent all their free time together, just like all steady teen couples did. The only difference was that their time together was magnified for Mary Jo, because it wasn't just Dick she was looking for, she needed a family. She was looking for people to embrace her and love her with that unconditional, all-inclusive quality that love should really be. This was especially true after the blame and emotional pummeling she took from Dick's family; it had ripped her apart. She felt so alone during that time, and finally Dick realized that he didn't want this woman to be alone. He loved her. Perhaps with someone else the courtship would have gone on a few more years, but with Mary Jo he just knew, so why wait? He was already independent. He'd been paying his own tuition and expenses since high school. He had always been alone, emotionally, until Mary Jo came along. He had needed that bond as much as she had. He loved her caring heart, he loved that she put so much of herself into what she did, and he couldn't think of anything better than being married to her.

Of course, Dick's family was against this idea. And Mary Jo's grandmother and aunts were against it. The Hamiltons were against it. Father Leonard was against it. It was clear, however, that Mary Jo and Dick were going to do exactly what they wanted to do. Mary Jo moved in with her friend Jill Hasselo that February and started planning an April wedding.

In 1961, every Catholic family expected its children to have a church wedding. So despite what everyone was really feeling, the two families gathered on Monday, April 3 at St. Patrick's Church in Edina, Minnesota, for a bizarre wedding. Dick's friends circled around the bride and groom. In another corner was a circle of Mary Jo's parents, her gossiping aunts, and other relatives. And all of Dick's relatives circled around Dick's mother. Nobody mixed with one another. Nobody interacted at all. It was like being at a child's tea party with stuffed animals and dolls with plastic smiles. Mary Jo and Dick didn't care about anyone else. They were married, and they were happy.

5

Mary Jo and Dick returned from their three-day honeymoon in southern Minnesota and moved into their first apartment in south Minneapolis, a very small one-bedroom in the 2700 block of Girard Avenue. Most of the tenants in the sixteen units were older couples who were thrilled with the energy that the newlyweds brought. The caretakers, the Calans, lived in the apartment across the hall.

When Mary Jo and Dick first moved in, they had no furniture, no dishes, no pots and pans. They planned to buy things a few at a time, as soon as they could afford to. The first week they were there, Mr. Calan told Dick that he and his wife were getting new furniture and offered to give Dick and Mary Jo their old furniture.

"How much do you want for it?" Dick asked him. Mr. Calan said that they would talk about it later and that he wanted to start moving some things out right away.

When Mr. Calan said he was getting all new furniture, he really meant it. They moved everything—the bed, the tables, the chairs, sofas—across the hall into Mary Jo and Dick's apartment. When they finished, Mr. Calan wasn't going to let Dick pay him anything, but Dick insisted.

Mr. Calan finally said, "Okay then, fifty bucks for everything." Dick gave him sixty-five. It was all they had.

At last, they were set up in their first apartment. They had a little Volkswagen, Mary Jo still had her job as a nursing assistant at St. Mary's, and Dick had his job on nights and weekends at the *Minneapolis Star* and his classes during the day at the University of St. Thomas. When school was out during the summer, he worked full-time for a corporate mail service and kept his part-time hours at the newspaper. Just when they thought nothing could make them happier, Mary Jo discovered she was pregnant.

Raising a family was the thing they had talked about the most, and they both wanted a big family. They were still very young, but neither of them considered that to be a problem. They felt lucky to have the chance to start their dream early in their lives. It would be a lot of work; they didn't have any support from either of their families. They were still in contact with Dick's family, but essentially Mary Jo and Dick were on their own.

Dick picked up another job delivering office supplies between his classes, and Mary Jo kept her job for as long as she could. About six months into her pregnancy, Mary Jo had developed toxemia and was too sick to continue working. In between the excitement, nausea, and exhaustion, she busied herself with organizing the house, getting the nursery ready, and taking care of Dick. On February 7, 1962, after two days of hard labor, Mary Jo delivered a healthy baby girl, Therese Copeland. Mary Jo and Dick fell in love with her immediately.

While Mary Jo and Dick reveled in the joyful experience of parenthood, stress loomed right around the corner for Dick. Rumors of a strike at the *Minneapolis Star* came to fruition just after Therese was born. Dick certainly could not afford to go on strike now, but as Mary Jo constantly reminded him, God does not close a door without opening another. She wasn't worried.

There was a new discount retail store about to open at that time, so new that it was still under construction when Dick applied for a job. He went to his interview at a construction trailer near Knollwood Mall in St. Louis Park for this new discount chain called Target, part of the Dayton Hudson Corporation. A job in retail was not something Dick had ever considered before, but he had a feeling that this company was going to do well. The first store in the chain had just opened in St. Paul, and it was already doing good business.

Dick started working full-time with the receiving manager at the Knollwood Target, organizing and coding the merchandise that came in. He realized that he could not keep up a full-time job and full-time school and a wife and a baby. There just wasn't time. His classes at St. Thomas had to go. He dropped his classes that spring, intending to start again in the fall semester. But when the time came for him to re-enroll, he had been offered a promotion at Target. He decided it was more important to work right then instead of going to school. The reason he had been going to college in the first place was so he could get a good job, and the way he saw it, he already had one. He accepted the promotion and the pay raise, which he definitely needed, especially with the newest development. Mary Jo was pregnant again.

Her second pregnancy went much more smoothly than the first. Although she was very tired, she was thankful not to have toxemia this time. The exhaustion didn't really get to her either; she was having too much fun being a mother. In March 1963, scarcely a year after Therese's first birthday, Mary Jo delivered another girl, Andrea Mary. There couldn't have been two little girls more different from each other. While Therese had been running all over the house at ten months, Andrea was a very quiet and contented baby.

By that summer the Copelands' little apartment had become a bit too cozy. Mary Jo had converted the small dining room into a nursery, but that wasn't going to be room enough for much longer. That August she became pregnant again. They loved the Girard apartment, but they had been there more than two years, and it was time to say goodbye to the Calans and their other neighbors and look for a bigger place.

Mary Jo never procrastinated. That October, while pregnant and with two babies, she packed up everything they owned and got ready to go. Soon after moving day, everything was put away and set up. Her well-oiled machine was running as if nothing had changed.

Their new home was a two-bedroom in an apartment complex near Mary Jo's old high school. The biggest advantage they saw with the place was that it had a pool, and they knew that it would be great for their children. The problem they discovered soon after they moved in was that the place was not very family-oriented. Unlike the Calans and other residents at the Girard place, the residents here were not very welcoming. Apparently, this wasn't going to be the right environment for them, especially when their family was going to get bigger.

They stayed in that apartment for only a couple of months, just through the end of the year. They were in and out so quickly that neither Mary Jo nor Dick remembers much about being there. There was one day, though, that Mary Jo does remember vividly. It was cold outside, and she was inside with the girls, listening to a song on the radio. Then " . . . we interrupt this broadcast for the following important announcement . . . reports have been confirmed that today, while riding in a motorcade through downtown Dallas, the thirty-fifth President of the United States, John F. Kennedy, was shot and killed. I repeat, President Kennedy has been killed . . . the entire nation is in shock and mourning at this horrifying act of violence . . . Minnesota lawmakers have joined together in expressing their deepest grief on the death of our beloved President . . . in the words of Senator Humphrey, 'Today, America has lost a great President. The world has lost a great leader. And I have lost a good friend . . . '"

Mary Jo took a deep breath, her eyes lingered over both of her children, and she held on to her pregnant belly. What an inexcusable, senseless crime, she thought. It didn't need to happen. She was sad, along with the rest of the country, but more than that she was angry about this kind of escalating violence. Her convictions grew a little stronger that day. If she was only put on this earth to accomplish one single thing, she was going to teach her children to make this world a better place.

....

Mary Jo and Dick found a new townhouse development called Nicollet Court not far from where they were. The townhouses had two upper levels, a finished basement and a yard big enough to plant a garden. Mary Jo loved it. She was really looking forward to spring when she could spend her days with the girls out in the yard and garden. She was still tired a lot of the time, but she stayed focused on the fun they had. She was having such a great time being a mom, and she could hardly wait to meet baby number three. In May 1964, just a couple of months after Andrea's first birthday, Mary Jo delivered a boy. They named him Michael, and by all accounts, he was the loud one, which did not please either of his sisters. The sibling rivalry had begun.

Although Mary Jo was flourishing in motherhood, she still had some leftover emotional problems that were draining her. She was spending a lot of energy on trying to please Dick's family. She really wanted to try to turn things around after his father's funeral; she wanted to convince Dick's mother to give her a chance. They never did talk out what happened at the hospital, that she had blamed Mary Jo for Dick's father's suicide. That had torn Mary Jo up. She supposed that his mom was too embarrassed or too grief-stricken to acknowledge what she had said, let alone apologize for it. At any rate, Mary Jo went out of her way to be nice to her and to the rest of the family. She baked things for them; she bought them little presents every time they visited. She tried so hard to win them over, and it was heartbreaking for Dick to watch. He knew that none of it would work. They would not openly reject her, but nothing she did would make them accept her. She just kept giving them things and praying for them, until Dick finally had to tell her to stop—one of the hardest things he'd ever had to say to her. "Mary, stop trying to make them like you. They don't want that. They don't want anything you give them."

Seeing how much that hurt her was hard for him, but Dick knew it was better than watching her chase after their approval for the rest of her life. She didn't understand how his family could treat anyone that way. He did the best he could to explain them to her, but the more he did, the more he realized that he didn't understand them himself. Although this was a difficult issue for both of them, Mary Jo felt the rejection more than he did. Dick had never been emotionally connected with his family, and he certainly wasn't dependent on them, so it was easy for him to walk away from it. But Mary Jo internalized the entire matter. For someone else, the situation may not have been as bad, but for her it was torture. A large part of her self-image was still wrapped up in what other people thought of her. She did stop trying with Dick's family, but whenever they visited with the children, she felt their disapproval and came away troubled and discouraged.

By December 1964, Michael was seven months old, and Mary Jo was pregnant. Clearly, no apartment would be big enough for all of them; they needed to start looking for a house. Although Dick was doing well in his position with Target, the steady growth of the family had kept them from saving enough for a down payment. In the meantime, they started looking for houses to rent and found a perfect place in Golden Valley, on a hill across from the Hennepin County Sheriff's Department. They scooped it up right away.

Not long after they moved in, Dick was noticing that Mary Jo still seemed to be very isolated and was becoming even more so. He had hoped that she would begin to come out of her shell a bit as their family grew, but it was just the opposite. She still wasn't comfortable interacting socially. When he had taken her to parties in high school, she could laugh and have a good time, but she wasn't really "there." She had never connected with her high school friends the way she had with Dick. And now, as a mother, she wasn't doing things with other mothers, only with her children. She just wasn't into having lunch or coffee by the pool with the ladies. She didn't enjoy that. That's what her life was when she was a child, surrounded by adults, being controlled by them. She was still more of a person who stood on the outside, waiting to be invited in. It seemed like too much work for her to try to make new friends. She wasn't even aware that she was missing that then. At the time, Mary Jo was hardly aware of what year it was; she was too busy. In February 1965, Therese turned three, in March, Andrea turned two, in May, Mike was a year old, and in September they brought home Cathy, their fourth baby. Mary Jo was twenty-two.

That Christmas, Mary Jo and Dick took all of the children to visit with his family, but his mother still kept up her same standoffishness. She acted as if they were all one big happy family, the whole time hardly speaking two words to Mary Jo. Dick saw how much this gnawed at Mary Jo and decided it was time to put a stop to this behavior. He pulled his mother aside and said, "Look, if you want to continue to be a family, then you're going to have to be a family all year long. Make an effort to be close like a family. You need to start giving Mary a little respect. You've never treated her right, and she's never done anything to you to deserve that, and you know it. You just continue to cause problems."

It was the first time Dick ever stood up to his mother or said anything against her, and she did not receive it well at all. His mother reacted as if she didn't have any idea what he was talking about. Realizing that he was getting nowhere, he said, "Okay, I can't do this anymore. Mary and I are not happy with this situation and we're tired of trying to make it better. If you can't find a way to be a positive part of our lives, then maybe it's best if we just leave each other alone." Dick hoped that hearing him say that would make his mother realize what she would be missing out on. It didn't work.

When Dick's father died, his estate was set up in trust funds for Dick and his brothers as a way to avoid paying estate taxes. This was about $60,000 for each brother, and over a five- or six-year period, they were each supposed to give it back to Dick's mother. There were many times that Dick wondered why he kept giving that money to her. Legally, he didn't have to. That was a great deal of money then, and he and Mary Jo certainly needed it more than his mother did. But what was right was right. His father wanted her to have it. It wasn't Dick's money; it was his father's. So he gave it all back to her, every penny. And after he made the final payment to her, she had nothing more to do with him or Mary Jo or any of her grandchildren.

Mary Jo and Dick also kept their distance from her side of the family. Gert occasionally gave them money or clothing from the apparel shop she had opened, but she was still living with Woody's abuse and dementia, and Mary Jo didn't want any more exposure to that. Certainly, she didn't want her children around it. Gert remained in denial and lived with it until Woody's death in 1986. After that, she continued coping in a chaotic environment with her son John, Mary Jo's brother, who had been diagnosed with paranoid schizophrenia. Gert repeatedly pulled him out of institutions to care for him at home until her death in 1996. John remains in the custody of Gertrude's extended family.

Mary Jo and Dick planned to stay in the Golden Valley house for a while, but after only about a year and a half, the owners decided to sell and they had to move out with only one month's notice. In five years of marriage, they had four children, and this was going to be the fifth time they had moved—and baby number five was on the way.

A beautiful four-bedroom, one-story house was for sale on 55th Avenue in Brooklyn Center. The backyard was huge and filled with lilac bushes and lilies of the valley. Mary Jo loved it. The owner of the house was willing to sell it to them on contract, which was the only way they would be able to get into something permanent.

They were thrilled. For the first time, the Copelands had their own home. It seemed as if they almost had more room than they knew what to do with. Almost. They moved in at the beginning of

January 1967, just in time to set up a nursery for the first blond Copeland, Jenny, born on March 8.

By this time, Mary Jo and Dick had both developed very strong parental styles. With five children, they didn't have time to worry about which way to do things, they just made decisions and acted upon them. Mary Jo was the one who got upset over the little things— people not picking up after themselves, for instance. She didn't put up with that. Not for one second. Not from a five-year-old and not from a twenty-eight-year-old. She did give a little leeway to those who couldn't walk or talk yet, but whether they were able to talk or not, everyone in that house knew that "no" meant "no."

Whenever something major would happen, however, Mary Jo stayed calm. After what she'd been through and seen in her life, there really wasn't much she couldn't handle. Dick was the one with a quick temper. They were both very vocal, but the children figured out early that when Dad yelled it really wasn't necessarily so serious. As they got older, the children learned that they could be in and out of trouble pretty quickly with him. But when Mom said they were grounded, those children did not leave their rooms. There was always consistency with her. The children always knew the rules, and they always knew exactly where they stood. With that system in place, they brought home baby number six, Mark, born in April 1968, a month after Jenny's first birthday. His older brother Mike, now almost three, was more excited than anyone. After being surrounded by all these females, finally, another boy in the house.

As Mary Jo's job at home grew more demanding, so did Dick's career. He'd been offered another promotion at Target. He was also offered a job and quite a bit more money at Donaldson's, a competitor of the Dayton Hudson Corporation. Although he learned a lot at Target and had planned to stay with them from the beginning, he had to think about his family first. At age twenty-eight, he had a wife and six children and a house to pay for. Not to take the job with the higher salary would have been a mistake.

Dick knew the job transition was not going to be easy, but he certainly did not expect what it led to. His new position as a cosmetics buyer for Donaldson's was a field he had no experience in. What he knew was merchandising. What he lacked were the industry contacts in New York that his counterparts had. The larger problem was that Donaldson's as a whole was not doing very well. Despite his lack of experience, Dick ran his department extremely well for more than a year. Then Donaldson's decided to overhaul the management team. No one got fired, but Dick's job was slowly being eliminated. He ultimately confronted his boss, demanding to know what was going on, requesting that his authority be defined or he would leave. That was the day Dick Copeland learned the value of patience—and to wait for an exit package the next time.

He drove around for the rest of that morning, trying to decide what to do next. He was in shock. He finally went home.

Mary Jo had just put the children down for a nap and was in the middle of her twenty minutes of afternoon relaxation when he came in. "Hi honey!" she said with her usual exuberance. And then, "What are you doing home so early?"

"Mary . . . I've lost my job."

She didn't even flinch. "That's all right," she said. "We can finally spend some time together."

Dick was dumbfounded. "Don't you understand? *I don't have a job!*"

"So? You'll find another one. In the meantime, you can paint the house."

6

Dick had never imagined being out of work. His whole life he had worked hard and paid for his own way. Anything he had ever wanted was attainable by working hard and being productive, and when he could no longer do that, he was devastated.

A month went by before Dick discovered what his former employer had stooped to. Dick had an excellent track record, and he couldn't understand why he hadn't secured a new job yet. Finally, one of the people he was interviewing with said to him, "I don't know what Donaldson's has against you, but they sure aren't giving you much of a reference." Every person he interviewed with had called Donaldson's, and Donaldson's was blackballing him. They didn't want him working for the competition. They apparently didn't care that he had a family to take care of.

Since he could do nothing about it, Mary Jo kept telling him to just forget about Donaldson's, but he didn't see how he could. He needed a job, and they were preventing him from getting one. The more hopeless and frustrated he became, the more fervently and constantly she reminded him about trust and faith. They had a house to live in and food to eat and clothes to wear, she said. "God has always provided what we need, one way or another, so stop worrying." Dick knew all this too, but he still worried.

A short time later, Dick received an envelope in the mail from a contact and good friend he'd made in New York named Sam Saul. Sam had heard about what Donaldson's had done to Dick. Inside the envelope there was a check for $2,000 and a note instructing him not to jump at the first offer but to use the money to wait for a good job.

"See?" said Mary Jo, "we get what we need when we need it." Dick wasn't looking at it that way, though. He didn't want to accept the money. He hung on to that check for a long time. He didn't want to cash it. For him, the larger issue was still looming: he didn't have a job.

What else could possibly be piled on to the stress of this situation? Well, Mary Jo was pregnant. Dick was happy about it, but another baby was just coming at a very hard time. He felt that everything was slipping away from him and that he had no control emotionally or with anything else. He couldn't believe what had happened. He couldn't bring himself to go down to the unemployment office, and every day that went by, he felt more and more squeezed into a corner. He began to think he was never going to get another job. The last thing he wanted was to put any of this stress on Mary Jo or the children, but nobody can keep that kind of pressure bottled up. For a while, he was very difficult to live with, and not even Mary Jo's optimism could make him feel better.

In 1969 the economy was muddling along, and the job market was good for the most part, but Dick could not secure a job in retail in town no matter what he did. He knocked on every door until there were no more left. He was even considering a job offer in Florida but ultimately decided against moving the family across the country. With no more options or time left, he realized that he was going to have to work in another industry. He had to get some money coming in, so he took a job as a buyer at Univac. He was being paid less, and his abilities were not being utilized, but they needed the money.

Still there wasn't enough money to cover the bills. There was no one better than Mary Jo at cutting corners and clipping coupons to save money, but they weren't making it. Going through a hard spell and putting off bills for a while was one thing, but this had gone on too long, and it was getting to the point where they would have to declare bankruptcy. Dick couldn't even think about that. To put down on paper that he couldn't take care of his family was just too much.

Mary Jo had a lot of emotional scars, but burdened by pride and ambition she was not. She finally said to Dick one day, "You've been putting this off and living with all that pressure for months. There's no reason for it. If we need to file for bankruptcy, then just go do it. Letting all this time go by isn't helping anyone. Just go file and get it over with!" It was just paperwork to Mary Jo. Not so for Dick. He still wouldn't file.

One bright spot in all this was that in the late 1960s, real estate values were on the rise. In only a couple of years of living there, the property value on their house went up 20 percent. If the circumstances had been different, they would have hung on to the house for a little longer, but their contract had a $3,000 balloon payment that was due. With their mound of debt and Mary Jo about to deliver another baby, the only way they could make that payment was to sell the house.

The profit they made was enough to get by on for a short time and to make a down payment on another house. Their new home was just a few blocks from their old house, just on the other side of Shingle Creek on Newton Avenue. Right across the street was a great park that had baseball and football fields, an ice rink, warming house, picnic areas, tennis courts, and a pool. It was perfect for the children. The thing that sold them on the new house was that, although it was much smaller than what they were moving from—only two bedrooms and one bathroom—the space was laid out well. The attic was finished in knotty pine and had built-in dresser drawers all along one wall. On the other wall was a walk-in closet, and there was a crawl space with plenty of room for storage. The attic would expand into a third bedroom where three or four beds would fit.

Some of the financial pressure eased after the sale of the house, but making this move was tough on Dick. He had taken his wife and six children from all that space—four bedrooms, a huge backyard—and put them into this 898-square-foot house. He was ready for some good news.

In September that year, 1969, just a month before Mary Jo's twenty-seventh birthday, they brought home baby number seven, Barbara. Her oldest sister Therese was now seven. Andrea was six, and insisting that everyone start calling her by her middle name, Mary, as if there wasn't enough confusion in that house. Mike was five, Cathy was four, Jenny was two, and Mark was one.

....

Although they were not far from their old house, now the Copelands were in a totally different neighborhood. All the neighbors knew one another well, and it was difficult for the Copelands to try to fit into that. They had purchased their house from the Jonquists, and in the beginning they were known as "the new people living in the Jonquist house." The neighborhood was very family-oriented; almost every house had children. The Copelands had more children than any of them, though, and even if she'd wanted to, Mary Jo didn't have time to become involved with the other moms. She was never one to get hung up on "what the neighbors must think," which probably helped them to be labeled as outsiders.

The Copelands squeezed into their new surroundings. Mary Jo and Dick had one bedroom. They put the oldest children up in the dormer bedroom, and the two youngest had bunk beds in the room across from their parents. There was also a crib in the downstairs room for Barb, but she wasn't going to stay in it very long. Mary Jo was pregnant again.

The Copeland children all had their own quirks and needs, yet Mary Jo managed by treating them all the same. She focused on the basics. Every day, every one got a kiss and a hug, a home-cooked dinner, fresh clothes laid out for the next day, a bath before bed, and a prayer. She never strayed from her daily schedule that allowed her to keep the day under control and to sprinkle it with games, songs, and treats. No matter what came up, Mary Jo made it fun. If it was raining or cold outside, she made a carpet picnic in the living room. Whenever someone got sick or hurt and had to go to the doctor, they always stopped at Dairy Queen on the way home. Every birthday, every Halloween, every holiday there was an array of art projects created to decorate the house. She even made the housework into a game. One household rule was that everybody got fresh sheets on their bed every week. The game that went along with that rule was called "chocolate eclair roll-ups." The children would lie across one end of the bed, gather up the sheets and blankets from the corners of the mattress, and just like opening a can of sardines, they rolled to the other end of the bed, taking the bedding with them. The winner was the first one to get the sheets off the bed and jump up to declare themselves a "chocolate eclair roll-up!" On bed sheets day there were always a bunch of happy little Copelands, giggling and hopping around the house.

Mary Jo put a lot of effort into making sure that there was no chance for her children to go through the hardships that she went through as a child. Every day, no matter how tired she may have been, they were fed good meals. Every day they wore clean clothes. They may not have lived in a big house, but every day they came home to a safe, clean place. Every Sunday they went to church, not always on time, but always they went. She made sure that none of them would ever be lonely like she was and that every one of them went to sleep at night knowing that they were loved. Mary Jo felt almost as if she were having her own childhood over again—the right way.

Along with a lot of love, the Copelands were given a lot of medical attention while growing up. Having all those energetic youngsters packed into one little house made trips to the emergency room inevitable. Mike (number three) held the record for the most visits to the doctor. The first set of stitches in his head came from his standing on the back of a high chair to reach a banana. Another time he was in the garage with Mary (Andrea, number two) breaking down cardboard boxes, and he decided to jump on top of a box at the same time she decided to swing a hammer at it. He got a mass of stitches above his eye for that one. Once when he was diving into a pool, his head somehow managed to make contact with the cement instead of the water. More stitches. Still another time, he was in the basement, spinning around in circles on his knee for some foolish reason, and smacked his head into the corner of a table. Stitches.

While the sight of her children bleeding was surely alarming, Mary Jo still handled all the household injuries with the same calm grace and common sense as she did everything else. And when a malformation in baby Mark's hip socket was discovered, Mary Jo's strength and determination helped bring him to a successful recovery.

The first sign of the problem with Mark's hip developed when he was learning to walk. He was extremely wobbly and fell over all the time, more than a normal toddler. When they brought him into the doctor, x-rays revealed that the bone going to his hip was detached from the socket. This commonly happened during labor, but the doctor hadn't caught it after Mark's delivery, when it could have easily been put into place. Now the only way the doctors knew how to correct the problem so he would be able to walk normally was to put Mark in a lower body cast that kept both his legs separated. He looked as if he had two broken legs, with the cast covering both legs and his hips. He was only two years old then, and the cast put about ten extra pounds on him and made him nearly immobile. Originally, the doctors had recommended that he be put in traction for six months, but Mary Jo protested that treatment. It did not make sense to her that a child who was already learning to walk be suddenly immobilized, not to mention having him separated from the family. She simply refused to put her son through that. The doctors insisted that the only other way for his hip to set and grow normally was the body cast.

Of course, Mary Jo and Dick were upset about their son's condition, but the mistake had already been made, and there wasn't anything they could do about it. Neither the hospital nor the doctor who delivered Mark would take responsibility for the oversight, and Mary Jo was not inclined to waste her energy with a lawsuit. Her only goal was to keep moving forward with Mark's progress, cast or no cast.

Dick built a special chair so that Mark could be perched up at the table, but Mary Jo did not agree that he should just be sitting there all day, getting frustrated by his immobility. She set Mark out in the middle of the carpet one day and said, "Okay, kiddo, you're just going to have to learn how to get around, and that's all there is to it." Soon Mark was pulling himself up and swinging himself around. He couldn't go very fast, but he could get from room to room and toy to toy on his own. While playing out in the backyard, he learned to scoot himself up and down the slide, especially when the neighbor's dog came bounding and barking at him.

After about six months of having Mark's cast replaced every four to six weeks, Mary Jo began to question the need to have him in such an extensive and weighty cast. She knew it would be a lot easier on him if he could have the load lightened. She asked the doctors why he couldn't have just one leg in the cast, since the problem was only in one hip, but they said this wouldn't work. This was the only way the problem would be resolved, they said. They had never done it any other way.

Mary Jo still protested. She wasn't trying to be difficult. She did not claim to know more than the doctors. But she was not one to accept difficult circumstances for what they were either. She survived through all of her tough times by finding new ways to adapt. She felt that if the doctors had never tried the treatment for Mark the way she suggested, then how did they know it wouldn't work?

They finally agreed to try the cast on just one leg. Being only half as restricted, Mark started running. After the cast, they went to a brace. By the time he went to kindergarten and had several surgeries, his hip grew around the bone, and he didn't need any further treatment. Doctors said, however, that he would probably have trouble with sports and other physical activities. Again, Mary Jo questioned this forewarning. The only thing she was sure of was that if a child grew up being told that he was limited, then he most certainly would be. She never told Mark that he would have trouble physically or babied him. She and Dick both continued to treat him the same as all the other children, and he grew up just as athletic as the rest of them. He played football in high school and became a championship weightlifter after he graduated.

In April 1971, Mary Jo delivered her eighth child, Steven, who became the great showman. The older Steve got, the more he loved to be the center of attention, which was obviously not the easiest thing to achieve in the Copeland house. His arrival brought a lot of joy, as all of the babies had, but it also meant another large hospital bill. Adding that to the previous medical bills, credit card bills, mortgage, and everything else they had to pay for—and that the savings they had been living on had run out —it was just about the end of the line for the Copelands financially. They had stretched things out as long as they could. They had to file for bankruptcy. It was the hardest thing Dick ever had to do. They only owed somewhere around $4,000, but it might as well have been $1 million; they just didn't have the money. Dick had been fighting so hard and paying things back little by little, just so he wouldn't have to go through bankruptcy. In the end he had to file anyway. But as it turned out, Mary Jo was right again. They could now reorganize their debts to make repayment manageable. Eventually, Dick came to see that things continued exactly as they always had, just without all the stress. Mary Jo got pregnant again.

One day that certainly helped put their financial concerns into perspective was the day the house caught on fire. While Mary Jo was vacuuming, a short in the cord sent a spark into the drapes. Flames shot up instantly and raced up the living room wall. The blaze was too big for Mary Jo to put out, and she immediately went for the children. Therese, Mary, Mike, and Cathy were at school, and she grabbed Steve, Barb, Mark, and found a terrified little Jenny hiding in a closet. She got them all out as smoke poured through the house.

The good thing about the Newton house being so small and closed up was that it did not leave much oxygen for the fire to survive. None of the windows were open, so the fire stayed contained in the living room, and then burned itself out. The smoke damage, though, covered the entire main floor and the upstairs.

The insurance money they received was enough to cover a hotel stay while everything was replaced and repaired, but between the diapers and laundry and meals and everything else that needed to be done in a day in order for Mary Jo to function, a hotel was the last place she wanted to be with eight children. The basement rooms had been undamaged in the fire, so while the rest of the house was being refurbished, they bunked down there—all ten of them. It had become more than evident by now that there wasn't a lot that was going to slow Mary Jo down—not an injury, not a bankruptcy, not even a house fire. She was just going to keep praying, taking care of her family, and moving forward no matter what they faced.

This same strong will carried her through their next challenge. As much as Mary Jo loved being a mother, being pregnant for almost twelve straight years was not easy. This time she suffered more than enduring discomfort and fatigue. She had developed placenta previa, and the doctors feared she would lose the child. They wanted her to stay in the hospital for the rest of her pregnancy, but that was impossible. Who would take care of the children? Mary Jo and Dick had worked out their routine so that Dick took a week of vacation to stay home with the children whenever Mary Jo was delivering a baby, but she never had any other help.

Mary Jo compromised and agreed to stay in the hospital overnight sometimes on the weekends so they could monitor her. She also tried to take it easier at home. She was almost able to carry to full term but had to have an emergency cesarean delivery. She didn't like that she wasn't awake for the birth, but she did like her new baby boy, Jimmy. It was August 1972. Therese was ten, Mary was nine, Mike was eight, Cathy was seven, Jenny was five, Mark was four, Barb was three, Steve was one, little Jimmy was brand new—and Mary Jo, nearly thirty, was exhausted.

The next year, Dick started working at May Company Wholesale Foods, a distributor for local supermarkets. He was starting over again in a new industry, but with the size of his family, he needed to move to a company he could grow with as well. He settled into his new job, and Mary Jo settled into the new routine at home. Every time a new baby came in, things shifted a little. The girls shared the dormer upstairs; the boys had bunk beds in the downstairs bedroom. Every time a new baby came home, whoever was in the crib got moved to a bed, and the daily schedule went like this: The house woke up around five o'clock in the morning, and every child had a chore to do. To prevent the dust bunnies from being swept under a rug and the toys and other belongings from being stuffed where they shouldn't be, Mary Jo had them clean one another's rooms instead of their own. While Dick got everyone cereal in the morning, Mary Jo would get a load of laundry going; she did ten or twelve loads a day. After breakfast, the children who were going to school washed up, got dressed, picked up a bag lunch and backpack, and out they went. Then Dick would leave for work, where he'd be for ten hours a day. Mary Jo would get the younger children up and dressed and fed, keep the laundry loads going, change a baby, feed a baby, and do another load of laundry while they played together. The rest of the morning and afternoon would be filled with the same, along with folding and cleaning. When the children came home from school, she had a snack ready for them while they watched *Lost in Space*. Dinner was also on a schedule. Sloppy Joes one night, Salisbury steak night, macaroni and cheese night, and so on. Dirty dishes got to be endless. There wasn't any room in the schedule for dirty dishes, so Mary Jo switched to paper plates. When Dick came home from work, he would make dinner for himself and Mary Jo, and they would have an hour of "quiet time" together while they ate. After dinner they helped the children with homework, spent time with them, played with them, prayed with them, and got them to bed. That was the schedule, and they stuck to it. It was the way Mary Jo kept things on track.

Mary Jo's tenth pregnancy wasn't quite as difficult as the last, but she still had to be careful and required another C-section delivery. Jeff was born in July 1974, healthy and happy.

Just then, someone blinked. A year and a half later, another baby arrived, Matt. His arrival meant there were now more boys than girls in the house for the first time in Copeland history.

7

With all of the activity that was going on each day, no one knew what was going on with Mary Jo. Physically, she was exhausted from all the pregnancies, but she still kept going every day. She didn't have a choice. Mentally, she was rundown. But she still kept the house on schedule and on budget and kept a smile on her face. Overall, she was happy. This was exactly the life she wanted. But even with all the blessings she'd been given, there was a part of her that still felt scared and isolated sometimes, just as when she was a child. She still carried with her the images of her mother, bruised and bleeding. At times she could still hear the angry, hurtful words of her father, telling her how worthless she was. She still felt rejected over the alienation by Dick's family. Pain like that never goes away.

She had been stifling these feelings for years, praying through them as she always had. Most of the time she was able to stay focused on what was in front of her and how happy she was instead of the neglect and abuse of her past. But still there were moments, and as her days became more hectic, the more difficulty she had suppressing her feelings about her past.

Valium was a popular prescription drug at that time for people with stressful lives. It was sort of the Prozac of the 1970s, except that instead of taking it as prescribed, people took it whenever they felt they needed it. Shortly after Barb's birth in 1969, Mary Jo's doctor prescribed Valium for her. It did help her to cope with endless days of crying babies and having to focus constantly on everyone else's needs. It also dulled the emotional pain from her past. Valium seemed to be the perfect solution, but after delivering four more children after Barb, three of those by C-section, continuing to raise the ones she had, and now having yet another one, number twelve, on the way, she had become entirely too dependent on "mother's little helper," as the Rolling Stones named the popular drug. She was taking Valium pills every day, sometimes throughout the day, sometimes coupling them with pain pills to help recover from her C-section surgeries.

In 1976, she somehow knew that this would be her last pregnancy, and her body started reflecting what had been going on emotionally. She went about her days as before, but she knew clearly that there was something terribly wrong. She couldn't sleep, she couldn't eat, and she was losing weight steadily. Dick kept taking her to the doctor to find out what was going on, only to be sent back home. The doctor said she was fine and that the baby was fine. The problem was that the doctor was only running tests on the baby. No one was checking Mary Jo's blood sugar or heart rate or other vital signs. Dick was furious.

"The baby is connected to the mother, if you haven't figured that out, and the mother *is not* fine!" he pointed out. Mary Jo was down to 120 pounds, and her hair was falling out. It was all Dick could do just to keep two bites of food in her. He was losing his wife, and no one would do anything.

Mary Jo's health continued going downhill, and during her third trimester she began hemorrhaging. When she was pronounced out of immediate danger, she returned home from the hospital, but she was back within a month. Aside from her malnutrition, there was a weakness in the lining of her uterus. Her only option now was to stay in bed or she would lose the baby. She stayed in bed for about six weeks. Being cooped up like that made her feel as if she would lose her mind, but she did not lose the baby. On May 28, 1977, by her fourth C-section, Mary Jo delivered baby number twelve, Molly. This would be her last child. She bled so much during the operation that doctors had to remove her uterus.

Mary Jo had carried the baby to full term, but within days of her birth, Molly was showing the same kinds of symptoms as if she had been born prematurely. She wasn't responding to normal stimuli, and she wasn't able to eat. The same doctors who had reported that Molly was doing fine in the womb were now saying that she was mentally handicapped.

The anxious parents consulted several specialists and pediatricians and learned that there was no way to determine this early that Molly was anything more than underdeveloped. Although Mary Jo had carried her to full term, Molly's development was slowed because of Mary Jo's weakened condition during the pregnancy. Mary Jo and Dick believed that all Molly really needed was extra care and love. They believed that, just as with Mark's hip, Molly's growth would catch up, and she'd have a good chance of developing normally.

When Dick and Mary Jo brought Molly home, once again the rules and the schedule changed. When Mary Jo was in the hospital, the family all pulled together to keep the house going. The older children alternated taking half-days off from school to help take care of the younger ones. Once at home, Molly needed to be fed every two hours, and the older girls would take turns getting up in the middle of the night to help feed her. The children were always excited when a new baby came home, but even more so with Molly. The novelty of her never wore off. Everyone embraced her. Everyone wanted to take care of Molly.

Mary Jo was given heavy doses of Valium to help her recover, and this time the emotional effects on her were deadening. Her feelings about not being able to have any more children were constantly vacillating. She felt more than fortunate for the family she'd been given. At the same time, her ability to mother children was what she valued most about herself, and coming to the end of that for her felt like coming to the end of life itself.

Again, the doctors advised that Mary Jo's depression was normal. "Don't worry about it. It will pass." But Mary Jo's body was shutting down, and the depression started overwhelming her. Her hair was thinning, her appetite was gone, she couldn't sleep, and she felt she had no purpose anymore. She wanted to die so it would all be over. This was definitely *not* normal. Not for Mary Jo, the woman whose bright spirit consistently carried her and everyone around her through the worst of circumstances. But now it was as if all the negative forces in her life that she had struggled against were finally winning. The spark that everyone loved so much about her was gone. For the first time in her life, Mary Jo didn't know how she was going to survive. She didn't believe she could. She'd lost her will and felt that all that was left was for her to go home to God.

She floated through each day taking pills to ease her pain, taking pills to cover her depression, taking pills to substitute for the food she couldn't keep down. There was still something remarkable going on though. The fact that she had become so worn down and addicted to pills did not change the fact that she could keep up with the demands of a husband and twelve children and a house to run. She didn't understand why God had not taken her home to heaven yet, but until that time, there was laundry to do. She just kept going.

More than a year went by, and the depression still shadowed Mary Jo. She also started experiencing periods of anxiety, and often when it kept her up at night, she'd grab a can of wax and start cleaning the kitchen floor. Throughout the day, whenever she'd start to get upset about something, she would find something to clean—the beds, the clothes, the baby, the walls—anything.

There was certainly enough to keep her busy inside, and as the family grew over the years, Mary Jo had become even more isolated from anything that wasn't Copeland. During her months of depression, most days she stayed in her housecoat and never went outside the 868-square foot house. She stayed in the house and worked. The only exposure she had to the rest of the world came when Dick and the children came home to tell her about their day.

On weekends, Dick was the one who took the youngsters out on excursions. The babies and the younger ones stayed home with Mary Jo, and Dick would pile the rest of them into the station wagon and take them to the Civic Center swimming pool. It was very cheap entertainment, and they got their money's worth from the family membership.

Dick would spend time with each child in a swimming lesson, and for the rest of the day, they played a game they called "Touchdown," where all of them would try to stop Dick from going from one end of the pool to the other. Dick's six-feet-two-inch frame and sturdy build forced all the children to gang up to try to knock him over. A few of them would grab his arms, some of them were underwater trying to pull his legs out from under him, some of them were jumping on him from the edge of the pool. Dick would grab whatever child was within his reach by the trunks and toss them. He had as much fun as they did.

Another way Dick gave Mary Jo a break from having a full house was to take some of the children along on the Sunday grocery trips. After sitting in church all morning, the children would usually be restless in the car, but Dick became very skilled at the over-the-seat swat. Everyone within arm's reach learned to behave in the car. Dick had very long arms. At home Mary Jo kept making up new games for the children. Anything that kept her focus on the positive instead of her depression was what she did. The pastime that became the biggest hit was the children's singing and dancing contests. Steve was the biggest showman and insists to this day that he was the winner of every contest they had. He went on a long crusade to get all of his brothers and sisters to start calling him "The Great Eight" (being the eighth one born), but none of them ever did. Mary Jo and Dick were partial to the music of Johnny Mathis and Crosby Stills and Nash for these contests, but the youngsters all wanted to sing along and imitate the local rock station. Mary Jo would shout from the next room, "Turn off that acid rock!" But Steve convinced her to sit down and listen to it one day, and she got hooked on Devo. She started bouncing along and singing, " . . . *and I say, whip it! Whip it good!*" She loved it, and for a long time after that, Devo boomed from the stereo during the morning housecleaning. Seeing her opening her front door while boogying and calling to the paperboy in the street to *"Whip it!"* (the newspaper) to her, made it difficult for anyone to tell how sad she really was inside.

When he was ten or eleven, Mike decided that he wanted to get a paper route and start earning his own money. This worked out so well for him that his brothers and sisters started getting their own routes too. Soon the Copelands controlled every route in the area, and none of the other neighborhood youngsters could get a route. As the Copelands grew older and started working part-time jobs, they would hand their paper routes down to the next younger brother or sister. The Copeland family had a monopoly on the North Minneapolis paper deliveries for many years.

Behind all the singing and dancing and fun, Mary Jo was still in a constant battle emotionally. The sadness that fed her Valium addiction grew more pronounced than the pills anesthetizing it. Dick was the only one who really knew how much she was suffering, and nothing he did could reach her. She had grown stubborn and defensive with him. He would try to bring up the subject sometimes after all the children were in bed, but she'd just snap at him, "You can't help me! Leave me alone!" He really missed his wife.

Although she tried, Mary Jo couldn't keep her problems hidden from the children all the time either. One day Barb and some of the younger children came home from school and found Mary Jo sitting at the kitchen table, sobbing. Her arms were bleeding. She had inadvertently made cuts in her skin with a can opener. Barb didn't know what to think; she was so scared that she started crying too. She went over and hugged Mary Jo and kept telling her it would be okay.

New cuts and bruises were showing up on Mary Jo frequently. This self-mutilation is a common manifestation in people so emotionally tortured, but no one understood what was going on with her at the time. She had been walking around with so much pain bottled up for so long that she started taking her past out on herself—it was her parents rejecting her, her grandparents rejecting her, the children at school rejecting her, Dick's parents rejecting her. The more these painful memories kept flooding over her, the harder it became for her to function. She felt she had no purpose anymore. She had been walking around feeling worthless for so long that she just couldn't stand herself sometimes. It would take her a long time to realize what she was doing.

Mary Jo had been in such a dark place for so long, and Dick knew that nobody could survive like that forever. Although she tried hard to hide what she was going through, he hurt to see her in such pain. He wanted the girl he married back. Since Mary Jo refused to see any more doctors and didn't feel comfortable about going to a therapist, he decided to try what had worked in the beginning. He asked her out on a date.

Only after much convincing would Mary Jo agree. She still focused on all the work in the house. Of course, she couldn't leave, she said, she had dinner to make. She had to give the kids baths. She had to do the wash. There was just too much to do. But Dick wouldn't give up. Like a persistent teenager, he kept asking her out. He finally convinced her one day to get dressed and go with him to get a burger. "Okay, but just for something to eat," she said, "and then I have to get right back."

The older children were left in charge, and Mary Jo and Dick went to a little corner bar near their house. Mary Jo was uncomfortable. She felt completely out of place in public now. She thought everyone was staring at her. They settled into a booth and ordered. With her feeling like such a foreigner being out of the house and away from the children, talking about them and their activities seemed to put her at ease. This was their first break from parenting in years, and all she wanted to talk about was the children. Dick didn't mind. It was working.

Dick continued trying to take her out to eat or shopping or for walks. He didn't push too hard; he just kept giving her gentle reminders of how important she was and how important their love was. Each time they went out was difficult, but each time she made a little progress. After about six months, she was starting to allow herself to enjoy that time they had together. Little by little, day by day, she started to regain some confidence. Friday nights became sacred for them. Friday night was date night. Sometimes they would go out on Saturdays too, if they could manage it. When they were teenagers they had always loved to go dancing together, so they started doing that again. Any bar that had live music was where they went. Mary Jo was getting her smile back.

Life continued just the same at the Copeland house, and for Mary Jo it was finally getting better. Although her problems had not disappeared, she and Dick had found a better way for her to function by taking a break on the weekends. She was still taking pills but not as many. She was still inside the house most of the day, but she started gardening again. She still felt an enormous hole in her life, but she was on her way to recovering. She was praying for that more than anything.

Although the neighbors had always considered Mary Jo and Dick strange and reclusive, the Copeland house had now become a hot spot for all the neighborhood children. When the children would bring their friends home from school, none of them could believe how much food the Copelands had. There was none of that healthy snack nonsense going on there either—they had the good stuff. There was a constant supply of chips and Fritos and pop and candy available out on the picnic table. All the children would come over from across the street at the park and visit the Copelands when they got hungry.

One day Mark brought a new friend named Robbie home with him after school. While most people lose sight of the childhood friends they make, Mark and Robbie stayed best friends through high school and on into their adult lives. On his first visit to the Copeland house, Robbie couldn't believe how much food they had. Or how many shoes were piled up at the back door. He came from a large family too, but he had never seen so many children. Mark introduced Robbie to some of his younger brothers with the comment, "Look, you can punch 'em as hard as you want and they don't even cry!"

The thing that Robbie would never forget that day was how kind Mary Jo was to him. Robbie had had a hard day. Mary Jo had her hands full, but she wasn't too busy to notice that he looked a little upset. Robbie told her about the kids at school who were being nasty to him, spitting on him, and harassing him, and that Mark had stuck up for him. He said he felt so happy to have a friend like Mark, but it was still hard on him to be the kid that everyone wants to pick on. Mary Jo sure understood that one. She sat him down gave him a big hug, and said, "Robbie, you're going to have to accept that you're not like those other kids. You're special, and God's got a special plan for you. You concentrate on that, and don't give them any more of your energy."

Robbie wasn't too sure about all that grand plan stuff, but from then on, somehow, all those mean kids at his school didn't matter to him so much. Whenever he was down about something, he went over to hang out at the Copeland house. And he wasn't the only one. Having a lot of children meant having a lot of your children's friends around. The Copeland house was where everyone wanted to be. Mary Jo and Dick now had about thirty children running in and out.

If the neighbors thought they were strange before, they must have thought the Copelands were complete lunatics now. Mary Jo didn't care though. It did a lot for her to have all those children coming over to talk to her and get her advice or just to say hello. It helped to make her realize that she was much more than just the Copeland maid, as she had been feeling. She was beginning to see that she had more than that to offer to her family and to other people.

Joey Maxwell was one of the neighborhood children who was spending a lot of time at the Copeland's house. His situation at home was so bad that he actually lived with the Copelands for a few months. For any other household, that would have been a big responsibility, but Mary Jo's attitude about it was, "At this point, what's one more kid?" The trouble it took to accommodate Joey was nothing compared to the difference it could make for him. It made her feel good to be able to reach out to him.

At night, the park across the street from their house had become a hangout for many teenagers doing drugs and drinking, but more and more these young people started hanging out across the street at the Copeland's picnic table with Mary Jo. Without lecturing them, without telling them what to do with their lives, Mary Jo was influencing these teenagers to live better lives. All she did was sit out at the picnic table and talk with them, sometimes until two or three in the morning if they needed to. She was genuinely interested in their lives. For most of them, that was all they really needed, and it was a lot more than they got at home. At the very least, the time they spent with Mary Jo was time they weren't spending getting high and getting drunk.

In addition to making such great differences with the kids, Mary Jo was having terrific fun. The little girl who grew up having no one to play with but bees and flowers was thriving on never-before-experienced popularity. There weren't very many people who didn't know a Copeland, or know where the Copeland house was, and where all the good food was. Mary Jo got a call one day from the *Minneapolis Tribune*, wanting to do a story about the remarkable Copeland family.

The four-page feature, written by Ruth Hammond, was published with family photos on August 30, 1980.

The article described a day in the life of the Copeland family, beginning at 5 A.M. and continuing through cooking and gobbling meals, overseeing the kids' 350 newspaper deliveries, cleaning the house, changing babies, doing twelve loads of laundry, laughing, playing, fighting, yelling, and a lot of praying. It read, not surprisingly, much like a day in Mary Jo's life today, with her love and attention being demanded from twelve different directions at once. In the interviews, the article captured the sense that the constant activity in the tiny house was normal, but Mary Jo and Dick both admitted that their choice to have such a large family was difficult. "There's no more putting up your feet at 8 P.M. and saying, 'Whooo, that was a hard day, but now it's over.' It's never over," Dick told the reporter. They joked about having their own television show, "Eight Is Enough, Twelve Is Too Many."

Each of the children was interviewed also, and, true to their independent personalities, they each gave a different take on what it was like to be a Copeland. "I really like a big family. Just the joy of coming home and seeing all those kids," said the eldest sibling Therese, then 18. Andrea Mary, the next in line, complained about the lack of privacy in the house and didn't want anything written about the family in the paper. Mike, 16, said he felt very close to Mary Jo and that he helped take care of the kids when his parents went out on the weekends. He said since the younger kids wouldn't listen to Jen and Barb "because they're girls," he took care of all the discipline. Cathy, 14, complained about sharing her room with four sisters and having to sit at the bathroom door and yell to get in there. She said if she had the choice, she wouldn't have so many brothers and sisters but understood that her parents chose to follow the will of God. Jenny, 13, said she didn't think religion had anything to do with her parents' choice to have a large family. "I know I'm Catholic," she said, "I don't pray every second; I think Mass is kind of boring, but I like it. I don't swear too much." Mark, 12, said even though they fought a lot, he liked being in a big family. He said he wanted to be a football player when he grew up, have three or four kids, and be as close as he could to his mom and dad, and maybe not anyone else. Barb, 10, said she'd rather be in a smaller family and that she planned to have two kids when she grew up because "it's not a crowd and it's not a mess." Steve, 9, said that a long time ago when he was a kid (when he was eight), he used to be afraid that his parents would die when they went out on the weekends, but he got over that. He thought it was fun in a big family, and fun getting about a million toys at Christmas. Jimmy, 8, said he liked playing with all his brothers and sisters. "They're all my favorites." He said when he's older, he would be a rich doctor and buy his mom a boat. Jeff, 6, said he was worried about starting first grade. "I don't know how to read. That's my whole problem." He said he hated being in a big family, but sometimes he liked it because he got to have his picture taken. Matt, 4, told the reporter about his life so far: he was born, and then they went to church and Therese (his godmother) gave him to God and he was "appetized," and then he grew up. Molly, 3, who was going to Courage Center for speech and physical therapy, had just said "Mom" for the first time a few months before. She was the family darling, and everyone loved taking care of her.

The three things that everyone agreed on in the article were that "their parents loved them, they loved their parents, and they all got enough attention."

8

At Courage Center Molly grew stronger with physical therapy and more articulate with speech therapy. She continued going there until she was six. She still had to work harder than the others, and it took her longer to learn, but by the time she was a teenager, she was essentially much like any other young person. On the days she was at Courage Center, her next oldest brother Matt was the only one at home with Mary Jo during the day until 1982, when he started first grade.

Mary Jo continued to grow stronger as well. Dick kept finding new ways to get her out of the house. He never pushed too hard, and very slowly the hurtful words and rejection she had suffered started slipping away. She had also started counseling with priests through her church. Eventually, her depression lifted, but it took time and heartache to get back to the happiness and purpose she once knew.

By 1982, all twelve of the Copeland children were in school and some of them had already moved out. This was the first time since she was pregnant with Therese that Mary Jo had spent any time alone, and the first time she had any consecutive hours to herself in more than twenty years. She finished cleaning up after breakfast and all of a sudden, she had all this time on her hands until the children came home from school. It was somewhat of a dangerous place for her to be. She started feeling the waves of inadequacy threatening again.

Dick was not going to watch his wife fall back into depression this time. "Mary, you've got to stop bottling all this up," he told her. "You've got more love in your heart than anyone I've ever known. You have to go out and share yourself with the world. Go be part of the rest of the world. You'll never fully recover from all of your pain if you don't, and you'll just wind up losing the gift you've been given."

That worked. Mary Jo agreed with him. It sounded logical enough, but what was it that she was supposed to do? She never went to college, and she hadn't had a job since the early 1960s. It seemed impossible for her to try to enter the job market now. She decided to look for some opportunities to volunteer. She had done some off-and-on volunteer work in the past, before she became so busy with all the children. Now that things had slowed down a little was the perfect time for her to become involved in the community again. She got out the phone book and started calling charities, leaving messages at outreach centers all over the city.

Mary Jo was thirty-eight years old, and she realized that from the time she met Dick twenty-three years earlier, she had hardly been anywhere without him. Since she started having babies, she had never been with any other people as just Mary Jo—only as Mary Jo and Dick. She had always had problems trying to manage the confusing bus schedules, and since she would be going out to volunteer on a regular basis, Dick suggested that it was time for her to get her driver's license.

"No way," said Mary Jo, "If I'm gonna share my time and my heart with the world, I'm gonna do it on the bus." Her stubbornness was as evident as ever.

Dick applied the tactics that had worked with her in the past, gently reminding her that she was capable of anything she put her mind to. But she resisted. "There's no point to it," she kept saying. "You take the car to work every day. What do I need my license for?"

"Why don't you look out the window?" Dick replied one day. Parked in front of their house was a little blue Plymouth Reliant. He tossed the keys and a driver's instruction manual on the table and said, "It'll be there when you're ready."

That husband of hers was infuriating. That little car sat out there, all shiny blue and happy, taunting her day after day. If she had been wrong about the antidriving thing this whole time, she wasn't going to let anyone else know about it. She started getting up in the middle of the night with a flashlight to study that driver's manual. There she was, a grown woman sneaking around in her own house under a blanket trying to hide her reading light. As her teenagers had learned when trying to sneak out at night, hiding anything in a tiny house with fourteen people in it isn't easy. But she was stubborn; she didn't want Dick to know. He did know, of course, but he was smart enough not to let on that he knew.

One day Mary Jo woke up and said, "Dick, I don't want any arguments. Take me for my permit test." And he did. And she failed. She was furious. She went back to take that test again and passed. Next was the driver's test, and again, she failed, and again she went back, and failed, and went back, and *voila* . . . she passed it. She was thirty-eight years old and for the first time, a legal driver. Dick hadn't seen her so happy in . . . well, ever. She drove around the block a couple of times when they got home, bouncing in her seat. Dick gave her some money, and she drove herself to Target. She couldn't believe it—she was shopping! The children were very excited too. "Look at that! Mom's *driving*!"

The day she got her license Mary Jo really started feeling like part of the rest of the world. Not being able to drive was one of the things that had been adding to the separation between her and other children's parents and even with her own children when they started driving. Dick and Mary Jo made sure that each learned to drive, and they bought used cars for them. They felt they should give their children their freedom, but inside, Mary Jo had felt as if she was the poor pathetic mother who had no freedom of her own. That little laminated card in her wallet was a very significant milestone for her.

Some of the charitable organizations that she had contacted began calling back. Catholic Charities, the first one she talked to, explained that their system was set up with different Branches of outreach programs located around the city. Branch II in downtown Minneapolis needed a lot of help. "That sounds great," Mary Jo said. "Where is it?"

She felt so good driving herself over there in her own little car, driving downtown just like normal people did. It was the first time she ever drove downtown. She got lost. After circling the one-way streets over and over, she finally found the place and parked.

She shook off the stress of getting lost and bounced in to introduce herself to the two Branch managers—Clarence and Harold. Clarence was an average-looking black man who seemed to put a lot of effort into dressing well. Harold was a Native American with a substantial build, enormous hands, and a long ponytail spilling down his back. Harold was the kind of guy no one messed with.

Both of them had been at Branch II for a long time, and neither of them took to Mary Jo very warmly. They seemed like nice enough fellows, but she could read the look on their faces . . . *Oh, look what we've got here . . . another little suburban flower, comin' down here to play Miss Goody-two-shoes so she can go home feelin' good about her cushy little life. She'll be gone within a week.*

Harold and Clarence gave her a tour of the place. She saw where the coffee pot was, some tables and chairs, a desk with a telephone, and some stale doughnuts. That's about all there was to it.

"What is it I'm here to help with?" she asked. They explained that the Branch was a drop-in center. When vagrants came in, they were referred to the community service programs that they were eligible for. The Branch would sometimes get donations of food or clothing, but since there was not a lot of that going on at the time, they had to ration out what they did get. Mary Jo asked them about the men who were there, sitting at tables. Harold and Clarence said most of the people would just come in and drink coffee and sit around. They don't have anything else to do.

Having nothing to do was a concept that Mary Jo Copeland just could not fathom. How could anyone have *nothing* to do? Oblivious to any fears about these hardened people, she had to find out. Her demeanor was almost laughable. There she was, hardly out of the house in twenty years, and she just walked right up to one of the men there, smiled and said, "Hello, I'm Mary Jo. What's your name? What do you do all day?"

Apparently, Harold and Clarence had never seen anything like that before. Harold leaned over to Clarence and asked what the hell she was doing. Mary Jo ignored them. Apparently, the man that she approached had never seen anything like that before either; he was looking at her the same way Harold and Clarence were. He was used to people ignoring him or being afraid of him. Mary Jo wasn't in the least bit afraid, but he was a little afraid of her.

"John Power," he finally answered her, shifting his position on the window ledge.

"How are you today, John? Have you been having a hard time?" she asked.

Of course, he had been having a hard time, but who ever cared about that? He wasn't sure what to think of this woman. He was waiting for her to tell him that he had to leave or something. Harold and Clarence watched her silently. They didn't understand why she was talking to him. When they asked her later, she said, "Well, he looked lonely."

Mary Jo spent the rest of the afternoon there, meeting and talking with people. She told Harold and Clarence that she would be back the day after tomorrow and then drove home, anxious to tell Dick about her day.

"Boy, Dick," she said, "I've got to get right back down there. I'm going back on Thursday. Those people really need a lot of help!" He just sat back and smiled at her.

Mary Jo became a regular volunteer each Tuesday and Thursday while Molly was at Courage Center. She became more excited about her work with Catholic Charities with every day she spent there. She was curious about the people there but regarded them with motherly sensitivity. Trying not to delve too far into any of their lives, she made sure to give personal attention to every person who came in, and they were responding to her. She remembers one day a man she was talking to asked her, "How come you look at me like that?" No one had ever looked him in the eye before. When he was out on the street, people didn't look at him at all, not even the ones who gave him pocket change. "I think sometimes they're payin' so I'll go somewhere else," he said. It absolutely broke Mary Jo's heart to see so much pain in people.

Another man she met there was living at the Fairmont Hotel, a roach-infested dive located downtown not far from Branch II. His name was Elmer Tillet. He was quite old and quite a drinker. After Elmer visited his wife in a nursing home every day, he would hang around at the Branch so that he wouldn't have to be at home alone. The Catholic Charities didn't have funding to give out money to people then, so Mary Jo gave him a couple of dollars out of her own pocket every now and then, whenever she could. Harold and Clarence both thought she was insane by now.

"Every bum in the city's gonna be in here wanting your money if you keep that up," they said. Elmer came into the Branch on the first of the month, and he continued to do so every month to pay back Mary Jo every dime she gave him.

Another volunteer named Charlotte worked at the Branch at the time. She had been there just a little while before Mary Jo started, and primarily she answered the seldom-ringing phone, poured coffee, and drank coffee. Charlotte was a short Native American woman with long wiry black hair who spoke with a lisp. Despite the deep wrinkles in her face that displayed where the world had cut its grooves, Mary Jo sensed that she was a kindred spirit. She and Charlotte would eventually become good friends, but in the beginning Charlotte didn't trust Mary Jo at all. Charlotte didn't like all of her questions and figured she must be after something or that she was completely nuts.

Before Mary Jo started at Catholic Charities, she didn't know what to expect, and she was not prepared for the effect it had on her. The experience felt a lot like the day she met Dick. She identified with these people and felt certain that this work was her destiny. She also knew that she could no longer accomplish everything she had to at home *and* accomplish what she wanted to at Branch II while she was still leaning on the Valium. She had known for some time that she wasn't functioning right, but now after seeing some drastic examples down at the Branch of people coming in, all doped up and addicted and without any means, she knew it was time for her to let go of her crutch.

She poured all of her pills down the toilet and endured weeks of withdrawal. She remembers vivid hallucinations of insects trying to attack her. Her face felt numb, and she was sweating day and night. Dick was with her through all of it. He stayed with her and continually reminded her of how loveable she was. She just kept praying until it was all over.

There was a part of her that had become soured on the medical community in general, for prescribing her so many pills in such high doses in the first place, and for continuing to prescribe them for years after her last C-section surgery. This was part of the reason she never opted for medical help to get off the pills. What she felt was right for her was to rely on God, on Dick, and on herself. She was the one who got herself addicted, and she had a will strong enough to be the one to stop it. She would continue her recovery in her daily communion with God and with regular counsel with her priest. She prays every day to have the strength to leave her childhood grief behind her and for the ability to conduct her life with the grace that God gave her.

Mary Jo's addiction is something she'd like to forget, but there is no question that overcoming the addiction helped make her strong enough to handle what would lie ahead. She became considerably more successful in surviving her own hardships by helping other people through theirs. Forgetting about all the pain would be easier, but she realized that it would always be an important part of her life and part of what makes her who she is. "No one likes to talk about their sad things," she says of her experience. "No one likes uncomfortable and difficult issues, but what kind of world would this be if all we had were rainbows and pleasantry, day in and day out?" As far as Mary Jo is concerned, there would be no meaning in that. There would be no passion there, no real love. There would be no soul in that world.

9

Neighbors from a half a block away could hear random shouting coming from the Newton house any time that Mary Jo and Dick were out on Friday and Saturday nights. *Gimme back my Fudgsicle! Stop punching me! Go clean your room! I'm tellin' Mom and Dad! Get out of my room! Quit hoggin' the bathroom! Can I have some candy? Mom said I could! Mom said for you to clean your room, so quit buggin' me! You brats stop that fighting!*

The Copeland children were beginning to understand what their mom had been going through. Every year, as one sibling got older, one moved out and the next oldest was in charge while babysitting. Being a Copeland teen wasn't easy. They were tormented by the younger siblings with the same reign of terror that they had enjoyed when they were younger.

All of them handled their issues differently. Like all teenagers, their main concern was for space. They wanted their space, and they wanted their privacy, and they wanted it now. Since that was the one thing they would never get while living in the Newton house, Mary Jo and Dick encouraged the older ones to get involved in things outside the house. Go out with friends. Get a job. Join the softball team. Go find your space. For some of them, this came more easily than others.

The family noticed a lot of things changing at home when Mary Jo started volunteering with Catholic Charities. Number one was that Mom was in a much better mood these days. Running the Copeland house was still hard work, but there seemed to be more oomph in her daily routine now. She was smiling again.

Number two was that the children were given more responsibility. Most of the older ones were involved in school sports or had jobs, and everyone was coming and going at different times. No way could Mary Jo cater to everyone's schedules, so she made some changes in the meal planning and buffet line. The new regimen specified dinner at five o'clock. Anyone who wanted to eat after that was pointed in the direction of the microwave.

Along with responsibility came more freedom. Within reason, the older teens were allowed to set their own curfews although there were times when some of them took advantage of this privilege. But it wasn't Mary Jo's style to get angry over things like that. She knew when they were sneaking in at a late hour, but rather than getting upset and waking the whole house, she just let them get the few hours of sleep they had left. If they wanted to suffer through their jobs and paper routes the next day on little or no sleep, that was their problem. They were old enough by then to know better, and Mary Jo let them make their own choices.

While this form of parenting may have been progressive in the 1980s, no one was going to tell a couple with twelve children how to raise their family. No matter what came up, the Copeland's philosophy was to do the best they could to get through each day, keep a clean and orderly house, teach the children what was right, and pray that they took the information with them. It worked for them, and it worked for the children.

Mike summed up his relationship with his parents while growing up. He was in downtown Minneapolis one day after school, waiting for the 5C bus to take him home. Even with as tight as their money was back then, giving the children a good education was more important to Mary Jo and Dick than anything else. They cut every corner and secured educational grants and financial aid in order to send the children to Catholic schools. A few of the older ones attended Benilde-St. Margaret's, and the rest went through Totino-Grace High School. There was no time in the mornings for Dick to drive children to school, so they all learned at an early age to use the public transportation system to get to school and other activities. For most suburban children, going downtown was a special occasion, but the Copeland children traveled through downtown every day on their way to school and were comfortable with it.

One day while Mike was waiting downtown to transfer buses, he noticed a little plastic baggie floating around in the street, being pushed this way and that in the tailwind of passing cars. He had a pretty good idea what was in that bag, and when he picked it up and took a whiff. Yep, he was right. A bag of marijuana.

Before he could decide what to do with it, his bus pulled up. He panicked, shoved the bag in his pocket, got on the bus, and then panicked even more. He thought for sure that the bus driver had seen him pick it up, that he and everybody else on the bus knew he had drugs in his pocket, and that the cops would come and raid the bus at any second.

When he got home, he knew there was no way he could keep the bag there, so he took it to a friend, who gave him $20 for it. The two of them climbed up on the roof of Shingle Creek Elementary School, assuming that was a safe place, and took out a small pipe to sample the goods. It seemed as if they had been up there for days, when suddenly the both of them were caught in the headlights of the park police. *Oh crap! How could they have known we were up here?* Somebody must have seen them and reported them. *Crap, crap!* There was only one way off that roof—by the same ladder they had climbed up, located directly beneath a brightly lit lamppost. They threw the evidence over a shadowed edge of the building, made their way down the ladder, and started strolling casually away, whistling innocently for effect. They didn't get very far. Suddenly, a police car appeared.

The two boys decided that the best course of action was to play dumb. The officer called them over to him. Holding the bag they had just thrown over the edge of the building, he asked them what it was. "What bag? I dunno. I dunno what's in the bag. What bag?" There was still a little bit of pot left in the pipe, and the smell was in their clothes. Mike's heart was pounding as they climbed into the back of that police car. He was hoping maybe they wouldn't be arrested, maybe they were just going to be let off with a warning and then no one would have to find out. *Maybe he'd give them a fake name*, he thought. *Yeah, that was a great idea. They'd never know.* Then the cop's partner looked over the back seat at him and said, "Hey, aren't you one of them Copeland kids?"

When they pulled up in front of the Newton house, Mike was trying to devise an escape route, but one of the cops stayed in the car with them while the other one went up to the house to talk to his parents. It was the longest five minutes of Mike's life. He thought he was having a heart attack. If he didn't have a heart attack, he knew this would be the last five minutes of his life because his dad was going to knock his head off. They finally went in, and the cops left. They weren't being arrested . . . but now there was Mom and Dad.

Without a word, Mike and his friend sat down in the living room with Mary Jo and Dick. Mike felt awful. He didn't want them to look at him.

Mary Jo's tone was calm and unfazed. "Michael, there is a lot of stuff out there that you are going to see, and a lot that you will do. There is even more that you will be offered. There will be drinking and gambling and heavy drugs and sex and violence—you're gonna get approached with everything. I can't say what you will or won't do. I can't be with you every second. Only God is with you every second. I've taught you what is right, and you already know how I will feel about everything you may question in the future, but I want you to know something . . . whatever it is that you do, whatever you get into, I want you to know that I'm still gonna be here. You can always come to me. I don't care what it is."

She continued talking, to both of them now, "You're in an experimental time right now, I know that. All I can do about it is pray that you make responsible decisions. You need to take **responsibility** for this and talk to your own parents," she said to Mike's friend, "but I want you to know, *both* of you, that there is nothing you can't tell me. There is nothing too severe in this world. There is nothing I haven't seen already. I don't want you to ever be afraid of coming to me. Not with anything."

Dick had been sitting silently beside Mary Jo the entire time. Mike thought for sure he was ready to break out his belt. But he didn't. That was all that was said. No long lecture, no yelling, no grounding till he was forty, just a very clear understanding.

"We're going back to bed now," said Mary Jo. "You can go back out if you want. Think about what I've said, but I want you back in this house at a decent hour. Don't wake up your brothers and sisters and don't leave your shoes in the doorway."

The boys went back outside quietly and walked across the street into the park. His friend finally exploded. "*Your Mom and Dad are so COOL!*" He couldn't believe Mary Jo let them go back out.

Would this kind of parenting have worked with other children in other situations? Who knows? It was right for the Copelands. This wasn't the last time Mike ever tangled with trouble, as he reported, but Mary Jo's voice of reason did stay with him and kept him from getting into anything serious. And it is the same voice that stays with those who come to her for help today. Her experience raising all those children on limited means served as her training ground for caring for the community's needy. She simply handles everyone the same way she handled her own children, as if they are her own children.

Meanwhile, back at Catholic Charities, Harold and Clarence were starting to find out that Mary Jo Copeland wasn't exactly the little mouse they had pegged her for. Mary Jo was also starting to find out that she wasn't so invisible in the world after all. For months now she had been going in to volunteer on a regular basis, talking to people, trying to help them out and causing quite a stir at the Branch. Harold and Clarence were right about one thing: The word on the street had spread, and now every bum in the city was coming in to see Mary Jo. She was still giving out money here and there when she could. She didn't have a lot of money either, but she tried to do what she could. Harold and Clarence finally told her to knock that off. "It's against the rules," they said.

"What rules?" Mary Jo asked. "It's my money. What difference does it make to you where I spend it?"

The point Harold and Clarence were missing was that all those people were not just coming in for Mary Jo's money; they were coming in for her attention. She paid attention to them. She talked to them. She listened to them. She genuinely cared about them and what happened to them. For most of them, it had been a long time since they'd had that kind of human interaction and connection. Some of them had never known that kind of love at all, and from her own childhood Mary Jo understood all too well how that felt. No one at Catholic Charities understood her motivations. They didn't know what she had been through or how sensitive that made her to other people's isolation.

Not only were the Branch managers opposed to the money Mary Jo was giving out, but also they didn't like the way she did things. She didn't seem to respect their authority at all. Most other volunteers just came in for the day, did what they were told to do, and then they wouldn't be seen again until Thanksgiving or Christmas. But Mary Jo kept coming back week after week, and they still hadn't been able to figure out what her agenda was. Mary Jo didn't have an agenda, but in fairness, they were right—she *didn't* respect their authority. In all forty years of her life, being told what to do and how to do it never sat too well with Mary Jo. Especially when she didn't agree with the way things were being done, and especially when it seemed there was *nothing* being done.

During one of those legendary Minnesota winters, someone had come in and donated an oversized box of scarves to Branch II. People were coming in from the streets with their fingers so stiff that they couldn't even hold on to a cup of coffee. Mary Jo wanted to give out those scarves right away, but the managers said, "We can't. We're saving them." Their policy was to ration the resources that came in as the managers saw fit. Yet, people were standing there with chunks of snow and ice hanging from their beards. Mary Jo was furious.

"What are you saving them for? A rainy day? They don't need scarves in the rain! It's thirty below outside, and these people are cold!"

"Mary Jo, those scarves were donated. They aren't yours. We're saving them. That's just the way we do things."

Mary Jo never did find out why the scarves were being saved because she went upstairs, collected the scarves, and gave them out herself. Harold was on the phone to the Catholic Charities office within seconds. A meeting was called among Father Boxleitner, who was in charge of all the Branches at the time, Sister Joan and Mary Kay (two other managers), and Mary Jo.

They were concerned about Mary Jo's repeated reluctance to be a "team player." They reminded her that the Branches were set up under a hierarchy and needed to be run that way. The operation of Catholic Charities was dependent on the resources supporting it, a combination of individual donations and several federal and state funding programs. When they explained the bureaucracy and documentation required for nonprofit organizations, Mary Jo didn't know how to relate to any of that information. All she knew was that those people were freezing.

A similar situation happened when a woman came into the Branch to ask for something from the food shelf. "The food shelf closed at three o'clock. You'll have to come back tomorrow," the woman was informed. Mary Jo volunteered to go down to the food shelf herself and get some cans of food together for the lady. "Mary Jo, the food shelf closes at three. That's just the way it is." Mary Jo went downstairs, took two cans of food from the shelf, and gave them to the hungry woman. Another meeting was called.

Not long after that, a girl named Dee was hired as an assistant to the volunteer coordinator in the main office. Her only job seemed to be to document the activities of Mary Jo Copeland. Every time Mary Jo gave out a pair of mittens, there was Dee, giving her a write-up. Every time Mary Jo gave out some money, Dee put it down in her log. Mary Jo started receiving letters instructing her to start following the rules. The intentions behind all these rules might have been good when they were set, but it was clear to Mary Jo that they just weren't working now. The people coming in had needs that weren't being met. The Branch managers kept trying to explain to Mary Jo that wasn't the kind of program they ran, but Mary Jo kept insisting that they needed to.

She finally became so frustrated with the hard time she was getting about using the resources there that she decided to use her own. She drove around collecting donations of needed food items, adding cans of food from her own kitchen. Dick was now working as a food buyer and had a steady supply of sample non-perishables coming in, so Mary Jo collected those too. She kept the stock of food in her trunk, and before she went into work at the Branch, she gave it all out from her car in the parking lot across the street. She also started picking up extra coats and shoes and socks whenever she was out shopping. Dick had been one hundred percent supportive thus far, but that was the point when he started to protest.

"Mary, we're feeding all of our children, and all the neighborhood children, and a good number of Minneapolis' vagrants . . . now we're buying shoes for people we don't even know? We can't spend that kind of money."

"Dick, it's snowing outside, and there's a man downtown who

doesn't have any shoes on his feet." There wasn't any more argument after that.

It didn't take long for the news about Mary Jo's makeshift mobile food shelf to spread. It became known among the needy that whatever the Branch wouldn't do for people, Mary Jo would. The work became even more demanding, her car was constantly stuffed with food and clothes, and more people were surfacing around that little parking lot food bank. Mousey's Bar was just across the alley, and at night all the drunks that were bounced out by the rough-and-tumble doorman would usually come wandering over to see Mary Jo. Dee, the assistant, was documenting all of it, of course. Before long, Mary Jo received another letter, listing all of her discrepancies and stating that if her behavior didn't improve, "we will have to terminate your position."

"Can you believe this, Dick?" Mary Jo said. "What position are they talking about? I'm a volunteer!" This situation had become impossible. But the Branch managers felt exactly the same way about her.

The warning did not deter Mary Jo's exhaustive outreaching to the poor. She loved those people. There was a part in every one of them that she identified with, and she believed that they deserved to be loved and cared for. She noticed that some of them were in need of medical attention, and she would encourage them to get to the hospital, or she would take them there herself. Some of them needed to go to AA, and she would point them in the direction of a meeting and encourage them until they went. A lot of the people coming into the Branch were chronically homeless, but there were also some who just needed emergency assistance. Sometimes the people would finally find a place to live, but they didn't have enough money to pay for a damage deposit. She didn't have that kind of money to give away, but if she had, she would have. She didn't bother asking Harold or Clarence for anything anymore; she knew the Branch would never pass out money for something like that.

This was when Mary Jo really saw what all of those years that she spent cooped up in their little house were for. She had twelve people to raise to be healthy, responsible, loving adults—but aside from that, Mary Jo was in training. When she started volunteering, part of her soul seemed to come bursting out.

She started to believe that what had been going on in that house and throughout her life was God's way of preparing her and giving her the tools she would need. Her difficult childhood had made her self-reliant. All of the yelling, the abuse, the insanity . . . the flowers, the jewelry selling, the dancing . . . the rejection, the sickness, the pain . . . the games, the treats, the laughter . . . the financial drought, the cramped space, the Valium . . . the independence, the twelve smiling faces, and Dick—all of it had been for her to learn with absolute certainty what she was meant to do. It had all been a gift. All of it.

Mary Jo knew it was wrong for people to come close to getting a home and then lose it because they didn't have a couple hundred dollars. One thing she learned while living in the Newton house was how to find and build resources. When you have only one income to stretch over fourteen people, you learn very quickly how to shop on sale, buy in bulk, and ask for help. To find apartment deposit cash for people, she started at the same place to get the financial aid that helped pay for her children's school tuition—her church. She called up not only her own church but also several local churches, asking if she could come to a church service to speak about the needs of the poor. She assured them that she was not coming to ask for money. She just wanted to speak to the congregation about the situation. Her goal was only to sensitize people to the needs of the poor, to remind everyone that the poor were human beings, in need and deserving of love. It worked; they agreed.

When it was time for her to get up in front of everybody, Mary Jo was nervous. She hadn't done anything like that before. Ignoring the butterflies in her stomach, she just got up and spoke from her heart. An electrifying public speaker emerged that day. She captivated her audience at every church she went to, and before she knew it, the checks started coming in. She was getting individual donations as well as volunteers coming in from the congregations she spoke to. She couldn't believe it!

This led her to start thinking about what else she might be able to accomplish. From what she had seen, the only thing any of the transients did consistently was sit around at the Branch all day, drink coffee, and eat stale doughnuts. "They come in every single day," she said to Dick. "There's no reason they shouldn't at least have a good meal while they're there. They don't get any nutrition from coffee and doughnuts." Mary Jo got back on the phone to those churches.

This time around Mary Jo discovered an entirely new skill she never knew she had. She never went to college; she never learned the intricacies of business and marketing, or how to dress up a product to make it more saleable. For her whole life, all Mary Jo had dealt with was what she had and what she needed to get. What she had was a group of malnourished, downtrodden, withered spirits, and what she needed to get was a healthy mix of good home cooking and TLC.

"Hi, my name is Mary Jo Copeland. I'm calling from Catholic Charities Branch II," she said to the churches she called. "I've got a group of guys down here who don't eat anything all day but old doughnuts and cold canned food at night. Can you get together fifty or a hundred sandwiches and maybe some coleslaw and some different fruits and five to seven people to help serve around noontime?"

Those telemarketing operations that were just beginning to boom should have taken a course from Mary Jo Copeland. No blather, no pitch, just what's what. Of course, most of the church secretaries didn't quite know how to respond to that kind of straightforwardness. Sometimes she would be put on hold. Sometimes she would have to leave a message for someone else to deal with her. Sometimes there would be a period of silence after she stopped talking, before they hung up on her. But none of it ever fazed her, and she never gave up. She didn't waste any time on the ones who said no; she just moved right on to the next listing in the phone book. There had to be some folks somewhere in this town who were willing to reach out to the community, and she was going to find them. She called every denomination of every church in the Twin Cities until finally, someone said yes. St. Edward's Church in Bloomington said, "Yes, we'd love to help." On every call she made after that one, she made sure to mention that St. Edward's had signed on. That seemed to be the miracle she needed because soon she had enough volunteers bringing in enough food to provide lunch for an entire week.

When the officials in the Catholic Charities office learned what she was up to, they were impressed with her accomplishments, but they still frowned on her tactics. "This isn't going to work, Mary Jo," they said. They disliked the fact that she had organized this program without going through the "proper channels."

"What do you want me to do, call all those churches back and tell them to forget it?"

Mary Jo had a church coming the following week with enough food for everyone at the Branch and all their friends. Catholic Charities wanted time to assess the situation. They needed to document this and that and authorize and supervise and organize. They just didn't want her to do it. Or rather, they didn't want *just* her doing this. But she never listened to meaningless excuses from any of her children, and she wasn't going to listen to them from these people either. She wasn't going to turn down all those churches after she'd worked so hard to get them in there. She was going ahead with her plans.

"Dick, I know you think I'm being stubborn, but they just won't agree with me!"

"I know, honey."

"I mean, what else can I do? These people need to eat!"

"Yes, honey," Dick smiled warmly. "I know." More than anything else, he was really enjoying watching her blossom.

"What are they gonna do, not let the volunteers in?"

The first day the lunch started, the church group showed up at noon with pans and pans full of hot food. They set it up along a table, and everyone got in line. It was working! Everything was happening exactly as she said it would. The people were so happy, so appreciative. The church volunteers were happy; they felt good being there. Mary Jo was absolutely thrilled. Even the Catholic Charities personnel were impressed . . . that is, until Mary Jo decided to say a prayer.

One of the major funding sources of Catholic Charities was United Way, a government-funded organization, which specified that there was no way to approve a meal prayer while operating on public money. Never mind that everything about the meal operation she was starting was donated privately. If an organization accepts any state or federal funds, there are guidelines against bringing in religion.

"But I'm not telling them how to pray or who to pray to," Mary Jo explained, "I'm just saying a prayer *for* them. These people are having a hard time, and I'm trying to show them that people care about them. I'm just wishing them well and sharing my joy." She was told again, "We can't approve of that. That's just the way it is."

If Mary Jo had been that sweet little goody-goody suburban housewife, maybe she would have backed down at that point. If Mary Jo had been a sweet little housewife, the lunch line program would not have been started in the first place. All she knew for sure was that taking away her right to pray was as offensive as whatever rule Catholic Charities was trying to protect. She wanted to tell them that they might as well take the "Catholic" right out of their charity. But she didn't. Instead, she continued to pray.

Meetings were called; phones were ringing; letters were written. All of this commotion was created because Mary Jo Copeland prayed for some homeless people before she fed them. While Catholic Charities scrambled around, Mary Jo went right on praying and running the lunch line, and for the second time, she made the news. The following article appeared in the *National Catholic Bulletin* on November 24, 1983, written by Mary Hanneman:

> "Where there's hungry people, God said feed
> them and love them," says Mary Jo Copeland, a

crisis counselor and advocate at Catholic Charities' Branch II, in Minneapolis. Last July, Copeland followed her belief and began calling neighborhood churches, asking them to feed the poor at her workplace. The result was the "Lunch Line," a hot meal service similar to the Loaves and Fishes Too free meal program in Minneapolis and St. Paul. Some 23 churches have begun providing and serving or planning to participate in the program, which began last month.

Copeland came up with the idea for the lunch line when she noticed that poor people dropping in at Branch II were relying on coffee and donated donuts for nutrition.

"I realized they can eat like my own family," said the mother of 12. "Many of these people have spent so much time in prisons and hospitals, eating institutionalized food. They need some good home cooking."

Food was the immediate, but not the only reason for the program, she added. "Besides the food, it's important for these parishes to come here for interaction" with guests. "The volunteers treat them like human beings. I see the women from the churches interacting with the 'drop-ins' and I see them so appreciative."

The guests are grateful for the meals, of course, which have included soups, sandwiches, hot dishes and homemade rolls, according to Copeland. Besides gaining a full stomach, however, guests also begin to gain back some of their lost self-esteem.

"If you had given those people five dollars apiece, instead of the meal, it wouldn't have been the same to them," she said. "They feel that, 'I must be important, because these people took all this time to cook me this food.'"

Prior to the Lunch Line, the First Baptist church and the Basilica of St. Mary parish, both in Minneapolis, provided hot soup and sandwiches to drop-in guests two days a week. Both churches now have signed up for the lunch program, and the Branch still operates a food shelf and provides free coffee and donuts.

The free lunches are served [from] 11 a.m.-12:30 p.m. Tuesdays-Fridays; despite the growing participation, not all those days have been spoken for in coming weeks and Copeland is still calling for volunteers.

Until the [center] brings its own kitchen up to code for cooking, the churches have been preparing lunches in their own facilities, then reheating the food at Branch II before serving. Participants are asked to provide enough food for 400–500 guests, and enough volunteers for serving. When possible, some of the food is served at nearby Branch III.

Copeland said she is overjoyed with the quick response from the local churches, and is optimistic that the giving will continue. "God said, 'Give us this day,' and we don't have to worry about much more," she said. "I think he will provide."

10

"Indians don't trust too many people," Charlotte, the volunteer, said to Mary Jo one day, "but I seen you in here now, I seen you givin' so much help to all these people. You don't have to do that. Other people don't do that. I don't know why you do. It's like you give their life back to them—you don't have to do that. I never met no one like that before."

Mary Jo smiled and gave her a hug, and Charlotte sat down and started telling her about her children. Her five-year-old daughter and one-year-old son were living on a Sioux reservation in North Dakota. Her son was only a few months old when she left there, and she hadn't seen them in more than a year. "I wanna see them, I wanna be with them, but I can't make it down there. There's nothing there, there's no way for me to live. My people don't know me. They won't help me. My aunt has my kids down there. They're keepin' 'em there, and I can't see 'em."

Charlotte had been living on the street all this time. She hung around with her friend Al on most days. They did a lot of drinking together. They were homeless together. They watched out for each other. Al spent a lot of time at the Branch too. That was all Mary Jo needed to hear. She made a deal with Charlotte that if she could manage to clean herself up, get sober, stay sober, and get herself into a stable place to live, she would help her to get her children back. Charlotte agreed.

This would not happen overnight. Charlotte struggled for many months straightening up, trying to build a healthy lifestyle. Mary Jo helped her through the maze of social services that qualified her for financial assistance, housing, and medical care. She served as Charlotte's advocate and character witness through her court battle against her family to get custody of her children. Everyone else had given up on Charlotte, but Mary Jo stood by her until she won. A couple of years later when Charlotte slipped from her sobriety, Mary Jo took care of Charlotte's children until she was ready to have them back again. No matter what happened, Charlotte always had a friend in Mary Jo.

In return, Mary Jo not only received the joy of helping a family reunite and progress on their journey, but also she gained the trust of a lot of people. Charlotte was right: Native Americans don't trust many people. But the ones who knew Mary Jo trusted her.

It took a year and a half for Charlotte to come to the conclusion that Mary Jo was for real, and once she did, Mary Jo had one tough street soldier on her side. Coming from the street, Charlotte knew the people on the street, and she started helping Mary Jo communicate with some who never would have trusted her otherwise. She also clued Mary Jo in on which people weren't ready for her help.

Although the success of the lunch line continued to grow, Mary Jo's popularity with the Catholic Charities officials did not. The more she tried to do for people, the more the officials fought her. To Mary Jo, it seemed that the only thing they wanted to accomplish in their organization was to figure out a way to get rid of Mary Jo Copeland. The heart of the problem was that Mary Jo simply had a different philosophy of service than Catholic Charities. Mary Jo wanted to do all she could for the drop-ins, and Catholic Charities wanted to stick to "helping those who help themselves." Mary Jo didn't think there was anything wrong with that philosophy, and when Father Boxleitner first started the Branches, it worked for them just fine. At that time needy people were showing up at churches because they didn't have anywhere else to go, or they didn't know where else to go. The need was for them to have a place to go to find out how to get help. When Mary Jo started working at the Branch, she saw people who needed far more than that. She believed that what they needed was love, and there was nowhere to refer them for that. The policy at the Branch was to refrain from giving "handouts" because it "enables" people. It was clear to Mary Jo that if the drop-ins were as healthy and able as that policy implied, then they wouldn't be there in the first place. What she saw were people who *couldn't* do anything for themselves. They *needed* someone to help them and hold their hand for a while. "You have to take people as they come to you, not as you want them to be," she kept trying to explain to them. Mary Jo's whole experience at Catholic Charities only strengthened her own philosophy: that the souls in this world will continue to flounder until their basic needs are met. They need services that are based on unconditional love, not bureaucracy.

On February 26, 1985, after two-and-a-half years and countless meetings and reprimands, Mary Jo received a very carefully worded, calmly toned letter from Catholic Charities, terminating her volunteer relationship. Her efforts did not follow the policies at Catholic Charities, and her defiant behavior would no longer be tolerated, the letter said. Her philosophy of service, they felt, did not benefit the people there. "Thank you for starting the lunch program," it read, "but your presence at the Branches is no longer permitted."

As shocking as this letter was, Mary Jo did not take it personally or let it stop her from believing that she was doing the right thing. She only gave it the energy and time it took to read the letter, file it, and move on. "They're right, Dick," she said. "I'm only getting in their way—and they've been in mine."

"Uh-oh." Dick had a feeling what she might be planning.

"They've been accusing me of trying to 'run my own show' down there for almost three years. There's no reason for me *not* to start my own place now."

"Now wait a minute, honey," he said. "You're a young woman, and we've still got eight children to take care of at home. You don't need all that responsibility of a whole place to run."

"I'm a *forty-two*-year-old woman, and I've been doing this with more than eight children at home. I can certainly do it now."

"Well, buying food and shoes is one thing . . . we don't have the money for this."

"Dick, there are people out there who need someone to depend on. They need a place to be. They need help. Who else is going to do it?" Again, Dick couldn't argue with that.

Within days, Mary Jo received a call from the Channel 11 news to inform her that she was one of the winners of the 1985 "11 Who Care" Awards for her work at Catholic Charities. There would be a presentation ceremony on April 17, to be broadcast live from the Carlton Celebrity Room. Before the event took place, Channel 11 wanted to get some footage of her at Catholic Charities, interacting with the poor.

"Wow. I guess Catholic Charities will have to lift the ban on Mary Jo Copeland for one afternoon, won't they?" she said to Dick.

"To make nice for a film crew? I'm sure they will." They did.

The night of the awards dinner, the entire Copeland family got dressed up and headed downtown. Until that point, most of the family didn't really know what Mom had been doing all this time. They knew she was out helping people, but they thought it was just something she was doing as a hobby. By the night of the awards dinner, they were starting to realize that this was sort of a big deal. For the Copelands to dress up for anything besides church was a big deal.

Upon arriving at the event, they were all introduced to newscast-
ers Diana Pierce and Paul Majors. Now the kids knew for sure—this
was *really* something! They were meeting celebrities! Wow, Mom!
Above everything else though, what really impressed them was when
Mary Jo went up to accept her award. For the first time, they heard
her speak in public, and they listened while she grabbed the hearts of
everyone there. She didn't waste any time gushing about how great it
was to win an award. She didn't say anything about Catholic Charities kicking her out. She spent her time at the podium talking about
the people who needed help. She shared stories about the poor and
prayed that she would be able to continue finding resources to help
them. She received a standing ovation.

Mary Jo and Dick started searching downtown Minneapolis rental
properties for a home for Mary Jo to start her own outreach program.
A short stretch of Glenwood Avenue came down at an angle from the
bus depot. A liquor store, a Chinese take-out restaurant, a sauna, the
Salvation Army, the Red Roost bar, a transient hotel, and a row of
empty storefronts with apartments above them were on that block.
Seedy, yes, but Mary Jo decided this was where she ought to be. She
wanted to be in the middle of the action. This was just the sort of
neighborhood that needed her help.

Mary Jo and Dick contacted the owner of the building about one
of the vacant spaces. Inside, the property was bigger than it looked; it
was basically just a one-room open space. The good thing about it
was that there was a loft office upstairs, which looked over the rest of
the space, a loading dock in the back, and a large basement with two
bathrooms. It was perfect.

They signed a three-year lease for $36,000, which in 1985 was
more than Dick's annual salary. They had not obtained non-profit status yet, so Dick had to sign a personal guarantee for it. They used
Mary Jo's award money to pay for the first month, and with what was

left over they put a coat of paint on the walls and had the name "Sharing and Caring Hands" painted on the front window. They picked up some used tables and chairs, ordered a phone line, put a couple of plants in the window, got a donated coffee pot, bought a supply of Maxwell House and Styrofoam cups—and Mary Jo was all set.

"All right, honey, there you go," said Dick. "You've got your place. Now what's your plan?"

"I'm going to help people, of course."

Dick paused for a minute and smiled. "Are you telling me that we're in this thing with all this money, all this time, all this liability, and the extent of your plan is 'I'm going to help people'?"

"Yeah . . . I'll just open the doors and see what they need, and I'll help them. What else is there?" Once again, her unwavering faith left him stunned.

Meanwhile, back at Catholic Charities, when the news got out about Mary Jo being "fired," Charlotte and Al started a petition to try to get her back. Every drop-in they talked to signed it. Mary Jo cried when she heard; she was so touched. She filled Charlotte in on her plans for Sharing and Caring Hands, and Charlotte and Al and many of the regular volunteers left the Branch to help Mary Jo get ready to open and continue working with her. On the first day they opened the doors, Mary Jo paused from her mopping to look around and visualize future possibilities for the place, "What do you think, Charlotte? You think this'll really work? You think we'll get some people in here?"

"Mary Jo, soon you're gonna have more bums in here than you know what to do with."

She was right. Within a couple of weeks, all the drop-ins were dropping in on Mary Jo—they just kept coming and coming. She was thrilled.

"Dick, I need more help!"

Not long before she started Sharing and Caring Hands, Mary Jo talked to her longtime friend, Father Bernie Reiser, about what had happened with Catholic Charities and what she wanted to do. With a calm smile, he said, "Mary Jo, if it is God's will for this to be successful, he will find a way for you. But one thing I can tell you . . . there can be no 'resurrection' without a Calvary. Get your resources in order."

She wrote a letter to all of the churches that had helped with the lunch line to tell them what she was doing now, and told them about the tremendous needs of the people that she wanted to help. She also went back out on her rounds to speak at the churches. Again, she didn't ask for money. Her goal was to sensitize people to the needs of the poor. The people she spoke to didn't know anything about her past or her family. They only knew Mary Jo as an advocate for the poor. Only a couple of years earlier, she had been at a point of not being able to leave her own house, and now she had become one of the most influential public speakers in the city. It seemed to have happened overnight, but she had this gift. She'd always had it; she just never had an outlet for it before. Her presence radiated determination and faith and love, no matter where she was or whom she was with. Those were the qualities that got her to a place where other women were not allowed, the podium at the Catholic Church. She met plenty of opposition trying to get there, but she just kept calling until she came across some of the more progressive priests. As more and more people began to know her and her work, she could get in to more and more churches more easily.

Some members of the Catholic community were repeatedly contacting Archbishop John R. Roach in St. Paul on the issue of Mary Jo speaking in churches where "lay people" were not supposed to be speaking. The Archbishop was not very confrontational, so whether or not he agreed with the way she did things, he would neither forbid nor encourage her. Only a handful of Catholic churches were against it, and by then it didn't matter because Mary Jo was also going to the Lutherans, the Methodists, the Presbyterians, the Jews, the Baptists—every religion there was, every church she could find, every church that would listen. And it wasn't just the churches. Mary Jo went to civic groups, school groups, community groups, and businesses. She just kept going out and talking about the poor.

"Every day of my life I am dealing with the homeless, the poor, the broken. Many of these people have reached this place by no fault of their own. They were once someone's baby, someone's son or daughter, just like we all were, and just like our children are . . . " Every weekend Mary Jo was speaking at a new church or community group. She was a captivating speaker wherever she went. She pulled people in. She pulled at people's hearts.

When Mary Jo wasn't out speaking or keeping things on an even keel at home, she was down on Glenwood Avenue, offering her friendship to anyone who wanted it, one face at a time. Her doors were open on Tuesdays, Wednesdays, and Thursdays. On the weekends while Mary Jo and Dick were out on speaking engagements, Therese and Cathy were there with the regular volunteers. Some of the younger Copelands would come in sometimes on their way home from school and on the weekends to help out.

....

Before long, dozens of churches were calling in response to Mary Jo's letters and talks to find out what they could do to help. People walking by on the street were stopping in to volunteer and donate things. Father Bernie stopped by to drop off a washer and dryer for the basement. A refrigerator and some more furniture appeared. Although Mary Jo didn't want to take away from the lunch operation she started at the Branches, she didn't want the people going away at night hungry either. There was only a small, makeshift kitchen, so she started bringing in bologna sandwiches, fruit, rolls, beverages—anything that was quick and easy and that the people could take with them if they wanted to. Mary Jo almost had enough money donated to put in some showers in the basement. Many of the people on the street had gone far too long without having anywhere to bathe. They didn't even have the privacy to change clothes, if they had clean clothes to change into, unless they could find an unlocked gas station bathroom.

There was something extraordinary happening on Glenwood Avenue. A new kind of bridge was being built between the volunteers and the poor. Sharing and Caring Hands was only one of many outreach programs available, but it was the only one that focused on serving dignity, love, and peace. Mary Jo promoted a positive, healing atmosphere among the volunteers and the poor. By her own example, she was demonstrating to other volunteers that it was okay to connect with the less fortunate—not just to provide them with things, but to make a real connection with them. She made a place where it was safe for volunteers to reach out and hold a hand instead of just putting a quarter in a cup. For the first time, other people were starting to experience what Mary Jo had been experiencing this whole time, the incredible feeling they got from making a real difference in someone's life. They could walk into Sharing and Caring Hands and come out realizing the truth about the people there. They weren't bad or lazy or pathetic. If those qualities were evident, they were only on the surface. Underneath they were lonely, they were unfortunate, they had been ignored. The simplest gestures made a stunning difference to them. Mary Jo didn't have a shortage of volunteers anymore because many of them became so addicted to the joy and energy they experienced that they couldn't help coming back for more, week after week.

Little by little, the word about Mary Jo Copeland continued to spread. More articles were published about her and about the people who worked with her and about the people they helped. One day she got a call from Dave Brunswick at Channel 5, who wanted to feature her on *Good Company*, a daily show that focused on the news and happenings in Minnesota. After the show aired, Mary Jo received even more money donations, more clothes, more food, and more volunteers. One woman came in and said she was about to make a donation to another charity, but seeing that show changed her mind. She gave Sharing and Caring Hands more than $2,000. Mary Jo called the contractors to start building the showers downstairs.

June Blanski had gone into Sharing and Caring Hands one day to volunteer with a group from her church. Although they had heard about the good work that Mary Jo was doing, they were all a little nervous about spending the day in such a depressed area of town. They were uncomfortable about what might happen there, and they didn't know what they would be expected to do.

When she first met Mary Jo, June was surprised at how young and full of energy she was. She had heard that Mary Jo had twelve children, and she knew that wasn't easy because she had seven children herself. June was impressed that Mary Jo had the ambition to run a place like this. Her apprehension was erased when her group arrived, and she saw the warm and bustling atmosphere. Piles of donated clothing needed to be sorted and washed. A stock of groceries that had come in was divided into separate bags, and whoever wanted to get in the food line would be given a bag of groceries. While all this work was going on, the volunteers sang and danced along to the music that played on the radio and observed and assisted Mary Jo as she addressed the individual needs of the people there—a bus token, a bandage, a jacket, a hug. June saw how people were drawn to Mary Jo. She radiated the kind of peace that most people look for and work for their whole lives.

June returned to Sharing and Caring Hands on a weekly basis because of Mary Jo and because of the other volunteers she met there— Tom Keene, a warm and gentle man who served as Mary Jo's assistant, Charlotte and Al, Mary Jo's children, and a man named Charles, another one of many that Mary Jo had helped get off the street. Now he dedicated his time to help others to get off the street. While June was there, she would help wherever she was needed—in the food line, sorting clothes, waiting on people, talking to people. Sometimes when people needed medical attention that went beyond changing bandage dressings or applying antiseptics (which they did there), June would take them to the Hennepin County Medical Center.

Another reason June kept going back was for a little alcoholic man everyone knew only as "Zone." He was very shy, very scruffy, and probably the most polite man she had ever met. June thought that he could have been very good-looking once. Even though his teeth were decayed and he didn't take care of himself, there was something amazing in his smile. He was always well mannered, a real gentleman. If anyone became noisy or boisterous or tried to challenge him, he would quietly step aside. He loved coming in and talking with the volunteers. June was one of many friends he made there, and each time he saw her, he would wink at her from across the room—his way of signaling the friendship they shared.

One day when he came in, he winked at her and then handed her something. It was a little shiny piece of shell, like mother-of-pearl, that he had found in a dumpster. There was a little hole in it and he had put a ring on it and made into a key chain. June didn't want to accept it at first, but he kept insisting. "Come on, you take it," he said to her. "It's so pretty. You do so many things for me. Please take it." Tears welled in her eyes as he closed her hand around the gift.

Darliss Wise was another volunteer who had befriended Zone and who became captivated by the energy at Sharing and Caring Hands. She went there one day with a friend from her church, and as many volunteers had before her, she went home so moved by the place that she cried. She was incredibly touched by the way Mary Jo reached out. One of the ways Mary Jo had started caring for people was by soaking and washing their tired feet, following the example of Jesus. She had seen many of the men coming in limping and dragging. She knew it had to be because of the old shoes they wore, and their socks, if they had any, were wet and never washed and encouraged infections on their feet. Mary Jo couldn't stand to see them in such pain. She started convincing them, one by one, to let her take care of them. She would get a pan of warm, soapy water and let them soak awhile, and then gently wash out their sores, and massage an antiseptic ointment over the sores before giving them new socks and shoes to wear.

Darliss cried when she witnessed this act of kindness, seeing the looks of gratitude on the faces of the men. She was one of the first volunteers to get down alongside Mary Jo and start washing feet.

Everyone who came in had special needs and special gifts. One man who had been coming in for months seemed to be more scared and dark and disturbed than anyone Mary Jo had ever seen. He would not let anyone near him. When he came in, he sat in the back of the shop near the back door, all alone. He wore a dirty Navy coat and had a thick, unkempt beard. Long, straggly hair came down from a black stocking cap pulled to the bridge of his nose. He couldn't have weighed more than 120 pounds and looked very ill. He had a backpack that he kept next to him at all times, and he never talked to anyone. When Mary Jo said hello to him, he ignored her. When she asked him what his name was, his eyes would dart in her direction, never directly at her, then he would quickly shift his eyes back to the ground and turn his back to her.

One day Mary Jo's daughter Cathy told her that while she was in back getting a box of food, she saw tears coming down this man's face. He made no sound at all, just tears. Mary Jo went back to where he sat and squatted down right in front him. He was crying. He still would not acknowledge her, but she did catch his eyes.

"I bet your feet hurt in those boots," she said to him. "Will you let me soak them?"

He didn't say yes, and he didn't say no. Mary Jo stood and motioned for him come with her. He picked up his backpack and followed her up into the loft, where she had her office. There wasn't anyone else up there. He sat down and let her take off his big, tattered boots and dirty, worn out, stinking socks. She gasped when she saw his feet. They were worse than anything she'd ever seen. There were bleeding sores, full of pus, covering his whole foot. "Oh, my God," she whispered. She had tears now too.

"I soak them in the river," he muttered, "but they never get any better."

He stayed sitting there, rocking back and forth while Mary Jo went to get a pan of warm, soapy water. She put his terrible feet in the pan and let them soak and gently washed out the sores. From down on her knees, she looked up into his eyes and asked him his name.

He was silent for a long time. Then finally he said, "My name is Brian."

11

Mary Jo soaked and washed and applied antiseptic ointments to Brian's feet every day, two or three times a day.
She gave him a new pair of boots, which he refused to
wear, and every day he got fresh socks. Then she said a prayer for him
and they'd say a rosary together, which he thought was pretty weird.
He had never prayed before. He didn't know why she was taking care
of him like this, but he was too tired to push her away. He just let her
keep soaking his feet and soaking his feet. He thought she was going
to soak his feet right off his legs. It took months of this constant daily
attention for the sores to heal, and Brian would only allow Mary Jo to
do this while he was up in her office, away from all the other people.
He didn't want anyone near him. He didn't want anyone talking to
him. He wouldn't even get in the food line to eat, so Mary Jo brought
food up to him. He usually sat quietly up there by himself. He sometimes fell asleep in his chair.

With Mary Jo down on her knees, soaking his feet every day, little
by little Brian started talking to her. That was how his story unfolded,
just a tiny bit at a time. Mary Jo asked him where he was from and at

first all he told her about was "the hole in the wall," the place under the bridge where he lived with a bunch of guys. He talked to her about some of the guys he knew and some of the places he had been. It took four months for her to find out why he was so tired all the time.

"I can't go to sleep at night anymore," he told her. "Every time I close my eyes, I picture my dad and my brother while they're smashin' my head against the bumper of the car. When I do fall asleep, I keep dreamin' like when I was little, sleepin' in my own blood 'cause I was too beat up to move. I'm layin' there bleedin' with my nose broken and my ribs broken from my brother poundin' on me with a shovel. I'm not even movin' and they'd just keep comin' over and beat me some more."

He rocked forward in his chair, and Mary Jo held him while he cried, "Why me, Mary? Why did they do that to me? What did I ever do?"

Mary Jo listened to him every day. She cried with him every day. When she looked into his eyes, what she saw was herself, a human being who had been tormented and hurt. She thought he must have seen into her heart too. She could think of no other explanation for his responding to her and opening up to her.

Mary Jo and Brian first became friends during the onset of 1987's frigid Minnesota winter. Winters were hard for Mary Jo, knowing that so many people were out in the cold. Brian explained to her how he was able to keep warm in a little box with a little fire.

"Brian, I don't want you living outside anymore. Let me find you some shelter." Brian didn't know how he felt about that. He was wary of shelters. He never went to them because he couldn't stand all those people around while he was trying to sleep. Mary Jo assured him that he would be in his own room, and no one would bother him. He gave in. It was really cold outside, and he knew he wouldn't survive much more of that.

Mary Jo arranged a room for him at the YMCA and got him settled in with his backpack and his few belongings. He lay there that night, tucked under a cozy warm blanket—it had been years since he'd slept in a bed—and he was wide awake. He stared up at the twelve-foot ceiling where a huge light bulb blasted away the darkness. His eyes darted around each of the four walls, waiting, restless. "This feels like a damn jail cell. I can't handle this shit." He stayed there for about two hours. Then he couldn't take it any more. He collected his bedroll and went down into the bushes across the street and slept.

When Mary Jo discovered that his room at the Y wasn't working out, she urged him to stay inside at Sharing and Caring Hands. "You can keep all of your things here if you want," she said, "and you can sleep right up in my office. You like it up there. We'll just make a bed for you next to my desk." He still wasn't too sure. "Besides," she said, "I need someone here at night. There's a lot of characters around, and I need someone to watch the place." That worked. Brian needed a purpose, and now he had one. He collected his things from the Y and made a little space for himself up in Mary Jo's office.

Mary Jo somehow managed to continue making time to reach out to Brian while still meeting the demands of her organization. The activity at Sharing and Caring Hands was growing. Two showering rooms were installed in the basement. So many clothes were donated now that the rest of the basement was piled with stacks of clothing for people to choose from. Mary Jo had no idea how much money her public speaking had been bringing into Catholic Charities until her inspired audiences started sending checks to Sharing and Caring Hands. Not only did she not have trouble making the rent and utility payments for her downtown space from the money donated, but also she was able to buy some new appliances and build a small kitchen in the back. With the lunch line still running at the Catholic Charities Branches, Mary Jo only intended to extend the supply of supplemental meals and food she gave out. She wanted to make sure that people got what they needed. If people came in hungry, she made them sandwiches and gave them items from the food shelf to take with them— no matter what time it was.

She also had enough money to help people get off the street and into apartments. For the career transients who never had a place to sleep, she teamed up with the YMCA to get rooms for them. Dick Webster was the vice president of the Minneapolis YMCA at the time, and Mary Jo convinced him to keep a few rooms reserved for her at a reduced rate. The number of rooms she paid for kept growing as more and more people discovered that it was possible for them at last to get off the street.

Although the support for Sharing and Caring Hands continued to grow, not everyone shared in the enthusiasm for the place. The two men who lived above Mary Jo's little storefront pounded on their floor, repeatedly complaining that their shower was cold because of all the showering going on in the basement. "The hot water is not on," they would shout down the stairwell. "We cannot tolerate this!" Mary Jo just kept doing what she could to placate them. She suggested that they come down and have a cup of coffee while they waited for the hot water to return. Maybe they could help out while they were at it, she hoped. They never came down.

Mary Jo's neighbors across the street were not thrilled about her presence in the neighborhood either. One woman, who worked at the Red Roost Bar, phoned Mary Jo on a regular basis to complain. "One of your bums just threw something in the street over here."

"Well, go pick it up then," was Mary Jo's answer. This was only the beginning of the "not in my back yard" syndrome, which would continue to be Mary Jo's toughest adversary in the years to come. People were assuming that what Mary Jo was doing attracted the "bad element" to the neighborhood. But the people who believed that didn't go in to visit Sharing and Caring Hands. They didn't witness the love that was being doled out or the difference that was being made. All they knew was that ever since Mary Jo's operation moved in, there were shabby-looking characters hanging around. If they had come inside to see for themselves what went on, they would have under- stood that Mary Jo was not attracting these people; they were already there. What she was doing was rounding them up from behind nearby dumpsters and bushes and bridges and giving them a refuge and a measure of hope.

Another adverse reaction she was getting was the same thing she got at Catholic Charities—the implication that she was enabling people to continue their vices and avoid taking responsibility for themselves. She didn't give much of her attention to that controversy either. She didn't have time to worry about what everybody thought; she had feet to wash. She didn't spend energy trying to point out to her adversaries that the people they were so concerned about her "enabling" were the same people that other agencies could do nothing for. If she hadn't been taking care of them, they'd be lying all over the sidewalks, breaking into buildings to stay warm, and stealing food to eat. The people whose opinions mattered to her didn't need convincing. They were already in there with her. She simply concentrated on her strong commitment to do God's work.

As time went on, more and more people began to understand that Mary Jo's philosophy of service wasn't so different, after all. She was helping people help themselves, as other agencies were. She helped people get off the street, sober up, get out of harmful relationships, find a place to live, stay out of the court systems and go on to healthier, more productive lives, as other agencies did. She helped any of those who made the effort to improve themselves. The difference was that Mary Jo also helped people who could not help themselves—the physically, mentally, and emotionally handicapped, who were unhealthy and unemployable. They were the in-betweens. They were the people who could not function in society, those who desperately needed psychiatric care but because they were not a direct danger to themselves or to others, would not be admitted to hospitals by the county. They were the people who were unable to go to work because of long-term illnesses and injuries, but because they were not bleeding to death or in some other life-threatening emergency, could not get the medical care they needed. They had no family to advocate for them. They had suffered years of neglect and abuse and spiritual bankruptcy. Mary Jo was dealing with the poorest of the poor. The city was full of Brian Philbricks who deserved to be loved as much as everyone else, no matter how difficult it was for her to do.

To report exactly how many people Sharing and Caring Hands helped in the 1980s or to what extent is impossible. Mary Jo didn't spend her time documenting how many people went in and out and what their situations were; she just did what she could to help them, one person at a time. There is no way to measure the impact of holding the hand and touching the heart of someone who had barely been acknowledged by another human being in months, if ever. Brian was just one of many people that Mary Jo reached out to and made a connection with. She and other volunteers estimate that there were about 150–200 people a day who came in for help. Some of them were the same people they saw every day; some of them were new faces that they would never see again. All of them, whether this was what they were looking for or not, came to Sharing and Caring Hands and found the individual love and respect and dignity that God intended them to have.

12

Incredibly, Mary Jo, that once-terrified little girl, was now running a full-time show at Sharing and Caring Hands, and still running her full-time show at home. She had heavy responsibilities in the community now, but she tried to make sure her family knew that she was still a mom too. Mondays became Mom-day at the Copeland house during the mid-1980s, one day out of the week when Mary Jo set aside everything else to spend time with her children. Even when she had started volunteering at Catholic Charities, she would try to spend every Monday morning taking the children to Crystal Lake to feed the ducks or to Como Zoo or out to lunch somewhere fun like Bridgeman's or Fuddruckers. On Monday nights she always made a big production of dinner. Everyone committed this one night to being together, so Mary Jo prepared a feast. She wanted Mondays to be special for everybody.

As the '80s moved along, the baby bottles and playpens were put away. Four of the older children moved out, but the Copeland house was now packed with teenagers, preteens and soon-to-be preteens. There was more fighting, shenanigans, and drama than ever. Although

Mary Jo and Dick were both very busy, there wasn't much that got past them. One night Steve managed to sneak out of the house to go TP'ing with his friends. Covering every tree in the yards of rival high school football team members with rolls of toilet paper had become a popular tradition in the suburban Midwest. Usually the TP'ers would go out and get the cheapest toilet paper available to use for this petty vandalism, but not Steve and his friends. Toilet paper was among the long list of things that the Copelands bought in bulk, and there were several cases of Quilted Northern out in the garage, just waiting to be dangled from trees. They discovered that the two-ply Northern hung on to the branches better than any other kind, especially when the morning dew formed. "It really glued it on there," as he put it. They covered one yard with an entire case, then went back for more and did it again until the whole yard looked to be populated with ghostly creatures.

Steve didn't realize until he returned home that he had forgotten his key to the back door. Sneaking back in was really going to be a challenge without that. His bedroom window near the back door was next to where his younger brother Jeff was sleeping in the bunk below his. Steve started tapping on the glass, trying to wake him up. He was tapping and tapping, and finally he saw the curtain on the window pulled aside. It was Mom. Oops.

"Steve? What are you doing out there?"

"Hi, Mom. Uh . . . could you open the door?"

"What are you doing outside?"

"Um, I thought I heard the newspaper truck dropping the papers off," he lied. Mary Jo had no time for this ridiculousness. She needed her sleep.

"I'll get your father," she said, leaving Steve standing outside. There was no escaping punishment after Dad was involved, and Steve learned again that you couldn't get away with much in the Copeland house, no matter how busy Mom and Dad were.

Trips to the doctor did not slow down either. When one of the children came home with chicken pox, they all had chicken pox. Then they all got strep throat at the same time. One day when Steve and Matt were horsing around in the back of the station wagon, Matt jerked back against the rear door, and it flew open, Matt fell out and the car behind them barely missed him. Being more concerned about getting left in the road than being hurt or scared, Matt ran for the back of the wagon and dived in just as Dick realized what happened and hit the brakes. The rear door slammed shut behind Matt, and they continued on their way. They didn't even stop traffic. As accident-prone as the Copelands were, nevertheless they all managed to grow up intact and accounted for.

Even when the injuries were more serious, Mary Jo refused to let her children grow up believing that any handicap or disability could stop them from doing what they wanted. Mark grew into quite an athlete, despite his dislocated hip. Molly came through her early developmental struggle as normal as any other child. And when Steve was diagnosed with a learning disability, Mary Jo and Dick fought to get Steve the extra help he needed at school. Mary Jo's positive attitude and unwavering belief that everything would turn out okay was instilled in all of the children. This was something Dick continued to learn from her too. While he tended to panic in times of home emergencies, she remained calm regardless. One time a neighbor child came pounding on the Copelands' back door, shouting, "Barb's been hit by a car." Dick panicked, but Mary Jo remained calm. "Okay, okay. I'm sure she'll be fine," Mary Jo said. "Just go on up and get her, Dick."

Dick jumped in the car and rushed about a mile up the road to the scene of the accident. Barb had been on her way home from picking up her paycheck from work, riding a moped, and the car had hit her head on. He hadn't seen her coming, the driver of the car said later. Barb was already on her way to the hospital when Dick arrived, but when he saw the condition of her moped, completely mangled underneath the car, he thought there was no way she could have survived that mess. He believed she was dead.

When Dick arrived at the hospital, Barb was in a lot of pain, but immediately she said, "Hey, Dad, where's my paycheck? Did you see it?" When the car hit her, she flew several feet and landed away from the crash, far better than being swept under the car as Dick had feared. She had a broken collar bone and some scrapes and bruises, but she was much more concerned about losing her $87 check. At $2.35 an hour, she had cleaned a lot of hotel rooms for that money.

The only thing that did change for the Copeland family came in 1988, when they moved to a new house. It had taken eighteen years, but they had finally paid off all their debts, and Dick now earned enough to buy a bigger house. They found a two-story, four-bedroom house with a spacious backyard and beautiful garden in Brooklyn Center, a suburb just ten miles northwest of downtown Minneapolis. It was exactly what they'd always wanted. It had two bathrooms—what a luxury! They moved during Barb's senior year of high school, so she and her five younger siblings were the only Copeland children who lived in the new house. Even though all twelve children had been born in rapid succession, the six youngest Copelands felt that they grew up in a completely different generation. Now half as many children were living in twice the house with twice as much money to go around.

Back at Sharing and Caring Hands, Brian was spending his days in Mary Jo's loft office. For several months he watched Mary Jo while she worked. Sometimes they would talk about his life, but mostly he just sat. When he did spend time downstairs with other transients and volunteers, he usually wound up in a fight. He still carried around a lot of anger, and the slightest thing would set him off. Mary Jo was the only person who could calm him down; she was the only one he would tolerate near him.

It was obvious to anyone who saw him that Brian needed psychiatric care, but he was a long way away from accepting that. He couldn't even sit next to somebody, let alone be examined by someone. Mary

Jo did not have training to deal with any psychological disorders, but what she did have was an amazing capacity to love. She knew that Brian was going to need plenty of that before he was ready for anything else.

She began just by listening to him. She encouraged him to talk about his life every day while she washed his feet. Sometimes he would be very open with her, but there were days when he was too upset to have anything to do with anybody, even Mary Jo. Although Brian would respond only to her, Mary Jo listened to more cursing and hateful tirades from Brian than she had heard in her whole life. Under other circumstances she never would have put up with such language, but she knew that there were times that Brian just needed to yell and "get it out." She demonstrated the same patience with him as she had with her own children.

She also continued making gentle suggestions for him to start doing things for her. He refused to do anything for himself. He would not change out of his ratty old clothes; he would not take a shower. But he was responding well when she asked him to do something for her. Just as she had always kept her home, she wanted everything to be clean and orderly at Sharing and Caring Hands.

"Will you look at this floor down here?" she mentioned one night, as she was locking up and saying goodnight to Brian. "I don't have enough time to clean up tonight. Do you think you could sweep the floor for me after I leave?"

Brian had never swept a floor before, and he had become so far removed from reality that he couldn't even think of how to do it. Mary Jo showed him where the brooms were, then demonstrated for him how to collect all the dust and dirt into a little pile and scoop it up in the dustpan. Then she showed him how to mop. And how to empty the garbage. And how to dust the windowsills and take care of the plants. Mary Jo came in to a wonderful surprise the next morning and every morning after that: Brian cleaned up everything. He experienced the joy of doing something for someone else. He liked seeing

Mary Jo's face in the morning, the way she grinned every single time, like she was surprised all over again. He got a kick out of how happy he made her. Although he still thought she must be some kind of fool for having anything to do with him, nothing had ever given him such a feeling before.

Mary Jo received a letter from the police department one day that there was a warrant out for Brian's arrest. Many of the people who came to Sharing and Caring Hands used the address there when filling out the paperwork to obtain identification, Social Security, disability benefits and so on. After years of spending his life invisibly, Brian needed to start establishing some documentation for himself. But when Mary Jo convinced him to go to the city's Department of Social Service, he caused a problem. He became involved in an incident between a security guard and the take-a-number machine. Brian didn't feel like taking a number and waiting in line on that particular day. What he felt like doing was shutting up that arrogant security guard with his fist, but he didn't. He became so frustrated with the guard telling him over and over to take a number (he was still triggered by anyone in uniform) that he decided to take all the numbers and smash the machine on the floor. He was arrested for disturbing the peace and damaging property.

Because he didn't show up for his court date, a warrant was now out for his arrest. Mary Jo tried to convince him to appear in court to get his record cleared.

"I can't go to court," he argued. "There's just no way. I ain't goin'. I can't sit there with all them cops watchin' me, lookin' at me. No way. I'd kill 'em. I won't go!"

"Brian, they have a warrant for your arrest. You have to go."

"There's a warrant for my arrest in probably twenty states. So what? I ain't goin'!"

After a couple of weeks, she convinced him, by promising she would go with him. On the day of his court date, Mary Jo and Tom Keene, the only other volunteer at Sharing and Caring Hands that

Brian did not fight with, drove Brian down to the courthouse. For more than an hour Tom struggled to convince Brian to get out of the car. He battled everything.

When they got to the courtroom, he refused to go in. "Come on, Brian," Mary Jo said. "Do you want to keep running from the police the rest of your life? If you are ever going to be free, you have to go through with this." Still he wouldn't go. It appeared as though his belligerence was winning out this time. Finally, one of the judge's assistants came out and said that the judge wanted to see Mary Jo in her chambers.

"Brian has a very bad history here," said Judge Pamela Alexander. "He drinks, he cannot get along with people, and he cannot relate to people. He is far from functioning as a member of this community, and he could very well be a danger to society. He could be a danger to you, Mary Jo."

The judge felt that the only option was to assign him to a hospital, but Mary Jo knew that having him locked up would destroy him at that point. He would have to be drugged twenty-four hours a day to keep him there.

"Pam," Mary Jo said, "Brian has been with me for a long time now. I've been working really hard with him, and I believe that if you just let me continue to help him . . . I think that what he really needs is for someone to care about him for once in his life."

"Mary Jo, he's wild with the police, he's wild with everybody . . . "

"But if you just let me take care of him . . ." Mary Jo interrupted.

The judge thought for a moment. "Are you telling me that you will take responsibility for him? You want me to release him to you?"

"Yes, if that's what it takes," answered Mary Jo.

Judge Alexander sat silently for a long moment. Finally, she sighed and shook her head in disbelief. "All right, Mary Jo," she said, "You have one year. If he gets in trouble, anything at all, we're going to have to put him away."

Mary Jo spent countless hours that year in the taming of Brian. Although this took longer than a year, that first year was the worst. He was twenty-six years old but still just like a little child. He had to be taught everything, which was both endearing and difficult. She finally got him to wear fresh clothes and start bathing and taking care of himself. She had to teach him to brush his teeth, brush his hair, and put on clean socks and underwear every day. He fought her every step of the way. He swore and yelled at her every day. "Fuck you, Mary Jo! You're not my mother!"

"Brian, stop swearing at me. I don't like it."

"Fuck you."

"I've listened to enough of that. Now be a good boy."

"Fuck you!"

The day she finally convinced him to let go of his ratty, stinky old boots was a major event. She knew that they had been causing his feet to sweat, which was why his sores kept coming back. Just to get tennis shoes on the man was quite an ordeal. He had never worn them in his life.

"These shoes are stupid!" he complained.

"They'll allow your feet to breathe, Brian. They'll be more comfortable for walking."

"They make me look stupid!"

He finally agreed to wear them, but he wanted Mary Jo to save his boots. Crazily, he wanted to bury his boots.

Mary Jo just kept working with him, listening to him, praying with him, feeding him, loving him, day after day. He stayed angry for a long time. He yelled and screamed at everybody. When she would come back from lunch, he'd have been in another fight and hit someone. She can't remember how many volunteers he chased off. Everyone griped about him. Dick started worrying about his wife spending so much time with him, as violent as he was, but Mary Jo never felt in the least bit threatened although Brian was very intense, and she went home exhausted every night. Some days she got sick of him, but she still never gave up. She knew he was a big marshmallow underneath, no matter how much it took to get to the marshmallow part.

The positive things about Brian developed as slowly as the negative ones disappeared, but they kept Mary Jo going with him. He had been eating out of dumpsters for so long that every meal he ate was as exciting as riding a roller coaster for the first time. Everything he tasted was new. Watching him eat was amazing. She wished that everyone could have that experience with meals every day. No one could savor a meal like someone who's tasted nothing but garbage his whole life.

Mary Jo's devotion to Brian constantly amazed the regular volunteers. With so many people to take care of, she could always make time for him. June Blanski saw her not only helping him through his emotional issues, but also sitting and talking and laughing with him. Brian used to sit on the floor of her office and pretend he was driving a car, making shifting sounds, and Mary Jo would giggle and play right along with him. June heard her say to him one day, "I bet you never had anyone to play with when you were little, did you?" She really identified with his needs.

Mary Jo's attention was starting to work. Small but significant changes began taking place in Brian's behavior. He started becoming very attached to Mary Jo—quite likely the first significant bond he had ever allowed himself—and very protective of her. He walked her to her car every night to make sure nothing happened to her. He always demonstrated a great deal of respect for her, even after one of his fits. Now he was offering to carry things for her and help out in any way he could. Finally, the marshmallow part was appearing.

Most of the volunteers knew Brian now and knew how fragile he was, and they all sort of tiptoed around him. He was definitely making progress, but he was still a loose cannon. He was still full of rage inside. He was especially disgruntled with the other street people, who knew it and even egged him on; they all were like children. It was a good thing Mary Jo had so much training at home.

He still had a hard time with his emotions. Just about any emotion to him meant danger, and his instincts were to run, just like an animal would. The path of least resistance was to run, and Brian threatened to leave just about every week. One day Brian was up in the loft when suddenly he started cursing and pacing around. This went on for about five minutes. He grew more and more agitated until he exploded completely.

"That's it! To hell with this place! I'm leavin'! I ain't puttin' up with this shit no more. I'm outta here!" He was upset because he saw a man pulling stuff out of the garbage can outside the back door, and dragging it in through the front door. He started collecting his clothes and belongings in his arms. "Damn fruit loop, draggin' shit all over the floor I just washed. I ain't stayin' here for that!"

"Brian, calm down now," said Mary Jo, trying to stop him from leaving. His clothing kept dropping from the bundle in his arms, making him even madder, "Goddamned underwear everywhere! Fuck it!" Standing in the front doorway, he threw his entire heap into the air and took off down the street, leaving all of his clothes scattered along Hennepin Avenue. Mary Jo was right behind him, gathering his things and calling after him, "Brian wait, come back . . . "

"Fuck off, I'm leavin'! I'm leavin' this place. I'm leavin' this city. I been here too damn long!" he screamed from about twenty feet down the sidewalk. Mary Jo went after him.

"Brian, please come back," she shouted, still following him.

"Fuck off!"

"God doesn't want you to live like this anymore," she called to him, trying to catch up.

"Fuck God!"

"Brian Philbrick!"

Brian continued trucking down the street, weaving in and out of the sea of midday pedestrians, repeatedly looking over his shoulder to check if Mary Jo was still coming, which she was, which made him swear some more. If the neighbors had questioned the sanity in her efforts before, this little scene must certainly have firmed up their assumptions. People were staring at them, moving back off the sidewalk, looking from their cars . . . Oh, look, there goes Mary Jo Copeland, chasing down one of her lunatics.

"Brian, come back!"

"Leave me alone! Stop followin' me!"

"Stop running away!"

"Damn, Mary! Stop followin' me!"

"Stop making me chase you!"

She kept after him all the way to the other end of downtown. Brian ducked over to Nicollet Mall and into the Woolworth's store in the IDS Center. In a few minutes, Mary Jo came in and took a stool next to him at the cafeteria counter. They sat together in silence for few moments, and then Brian said, "I needed some coffee." They talked about the weather for a little while and then headed back to Glenwood Avenue.

Every time Brian had a bad spell or one of his fits, Mary Jo virtually had to start all over again with him. She had to remind him that he was loved; she had to remind him that he had friends and Sharing and Caring Hands; she had to remind him of the relationship they shared with each other, over and over. It eventually took less and less time to get him back, but establishing any stability with him seemed impossible. Yet, Mary Jo would not give up.

After the first year or so of working with Brian, Mary Jo started raising the bar on his progress. She wanted to start trying to get him connected with the world again, outside of Glenwood Avenue. She took him to Bridgeman's restaurant for the first time in his life and taught him how to order from a menu and be polite to a waitress. "People are looking at me!" he kept saying. "No one's looking at you, Brian. They're looking at me. Now, what do you want to eat?"

He had the same paranoia on his first trip to Dayton's department store. Mary Jo tried to keep him focused on the agenda. "Brian, come here and feel this soft sweater." He had never put on brand new clothes before; he didn't know that new-clothes smell. "That guy is eyeballin' me. He thinks I'm stealin'!" he said. Being in a store felt like being put in a circus cage full of tigers to him, under a spotlight with everyone waiting to see what he would do. He just wanted to get out of there and go home.

Working on his anxiousness while he and Mary Jo were out made Brian aware of how comfortable he was at Sharing and Caring Hands. His outbursts while he was there diminished. Although Mary Jo wasn't immediately successful in getting Brian to be at ease with going out in public, these excursions were causing him to develop a sense of home—another first. He continually threatened to leave, but she knew he was starting to feel settled now. He knew he always had a place in Minneapolis.

The usual day at Sharing and Caring Hands now meant visits by two hundred to three hundred people. Most of them would be there for something to eat and some warm clothes. About five to ten new pairs of blistered feet came in each day, needing Mary Jo's care and concern. There was a new trend in teenagers flowing in and out. Some of them were volunteers; some of them were runaways. She gave out bus passes, bandages, rooms at the Y, money for bills, rent deposits, prayers, and hundreds of hugs. Many of the state agencies were starting to refer people to Mary Jo now when there was nothing they could do for them.

Had there ever been anyone in the city that was willing to take these people in, stop their bleeding, and give them the attention necessary to get at the root of their problems? Not like Mary Jo, there hadn't been. The police department was even rounding people up from benches and bridges and bringing them to Sharing and Caring Hands. Mary Jo will never forget the day she met probably the only police officer in the city who was not yet familiar with her work.

On a typical February afternoon in Minnesota, the extreme cold outside made it extremely busy inside Sharing and Caring Hands. A heavyset Native American woman named Elena came bursting into the crowded room, screaming for Mary Jo to help her. Elena had been struggling with a drinking problem and coming to Mary Jo for help for several months. Elena was having one of her bad days; she was drunk. In the same moment, the police officer who had been chasing Elena came rushing in the door, grabbed her, and threw her up against the wall. Mary Jo saw Elena's head smack the wall with a thud. A pause of disbelief struck everyone in that room before they turned their heads toward Mary Jo to see what would happen next.

Mary Jo dropped the foot she was working on, got off her knees, and marched right over to the ruddy-faced officer. Brian, watching from up in the loft, clenched his jaw and gripped the railing, trying to keep himself calm. Charlotte and Al and Tom and the rest of the volunteers and all of the people there were silent.

"Stop being so rough with her," Mary Jo said firmly. The officer ignored her. "You can't treat her like that," Mary Jo insisted.

They exchanged a few words, and soon they were arguing. The officer raised his voice above hers: "You say that again and you'll be arrested next."

"For what?"

"I'm warning you. I will arrest you."

"Go ahead."

The next thing Mary Jo knew she was in handcuffs and being escorted outside. Every jaw hit the floor as they watched Mary Jo Copeland being arrested for sticking up for Elena's rights. For Brian, it took everything he had not to rush over and choke that cop. He managed to remain calm. He took Mary Jo's coat from her office and went out in the below-zero weather to give it to her. When the officer spotted him coming out, he shouted, "Get back inside, scumbag!"

If only Brian had given the coat to someone else to bring out there . . . if only that officer would have just let him give Mary Jo her coat . . . if only he hadn't called him the same thing as the cops who almost beat him to death in California.

Brian completely lost it. He was yelling at the top of his lungs and started taking swings at the cop. Brian was wrestled to the ground, cuffs were slapped on him, and he was stuffed into the back of the squad car with Mary Jo. By this time, everyone on the block was standing out in the street.

"Hold the fort down, Charlotte!" Mary Jo called out as they pulled away. Charlotte rushed inside and called Dick.

Mary Jo would have taken comfort in the fact that she at least had her friend Brian, the seasoned jailbird, with her through this, except that her friend was in the middle of throwing one of his fits on the seat beside her. It wasn't one of his usual fits either. Brian was in a mood that Mary Jo had never seen before. He was banging his head on the Plexiglass in front of him and kicking and screaming and crying. He was trying to break out of the car.

"Brian! Brian, stop it. Stop this." She kept trying to calm him down. He was bleeding from his head and bleeding from his nose, and Mary Jo could do nothing. The officer put on his siren and called for backup. When he drove up to the county psych unit, eight other officers wrestled Brian out of the car.

After they subdued him enough to take him inside, Mary Jo told one of the officers that she was cold—she had never got her coat—and could they please turn the heat on in the car for her.

"Shut up," was the answer she got. She was left out there alone, freezing, while they took Brian inside. The original officer finally came back, got in, shut the door, and started driving.

"Where are you going?" Mary Jo asked as they passed right by the courthouse.

"Never mind."

He kept driving around a three-block square. Mary Jo couldn't understand it. She started thinking about all the stories Brian told her about how the cops beat him so badly. There was no one else in the car but her and that cop, and he apparently had no intentions of taking her to where there were some more cops, and he wasn't saying where they were going. She began to be really scared.

Finally, the policeman pulled up in the back of the courthouse where there was a loading area. No one else was around. Mary Jo was terrified. He came around and opened her door.

"Get out," he said. Mary Jo stayed where she was.

"Get out of the car!" he shouted. She got out and stood up and started reciting the Lord's Prayer. The cop took the cuffs off of her and then put a coat around her shoulders. She stood there puzzled for a moment, still scared, then he took her inside.

Apparently, reporters were swarming the courthouse. The police department was trying to avoid having pictures taken of Mary Jo in handcuffs with no coat, out in the cold.

In the booking room, they fingerprinted her, took her mug shot, and then she sat in jail and waited. A couple of hours later, the Minneapolis Chief of Police got wind of the situation, and the minute he did, Mary Jo's ordeal was over.

Since Police Chief Tony Bouza had spent twenty-four years on the New York City police force before he came to Minneapolis, he had observed enough good and bad in people to recognize this country's dire need for altruism. He acknowledged that the quality of life was better in Minnesota than in many other states—not a lot better, but from what he had seen, it was better.

One of the things that he attributed this to was that there were a lot of good people in Minneapolis, and that there were two extraordinarily good people in Minneapolis. One of them was Joe Selvaggio, a man who had spent the past fifteen years of his life developing Project for Pride and Living (PPL), a nonprofit housing program for low-income people and inner-city neighborhoods. The other one was Mary Jo Copeland, the downtown spitfire who recently had opened up her center of hope for the homeless and the hungry.

Tony Bouza understood the way the world worked, and he knew that when a city was fortunate enough to turn up not just one but two gems like Joe and Mary Jo, it had better take good care of them.

"What the hell do you think you're doing?" Tony said to the officer who arrested Mary Jo. "Do you really think it's a good idea to be arresting an urban saint? What's the matter with you?" The officer had no answer. "Let her go, right now."

The police department had managed to keep the press away from the courthouse, but when Mary Jo arrived back at Sharing and Caring Hands, she was met with television crews and newspaper reporters and an explosion of people cheering. There were a few reporters trying to lead Mary Jo into bashing the police department, but all she said was, "Look, I didn't like the way I was treated, but I'm sure no one who gets arrested likes it very much."

She knew there would be no benefit in pouting about the experience all over the media. Besides, she had already been vindicated. She spent her time at the jail helping two homeless men she met to get their charges dropped and wrangling the Chief of Police into coming down to volunteer one day; this led him to write a recommendation for a grant for Sharing and Caring Hands. It had been a good day. Even Brian's violent episode led to something positive. He was in the psych unit for seventy-two hours, then released under the agreement that he would undergo the continuing psychiatric care that he desperately needed on an outpatient basis.

In the two years since she opened Sharing and Caring Hands, Mary Jo had raised more than $240,000 in cash donations and an estimated amount equal to that in donated time, services, food, and goods. To help people with housing, medical services, utilities, food, transportation, and clothing required an annual budget of more than $120,000. Only a woman who had raised twelve children on a modest income could take care of hundreds of people on $120,000 a year. Like all mothers, she took no salary for herself.

Since her 11 Who Care Award, Mary Jo had received the WCCO Radio Good Neighbor Award, the Minneapolis League of Catholic Women Award, and the Rotary Hope Award for Extraordinary

Leadership. She received a personal letter of praise from Minnesota Governor Rudy Perpich and a letter from President Ronald Reagan, stating "It is always a pleasure to recognize individuals whose generosity and goodwill brighten the lives of others. You have made America a better place in which to live. Thank you for your contributions and God bless you." Police Chief Bouza sent her a thank you letter for her assistance to an officer in keeping an intoxicated suspect from getting the officer's revolver.

Despite being surrounded by despair and poverty each day, Mary Jo was happier than she had ever been. By all accounts, her little storefront endeavor had become quite a success. By June 1987, she had enough money and volunteers lined up to keep the operation running smoothly for a long time. That same month she received notice that the building that Sharing and Caring Hands occupied was going to be demolished to make room to build the Target Center, a $54 million arena to house the state's new pro basketball team. Her outreach program for the homeless was about to be homeless itself.

13

Mary Jo and Dick had to start looking for a new home for Sharing and Caring Hands at the same time that they were getting ready to move their family from the Newton Avenue house. Dick thought that his increase in salary was finally going to make things a little easier, but now their lives were more hectic than ever. Dick wanted to take his usual path-of-least-resistance approach to the situation and go with whatever property they could get the quickest and cheapest, but Mary Jo had very specific ideas about what she wanted. She was insistent on finding some property for sale instead of renting. She wanted to make sure that her center would never be yanked out from under her again.

They started looking into a few different locations around downtown Minneapolis: a little corner drugstore near Branch II, a building off Border Avenue near the Minneapolis Farmers' Market, and the one that Mary Jo really wanted, the old Twin Cities Group Insurance building on 7th Street and 4th Avenue. They contacted the owner of that long-empty building, to see what they could work out.

"Maybe we can get them to donate the building, Dick," she said.

Once again, her fearless optimism made him smile.

A donated building was not in the cards. The price tag was $240,000. The building also would need at least another $140,000 to $160,000 in renovations. To Dick, that was a big fat "no way." Even if he had the salary to support that kind of personal liability, which he certainly did not, he had just signed a purchase agreement for their new home. He knew there was no way they would qualify to borrow that kind of money. But Mary Jo had never let anyone tell her that what she wanted was impossible before—not her husband, not anyone. She believes that everyone is capable of getting what they want; it's just that some things are going to be harder to get. This was one of them.

Dick kept trying to sell her on the building near the Farmers' Market, which was a lot cheaper, but she wouldn't have anything to do with that. "I really think we should look at that Border Avenue building again," he said. "It's a much safer area there."

"No, Dick, we can't go in back there. No one will find us."

"I really think it's a better property, Mary. We won't even have to apply for zoning."

"No, we're not going in there. It's not even on a bus route! How will anyone find me?"

Mary Jo was absolutely sure that the 7th Street property was right for them. It had a parking lot and much more space, which by then she desperately needed. The Glenwood storefront had become too crowded to turn around in. The volunteer church groups that were coming in kept bringing more and more food to give away and serve. Soon a full-fledged lunch line was going every day. The lunch line at Catholic Charities was still running, but the Sharing and Caring Hands volunteers really wanted to serve—and the people really wanted to eat. Mary Jo certainly was not going to deny them that. She understood better than anyone that it was the interaction that occurred between the givers and receivers that everyone wanted.

With the lunch line, the foot soaks, the showering, the clothing, the food shelf, the waiting area, the dining tables, the desks, and the volunteers, Sharing and Caring Hands had run out of room for what the place was there for—the people. For all the new resources coming in, there were twice as many people who needed them. The problems were staggering. There aren't a lot of people who could be surrounded by that level of disparity and hopelessness day after day without eventually concluding that the problem was just too big and without feeling that their good intentions and hard work really weren't doing any good at all.

That was the difference with Mary Jo. No matter how discouraging the conditions, she never gave up. She kept a crystal-clear vision for what she wanted through everything she did. She kept her focus on what was right in front of her. Instead of watching the growing line of people who were waiting to see her, wondering how in the name of Jesus she would ever solve their never-ending problems, she focused her attention only on the person who was in front of her at the time. One face, one blistered foot, one bus token, one coat, one bandage at a time.

The problem in front of her at the moment was space. She needed more space for all of these people. The bottom line for her was fulfilling needs. She and Dick had signed a purchase agreement for the building on 7th Street without even having enough for the down payment. Mary Jo now had the task of raising a sum of money almost twice the total of what she had raised in the past two years. And she had to do it quickly.

While Dick continued looking for alternatives for a backup property, Mary Jo started her phone calling and public speaking campaign again. She was going to need a lot of help. She also decided it was time to start using her public stature more actively. Stories detailing her plight were run in the *Minneapolis Star Tribune, St. Paul Pioneer Press,* and in several community publications and newsletters. Following is an excerpt from a 1987 article by Fran Roth for the *Catholic Bulletin:*

Sharing and Caring Hands, a day shelter serving
the inner-city homeless of Minneapolis, needs a help-

ing hand to stay open. Mary Jo Copeland founded the shelter in 1985 to fill in the gaps in government and agency services and spread Christ's message of dignity for all.

"We must live in dignity and die in dignity. Whether rich or poor, we're all the same. The poor are not numbers or a business. They are hearts and souls," says Copeland. "Every time we open the doors, another Advent happens, another Christ comes in."

But Sharing and Caring Hands will close this fall, if money is not raised to buy and renovate a new building. Copeland said an estimated $400,000 is needed for a new building accessible to the people she serves, and $40,000 is needed immediately for a down payment . . .

The article went on to describe the services and advocacy Sharing and Caring Hands provided, and gave the following examples of people Mary Jo had helped:

Debbie spent six months on the streets because she couldn't produce identification to receive (state or government) aid. Copeland sent $6 to Debbie's home state for a copy of her birth certificate. $6 was all it took.

Three years ago, Kenneth Johnson was released from the hospital after attempting suicide. "I owe Mary Jo my life," said Johnson. "If I had anything to give her, I'd give it to her." Johnson said the hug he received from Copeland was the first hug that came with love.

After 17 years in the Stillwater State Penitentiary and two weeks on the streets, Bob Deckhart decided that he'd "pick up his gun again" if something good didn't happen to him soon. A year and a half later,

Deckhart credits Copeland with his new life.

Sharing and Caring Hands is a family ministry for the Copelands . . . Husband Dick and their children have an active role at the shelter. More importantly, Copeland said, "Dick is my St. Joseph. He takes care of me."

KARE-TV will air the documentary, "No Permanent Address," featuring Sharing and Caring Hands, from 9–10 P.M. this Saturday.

Mary Jo kept going out and speaking every Saturday and every Sunday, and every day that people would listen. She just kept speaking and speaking and praying and praying. In between, she kept her house and her family running (the children reported that they can't remember Mary Jo or Dick ever sitting down during this period), and she kept up business as usual at the Glenwood storefront. A man with a gunshot wound on his shoulder needed his dressing changed, a crate of a thousand pairs of gloves had been delivered, and Brian had been released from the hospital.

Even as traumatized as he was by the experience, Brian had been in need of psychiatric care for quite some time. During his 72-hour hold under supervision, the psychiatrists at the University of Minnesota Hospital were able to obtain a history and perform status exams and an assessment of his condition.

The day they brought him in he was too upset to be assessed by anyone. His admittance record reports that he was "withdrawn, crying, and talking like a petulant child. He was cowering in the corner of the office, crying, and sitting with his arms wrapped around his knees, and he later became frustrated during the interview, making violent gestures and raising his voice with incoherent speech alternating with crying spells."

After being left alone for a period of time, he produced the following statement, printed in pencil, with several sentences erased and rewritten, on the back of a YMCA rules and regulations sheet that he had in his pocket:

My name is Brian and I'm not a mean or bad Person I can never forget but I can try to forgive my father and my brother. My father was an alcoholic and He'd go to the bar room get drunk and come home and beat me up Have you ever: Had your father beat you up Or your Brother beat you up to the point that you would not see another day and really didn't care. They cut my hair in such a strange way that I was embrassed to go to school yet i kind of liked to go to school i guess I felt prety safe. After school I'd go down bye the Ocean and sit by myself becuause none of the other children would come around me becuase they seen me with black eye's and a bunch of bruise's and cut's I know my mother tryed her best to protect me from these to vicsios people. A family counselor came to the house and instead of solving the Problem my father blamed it on me becuase it was an easy way to deal with the problem   I was the only one in the family with blonde hair and they would tell me that i was not part of the family beccuase of this reason   I did not feel accepted becuase this is the reson I'd run away from home I will admit I have a lot of problems but i don't think I can deal with them I could go back and get revege but that would be wrong. I wake up all hours at night with bad dreams   Jan 7 was 10 year's from my 18 birthday for ten year's I've had this bottled up insid of me

Upon Brian's release, the following statements were issued in his outpatient evaluation summary:

. . . Because of his anxiety, for the past fifteen years Brian has been attempting to isolate himself from other people and from violence. He often feels a lump in his throat, palpitations, and "knots" in his stomach. He also notes tremors in his hands and lower extremities. He denies any sense of impending doom or feeling of going crazy that is often seen in panic attacks. Brian becomes anxious when he is around people, particularly crowds, or exposed to violence. He is particularly uncomfortable around police or security guards because his father was a uniformed security guard. He often avoids people for days because of his anxiety, but there are no delusional fears that I can identify. His only other stated fear is one of heights; he will not go above fifty feet.

Brian describes nightmares occurring from three times per week to one every other week. These nightmares usually involve beatings by his father or brother. During the day, Brian sometimes feels that he is reliving these traumatic experiences. During these times Brian can hear the voices of his father or brother telling him that he will be beaten. Sometimes the voices have a deprecatory content, but they occur only during a flashback. There are no command hallucinations. During one flashback he saw a vision of his father. When Brian sees police officers or security guards, he becomes quite anxious and it sometimes triggers a flashback. The same consequences have occurred when he sees violence on TV or in actual life.

Brian has felt sad and lonely all his life. He says the longest he has been happy is three to four hours at a time. He describes occasional crying spells and minimal interest or enjoyment. He engages in self-injurious behavior by hitting his head against a wall sometimes when he is angry. Once he lost consciousness

for perhaps 30 to 45 minutes because of the head banging. He says he hits his head because it keeps him from
acting on his rage and hurting someone else . . . ."

Brian's final assessment determined that he was "severely dysfunctional and socially withdrawn due to post-traumatic stress disor-
der with major depressive episodes and recurrent dysthymia, a less
severe form of depression." It also described severe muscle tension,
headaches, and severe flashbacks indicating paranoid schizophrenia.
The recommendation was for a trial period on antidepressants as well
as psychotherapy and group therapy to focus on the issues of abandon-
ment and rejection, although he probably would not tolerate group
therapy at that time.

Brian's medical reports were submitted to the Hennepin County
District Court, along with an affidavit stating that "in the interest of
justice, we respectfully move for a dismissal by the State of the charges
against Mr. Philbrick, the charges being disorderly conduct arising
from an incident occurring at Sharing and Caring Hands, a shelter for
the homeless in Minneapolis . . . in the result of an altercation there
were four arrests made, Brian Philbrick being one of the four. The
other three arrested were charged also with disorderly conduct, each
of those cases were dismissed by the City of Minneapolis on their
own Motion after consulting with the Police Department . . . Brian's
mental condition of 'severe paranoid schizophrenia' together with his
history of being abused as a child caused him to imagine that the
police were unjustifiably beating him and the others, similar to when
he received beatings as a child. His continued state of depression,
nightmares, and flashbacks are interrelated with the events which took
place on the day he was arrested and together with the medical information supplied, constitute grounds upon which a dismissal in this
case would be justified."

The judge approved the affidavit, and Brian's charges were
dropped. Even better news was that the severity of his medical assessment determined that his impairment met requirements to qualify

him for federal Supplemental Security Income. His monthly checks were made out in care of Sharing and Caring Hands, and just as she did for many others, Mary Jo kept an account for him, doling it out to budget for the things he needed. She also decided that Brian should have a place to live—a low-income apartment building in downtown Minneapolis called the Parkview. Brian was finally in his first apartment. He was twenty-eight years old.

Several months would pass, however, before Mary Jo was able to get Brian to see a therapist and several years before he would agree to take any kind of medication for his condition. Breaking through all his years of isolation and rage never got any easier. All she could do was go on loving him, day after day, and continue to encourage him to make little steps toward independence.

In doing this, the significance really wasn't just about Mary Jo helping to heal Brian; he was healing her too. People who witnessed her incredible patience and tenderness with him did not realize that his progress was a mirror for her own, in a way. Aiding him in his independence and sense of self was reinforcing everything she'd had to learn for herself. It strengthened her own confidence in who she was. Brian would always be a significant part of her life . . . no matter how difficult he was.

The day she took Brian for his driver's test prompted a considerable ordeal. He came out of the exam station after he failed and totally lost control in the parking lot. He kept swearing and yelling as Mary Jo kept trying to comfort him. "It's okay, Brian. I know how you feel. I went through the same thing when I took my test. It'll be okay. You just have to take the test again." He had his failed test in his hand and just kept swearing at it and threw it on the floor of the car.

"You're not supposed to throw it away. You have to keep it for next time," said Mary Jo. He ripped his test in half and threw it out the window. A few seconds later, there was Mary Jo, running out in the middle of the testing grounds, chasing down the torn pages that were being tossed around in the wind. A woman's voice shot out from the loudspeaker, "Ma'am, you're in the driving lane! No one's allowed in that area. You must vacate at once!"

Since she couldn't catch his test, they had to go back to get a duplicate made. Brian was upset and kept swearing and rolling his eyes. He was disgusted that he had to do this. He already knew how to drive, and he didn't see any need for a little plastic card to prove it.

Mary Jo thought he had calmed down when she got him back in the car to go home, but he got himself all worked up again, threw a tantrum, and started banging his head. She realized that this was one of those times that he just needed to scream and yell, so she pulled over on the side of the highway and let him out to throw his fit. There was Brian, pacing back and forth on the shoulder of the road, ranting and shaking his fists in the air. Mary Jo didn't know how long this was going to go on, but she waited patiently until he was finished. On the way home she reiterated a talk that she had already given him many times. She knew that eventually it would sink in.

"Brian, you've got to get off of the past," she said. "You keep getting yourself worked up about it, about people's looks, about people's attitudes, and it destroys your present. It destroys your future. You can't live in the past—you can't keep going over it. It's only going to continue to eat you up, and you'll stay completely self-absorbed in 'I'm this way because of this, and my dad did this to me and my mother never loved me.' You know what, Brian? I don't care about that. I can't do anything about what was done to you. You can't do anything about what was done to you. What I care about is what you're going to do about it now. What are you going to do with today? Everyone is affected by what's gone on in their lives—you're just like everybody else in that. Every environment in the world affects us, even the ones we don't know about. Where we work affects us. Who we are affects us. Everything. What's important is what we do with what we're in—whatever that is—a home, a workplace, a relationship. I understand how powerless you feel, Brian. I lived that way for a long time too. Getting control over it is simpler than you think. You just need to learn to make choices about how you're going to react. You always have a choice—you just have to decide to make it."

Eventually, Mary Jo got Brian to see a psychologist, Peter Demick, a trauma specialist at a local clinic. On the day of his appointment, he refused to leave his apartment. Mary Jo rescheduled the appointment, and on that day he went but he refused to go into the office. The next time he went in, but he wouldn't talk about anything; he spent the whole hour sitting in a chair. Anyone else probably would have deemed the situation hopeless, but Mary Jo credited every ounce of progress he made, even if he would only leave his apartment.

When he finally did start talking, Mary Jo was there with him for the first few sessions as he told his stories about riding the rails and about his family. She remembers Peter telling her how hard it was to listen to. "You almost get lost in it," he told her. It was hard for Mary Jo to listen to him go on too; the abuse was just so deep. Brian was so lost mentally when he talked. One time he got so wild while he was talking that he wanted to grab Peter. Mary Jo took Brian's hand and calmed him down.

After a while, Brian was able to be in there by himself while Mary Jo waited outside the office. The more he talked, the more the hurt got out of him. Mary Jo told him "it's like coughing when you have the flu . . . it's awful what comes up, but you just have to get the infection out of you." Through all of it, Brian was starting to learn that he had to help himself. That was the hardest lesson there was, and just like everything else, he fought it fiercely. Mary Jo still did not give up; she just kept reminding him over and over what was important.

"How many times can I tell you the same thing, Brian? I can tell ten different people the same thing ten different ways, but the bottom line is that it isn't going to be any different to them or to you. It isn't going to be any help to you until you choose it to be. There comes a point with everyone—and I've seen it a thousand times now with the people that come in—it's time to take off the BAND-AID. I will hold your hand and lend sympathy for as long as you need it, but you are done needing that now. It's time to throw out whoever you are using as a crutch, as your reason, your excuse, your blame, and just deal with it. That's the only way to get past it. You are the only one responsible for you, so take today and go. You have to walk. You have to move on. You have to live. You have to live until you are done. You are the only one who can determine how you are going to live while you are here. Everyone is here for a purpose. You have to get past this before you can figure out what that is. You will continue to suffer until you take control. There is a certain amount of time people need to take to figure this out and work it out, but eventually you will get to that point—and that point is different for everyone, Brian— where it's time to take action. I love you, and I will be here for you when you're ready. I will always be here."

....

Brian wasn't the only one doing the moving on. One day, two of the most unlikely people she'd ever seen popped in at Sharing and Caring Hands, and Mary Jo had the feeling that all her praying might be about to pay off.

As described in an article by Robert Franklin that appeared in the *Minneapolis Star Tribune* on December 26, 1987:

"It was an odd scene—an heiress in a floor-length black coat and a tall man in a business suit standing amidst people in jeans and parkas, some carrying all of their belongings in plastic garbage bags."

The article described Mary Jo's storefront charity as she guided the visitors through the crowd of homeless up to her office, talked to them about the shelter's needs, prayed with them, and then, as she does with everyone who comes through her doors, hugged them.

"The unannounced visitors were Virginia Binger, heiress to a 3M Company fortune, and Russell Ewald, an Episcopal minister and former Minneapolis jail chaplain," the article went on. "They are respectively president and vice president of Minnesota's largest giving organization, the $745 million McKnight Foundation, and their recent visit was typical of one way they like to do business."

Mary Jo remembers talking to Virginia and Russell about the desperate circumstances and great needs of the people she helps. If she was forced to shut her doors, many of those people would lose their only hope. Mary Jo told Virginia and Russell that she still needed to come up with a $40,000 down payment on the new building. The McKnight Foundation granted her the $40,000, plus an extra $100,000 to ensure that her good work would continue. It had been a good day.

Then-Texas governor George Bush visits Sharing and Caring Hands in 1999.
© 2002 *St. Paul Pioneer Press.* Reprinted with permission.

Mary Jo with Grandma Nellie
Copeland family photo

Mary Jo on dance recital day
Copeland family photo

Gert and John, Mary Jo's mother and brother
Copeland family photo

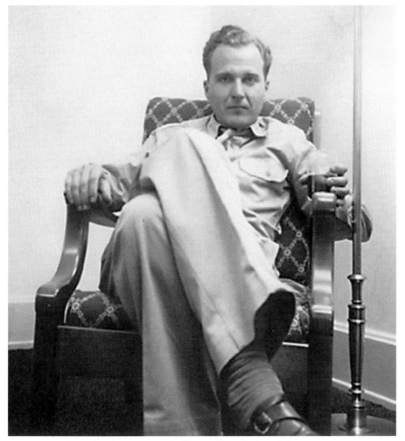

Mary Jo's father, Woody Holtby
Copeland family photo

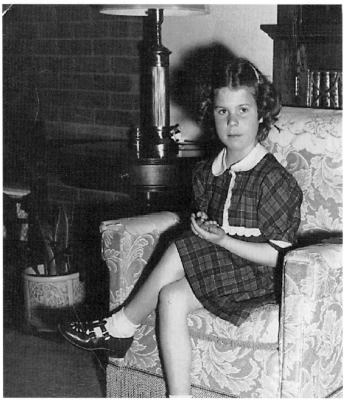

Mary Jo at age 6, trying to be perfect
Copeland family photo

Mary Jo and Dick Copeland at senior prom
Copeland family photo

Mary Jo and Dick's wedding day, 1961.
Copeland family photo

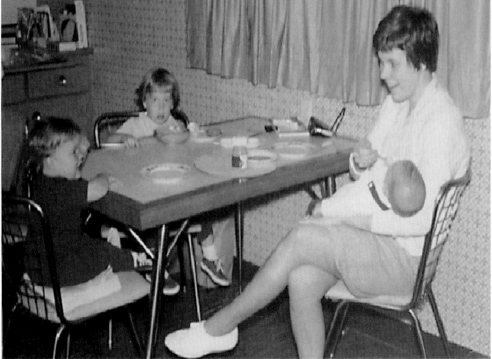

Mary Jo at Nicollet Court apartment with Therese, Andrea, and Mike
Copeland family photo

The Copeland Family, 1980

Standing, from left, Mike; Barb, parents Mary Jo and Dick; Mark, Therese, Cathy, Jenny, and Mary. Kneeling, from left: Jeff, James, Matt, Steve, and Molly.
© 2002 *Minneapolis Star Tribune.* Reprinted with permission.

Sharing & Caring Hands on Glenwood Avenue 1985
Copeland family photo

Mary Jo serves love with her meals.
©*Minneapolis Star Tribune 2002*. Reprinted with permission.

Every day Mary Jo washes the swollen, blistered feet of the poor.
Copeland family photo

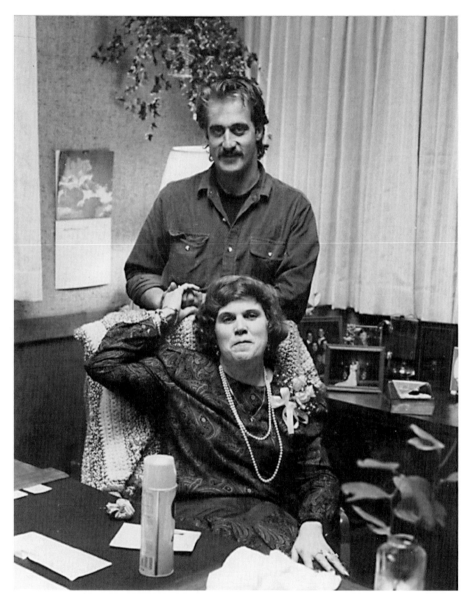

Mary Jo with Brian Philbrick
Copeland family photo

Senate candidate Paul Wellstone and Senator Rudy Boschwitz visit Sharing and Caring Hands at meal time.
©2002 *Minneapolis Star Tribune*. Reprinted with permission.

Mary's Place, a transitional housing shelter.
Copeland family photo

Mary Jo celebrates with her children on opening day of Mary's Place.
© 2002 *Minneapolis Star Tribune*. Reprinted with permission.

Minneapolis Vikings cheerleaders volunteer at Mary's Place annual Halloween party.

Copeland family photo

Girls' Choir in rehearsal at Mary's Place.
Author photo

Robbie Wills (center) supervises the Teen Center at Mary's Place.
Author photo

Mary Jo Copeland received the Presidential Citizens Medal at the White House on February 15, 2013.

(from left) Great Love author Michelle Peterson Hinck,
Father Cory Rolfing, President Obama, Mary Jo
Copeland, Dick Copeland, daughter Barb Copeland.

(Courtesy Official White House Photo Office)

14

Jeff Copeland came home from camp one day in the summer of 1988 to a FOR SALE sign in the front yard. "Whad'ya mean for sale? We can't move! I've lived here all my life!" he complained to his parents. He was more in shock than upset. The Copelands just weren't the kind of family that moved; they stayed put. The Newton house was home. But no one complained after they saw the new house. They were ecstatic when they found out that they each would have to share a room with only one sibling.

The transition didn't go as smoothly as planned. The closing on their new home in Brooklyn Park was contingent upon the sale of the Newton home, and just before the closing, just before the Copelands' scheduled moving date, their buyers found out that their financing didn't go through. There were the Copelands with the house packed and ready to go, and all they could do was wait.

Regrettably, they had to sell the Newton house back to the real estate dealers at much less than what they would have been able to get from a buyer. They didn't have any choice; they had to move quickly in order to get into the new home.

Years earlier, Mary Jo and Dick had established the house rule that once the children turned eighteen, they were on their own. The parents gave each one a few months' leeway and made exceptions for those who were in college, but other than that, age eighteen meant moving out of the house.

Most of them were happy to abide by the rule and get out of the Copeland sardine can, but there were a couple of reluctant ones. At the time they moved out of the Newton Avenue house, Mark was nineteen and needed a nudge out of the nest. He was in a situation similar to Mike's: He had a full-time job and spent the rest of his time at The Gym, Jesse Ventura's gym. Jesse wasn't involved heavily in politics yet; he was just "Jesse the Body" back then. He ran the gym where all the mammoth guys worked out, so of course, that's where the Copeland boys wanted to be. They worked out with Hawk and Animal, the Road Warriors, Rick Rude, and a lot of the big wrestlers. If Jesse had told anyone back then that he would run for governor one day, he probably would have been laughed right off of his own equipment. Mike and Mark remember that Jesse usually made an appearance every day, yelling out, "Hey, Copeland, where's your membership fee? Ya owe me thirty bucks!" as his way of saying hello.

Mary Jo and Dick made it clear to Mark that if he wanted to continue working and being a gym-head, that was fine, but he was going to have to do it somewhere else. "We're moving at the end of the month," they said, "and you're not coming with us. You're too old to be living with all these children. Go find an apartment."

They packed everything—all the beds, the furniture, the curtains, and Barb, seventeen, Steve, sixteen, Jimmy, fifteen, Jeff, thirteen, Matt, eleven, and Molly, ten. They left Mark in the Newton house with his bed, some food in the refrigerator, and thirty days before the realtors took ownership.

Brian Philbrick was the next one to move. He had not been in his apartment even a year, and he was unhappy the whole time. He had never had to deal with neighbors before, or caretakers, or spend nearly all of his disability income to live in a nasty little apartment. He thought whoever lived there before must have been an absolute pig. There was garbage left in the kitchen, urine odor in the carpet, and tobacco stains covering the walls. He was supposed to be getting a better apartment in the building, but when he got there, this was the only one available, take it or leave it. Mary Jo convinced him to take it, and they would clean it up. There just weren't any other choices for the poor. In better areas there were much better apartments at less rent. But someone like Brian needn't bother to apply; there were always more desirable applicants to choose from.

The manager of the place refused to pay for anything to be cleaned. Brian asked the caretaker if he could at least have some paint to paint the walls himself. When he went through that paint and asked for another gallon, the caretaker said, "No, you should have added water to the first gallon."

The caretaker had it in for him after that, and whenever Brian called for a repair, it went unfixed. When he called to complain about repeatedly coming home and finding used condoms in the hallway outside his neighbor's door, nothing was done.

One day when he came home, the police were waiting there to arrest him. Apparently, the caretaker had received a threatening phone call, and he pointed the finger at Brian. Even though Brian told the police that he had been working at the shelter, that he hadn't even been home, they arrested him anyway. That didn't even faze him anymore. "That's real original, havin' Brian Philbrick arrested," he said. "Whoop-de-doo."

When Mary Jo came down to bail him out, she asked him, "Did you call and threaten this guy, Brian?" He answered no, he didn't do it.

"Are you lying to me? Don't you lie to me, Brian."

"Mary, I didn't do this."

She was the first person who ever believed him about anything. She bailed him out and later got the charges dropped. She got him out of that place and into a better apartment in Brooklyn Center near their new house.

Mary Jo worked feverishly through the rest of the winter and into spring, trying to raise enough money for the renovations on the new building. Demolition of the Glenwood block was beginning in May, and they had to be out by April.

As Mary Jo continued speaking in churches and organizations, money began trickling in, but many prominent business and community groups she was talking to were skeptical of the kinds of numbers she was dealing in now. She had a hard time convincing them that she would be able to handle running an operation that was three times the scope of what she had run in the past. Prospective donors praised the work she was doing, but many of them felt this new plan was too big. And she didn't have a specific plan to give them. She didn't have charts to show them. All she knew was that the need was there and she intended to fill it. She never had a manual on raising a child, and she certainly did not have one for mothering twelve of them—she just did it. She took the same approach at Sharing and Caring Hands. For instance, she wasn't trained in the procedure for taking care of people's feet. It just occurred to her to do it, and so she did.

Whether they were churchgoing folks or not, there weren't many people who had the level of faith that Mary Jo Copeland did. Answering the question, "How will you ensure that this venture will be successful?" with, "If God wants it to be, then it will be" made people smile and nod in understanding, but that wasn't always enough to get their pens moving across their checkbooks. She had become a powerful speaker, but she had an extremely big chunk of money to raise and not much time left. The fate of her venture, and of all those people, was uncertain.

That's when she realized that the trick seemed to be getting people to come down to her storefront to see for themselves. For as much punch as her words carried, seeing her and others in action had time and again touched people as nothing else could. She spoke directly to people's hearts, but her actions jumpstarted their spirits. Everyone who had ever walked into Sharing and Caring Hands felt the spark.

Ginny Binger and Russ Ewald felt it. After their story hit the papers, that wonderful phenomenon of one person's giving spurring others to give kicked in. Piles and piles of checks came rolling in every day—individual donations of $200, $300, and $500 were coming in. Then, unbelievably, they started seeing checks for $2,000, $5,000, and even $10,000. General Mills and other foundations donated $50,000. A little girl sent in two dollar bills, her entire allowance. A man Mary Jo had helped off the street and into a place to live and a job came back in to give her what he could.

When it was time to leave Glenwood, Mary Jo had raised more than $200,000. That was in addition to the $140,000 McKnight award.

15

By the time the Christmas season was over, Mary Jo had raised enough money to buy the 7th Street building outright and pay the contractors in full for the renovations . . . and the checks still continued to come in. The Copelands gutted the building of its left-behind furnishings and old cubicles, knocked out existing walls and offices, and rebuilt to suit their needs.

The clothing operation remained downstairs and meal operations upstairs, as at Glenwood, but the new space was laid out to provide much more room. The kitchen was a full kitchen, not a few appliances and tables stuffed into a corner. Oversized refrigerators and freezers were purchased to store all the food that came in. Floor-to-ceiling shelves were built along an entire wall for the free clothing room. Food shelves were set up in a separate room. The dining room was packed with long cafeteria tables and chairs so that people would finally have enough space to sit and eat. A separate shoe closet stored boxes of new shoes, stacked up to the ceiling. Showers were installed, plus an office for Mary Jo and two more desks for administrative volunteers.

When the news first broke that the Target Center arena would force them to move from Glenwood, everyone at Sharing and Caring Hands panicked about what would become of them. But even though Mary Jo didn't know herself where they would go, she kept repeating to everyone, "You don't have to worry. Whenever God closes a door, it's because he's about to open a window." Mary Jo Copeland's little nonprofit venture now had $450,000 in equity.

There was a two-month gap between the time that Mary Jo had to close down Glenwood and when construction was finished and the new location was ready to open. Mary Jo and numerous volunteers worked diligently to keep to a minimum the time that the street people had to rely on other food shelves and shelters. Many of them left town when Glenwood closed. Mary Jo tried to get the word out about the new location before closing, but she still worried that some people wouldn't know where to go for help.

"Don't you remember, Mary Jo?" Charlotte told her. "You worried about the same thing the last time and look what happened. They'll find you."

And find her they did. On opening day the new Sharing and Caring Hands was packed wall to wall with people. The regular volunteers as well as the regular street people came back. The excitement that day was overwhelming as quite an assortment of characters reunited. Zone, the gentle alcoholic that volunteers June and Darliss had befriended, came in with his familiar wink and handmade gifts. A schizophrenic man named Donny came in, angry as always. He staked a claim to a chair in the corner, deposited his smelly bag on the floor, then scowled and barked at everyone who stood too close him, holding his hand up to shield himself from them. The cross-dressing man was back. No one knew what his name was, only that he had been so traumatized by his twin sister's death years ago that he had taken on her personality. There were scores of people who needed something to eat, something to wear, somewhere to rest, someone to hug them, and a large roomful of some very ripe folks who really needed a shower.

Along with the regulars, there were twice as many new faces as they had ever seen before. They were coming from other cities, from prison, from off the railroad, and from the suburbs. The word was out about Mary Jo Copeland's place, and people in need just kept coming.

Those who came in were all the same, no matter where they were from. They all had different stories and special needs, but their hearts were all the same. They all needed love and kindness. Every once in a while Mary Jo would come across someone in the crowd who didn't seem to belong there. These were people whose capabilities were intact for the most part, but for one reason or another, their lives had been lacking meaningful connections just as much as anyone else there. Many times, these people didn't even know why they were there. They hadn't come in with any specific needs. Just like most of the volunteers, donors, and street people, they simply found themselves drawn to the place.

Antonio Carnelli was one of those people. Having just returned from his hometown in Brooklyn, New York, when Mary Jo opened her new location, he decided to go over there to see what she had going. He didn't have a permanent home, but he never told anyone that. He had been going back and forth between Brooklyn and Minneapolis since 1980 and had known of Mary Jo since she began her work at Catholic Charities although he'd never met her. His friend suggested that they go in and get a cup of coffee one day before he left for New York, but he refused. Shelters or soup kitchens were depressing, he thought. But now for some reason, his curiosity got the better of him, and he felt compelled to "go see Mary Jo."

The first time he met her he realized what all the fuss was about. She had built up this place for the bums—and a really nice place at that, not grimy or depressing—and she had this big crowd of people to take care of, but, amazingly, she came right over to Antonio and asked why he was limping. No one ever asked Antonio how he was doing or how he felt. That just wasn't the way things worked in his world. Antonio was the neighborhood bulldog. No one tangled with him, and no one had ever worried about him before. He was six-feet-two with a solid, broad build and a dark, thick mustache, and he always wore dark sunglasses. He was the rough-and-tumble doorman who had bounced all of Mary Jo's drunks from Mousey's Bar across the street from Catholic Charities Branch II. That was his job before he left for New York.

"You know, I used to see you in that parking lot at Catholic Charities, passin' out hats and gloves and food from your car," Antonio told her.

"You did?"

"Yeah. I seen you out there every night, snow blowin' in your face. It was freezing out, and you're smilin' away, passing stuff out and huggin' everyone."

Mary Jo laughed. Back then was when she discovered the joy of helping the poor.

"Every night I was out in the back, kickin' someone out of the bar, and there you were, takin' them right in. I couldn't believe what I was seein'. I was supposed to be workin', but I stood there freezin' my buns off watchin' you, thinkin' who is this nut? I never seen nothin' like that before."

They continued talking, and before he knew it, Mary Jo was soaking his feet and washing out the bleeding ulcer that had opened up on his leg. "Well, this explains your limp," Mary Jo said when she found it. The blood circulation to his legs had all but stopped over the years, and Antonio was not very fond of doctors. He had never had his sores checked out. The condition was not helped any by his daily convention with his good friend Johnny Walker Red.

Although he hadn't come in asking for anything, Mary Jo knew he needed help and not just with his leg. This was the special talent she had. She looked right past people's dirty clothes, their addictions, their anger, their deceptions, and she only saw their hearts. What she saw in Antonio's heart was gold. It was suffocating inside a mass of pride, but gold was still gold, and she went after it. She had a feeling that he would never accept any kind of direct assistance from her, so she offered it another way; she asked him to come down and volunteer.

"Boy, you are nuts, ain't ya?" he said.

"I'm getting more business in here than I can handle ever since I re-opened. Antonio, why don't you come in and help me keep things under control?"

"I really ain't that kinda person," he told her. "I don't care about these people. These are the jerks that guys like me hav'ta throw out of the bars at night. You think I want to come in and see 'em all day too?"

The next day he came back and helped sort out some of the donations that came in, and he helped Mary Jo take care of some of the guys he knew. She made him sit down every so often so she could tend to his leg.

A few weeks went by, and Mary Jo kept working on him. His leg slowly began to heal, and his attitude began to change somewhat. Not on the outside, mind you; he was still as gruff as ever. He had an image to maintain, after all. But there was a reason he kept coming back every day. No one ever cared about him the way Mary Jo did. By treating him as if he was really something special, she made him feel that every little thing he did was important. The first time he met her, she genuinely thanked him for coming all the way across the room to talk to her. Even with the tremendous amount of progress she had made in her life, there remained a remnant of that isolated, lonely little girl. She was thankful for every friend she could get. Her humility was real. Antonio felt it.

Although he'd never say it out loud, Antonio knew that he was the one who was supposed to be thanking her. But what came out of his mouth was his usual griping, groaning, complaining, and moaning. Mary Jo never paid any attention to any of that. What she paid attention to were his actions, and they were beginning to follow her own.

One day, as they were wrapping up one of their most grueling days, Mary Jo called to Antonio, "I'm going to the kitchen . . . " He told her that he would be there in a minute. Not even a minute had passed, and Mary Jo's voice paged from the intercom, "Antonio to the kitchen, Antonio to the kitchen." When he arrived in the kitchen, there was Mary Jo, after a twelve-hour day, with her own house to go home to and take care of, standing in front of a counter full of dirty dishes.

"Antonio, we gotta do these pots and pans!"

"Now, wait just a minute, whad'ya mean *we*?"

They did all those pots and pans together. Then they wiped everything down in the dining room and swept the floor and mopped the floor—twice.

"What are we havin'? Breakfast on the floor tomorrow?" he said as she passed him with a mop. He'd never met anyone so clean before. They didn't get out of there until after eight o'clock that night.

" . . . The bar's been waitin' for me this whole time, and I'm over here mopping the floor with Mary Jo Copeland till dark," he griped as they were locking up. "I don't want to work with you no more!"

"See ya tomorrow, Antonio," she smiled, getting in her car.

Her compassion had blown him away from the start, but now he saw how hard she worked besides. She was in there getting her hands dirty all day long. He thought that she must be the only director of a half-million dollar operation that you wouldn't find sitting behind a desk. He told people who came in to see her, "If you want to find Mary Jo Copeland, roll up your sleeves and start scrubbin'. She'll show up right alongside you."

Mary Jo thought that all of the re-opening hoopla would die down after a couple of weeks, and then she would be able to get the tangles worked out of the new operation. Mary Jo could not have been more wrong. The crowds never slacked off. Days kept getting busier and busier.

They did the best they could to accommodate everyone, but even with all that new space, Sharing and Caring Hands was more crowded than it had been on Glenwood. The free clothing store and the showers downstairs had to run in shifts because it was so crowded. She started a morning meal as well as the lunch meal in an effort to ease the traffic upstairs. Now there was a separate resting area for all the people getting their feet soaked so that everyone could stop tripping over one another. No one could believe there was already a need for more space. They had only been open for two months.

The most disturbing trend was not just the growing numbers who needed help, but the people themselves who were coming in. Mary Jo was still taking in the traveling hobos, the drunks, the handicapped, the elderly, the unemployed, and the runaways—just as she always had. But now she was getting young mothers coming in with their children. They had no place to go. All those little faces—she couldn't stand it. Some of the families coming in did have some income for an apartment, but the only places they could afford were rundown apartments in bad neighborhoods. Others crowded in with relatives or friends. They were constantly living a week or two away from homelessness.

On top of this, Dick Webster of the downtown Minneapolis YMCA notified Mary Jo that the organization was shifting its focus to promote a stronger family environment and would no longer be providing rooms for rent. Mary Jo was renting fifty or sixty rooms from them at a time, and now all of those people suddenly had nowhere to sleep.

To Mary Jo, this situation was unacceptable. She started phoning around, looking for hotels and motels that were willing to make a deal with her. The first month after the Y program closed, Sharing and Caring Hands spent more than $8,000 on motel rooms. Mary Jo had no choice. Those people needed a place to sleep.

16

E ven with the hundreds of lives Mary Jo touched every day, she recognized that hunger and homelessness were not going to diminish anytime soon. She was only one woman in one city. Although she did have a growing body of support from volunteers and from the community, she could only help one person at a time, and people were lining up like never before.

The 1980s surge in the "buy now, pay later" mentality bankrupted thousands and left many in the lower income brackets even poorer. The definition of poverty was changing. Working families were losing their homes. More and more people needed public assistance, but they did not qualify to get it. More and more battered women were finding the courage to leave their destructive relationships and needed a place to go for help. There were more alcoholics and addicts needing help to get clean, and more children being born to parents who refused to get clean. All of these factors contributed to the increase in Mary Jo's workload. Sharing and Caring Hands was completely packed with people—again. The building couldn't hold everyone who came in for help every day. The early morning volunteer cooks remember people lining up around the corner beginning at six or seven o'clock. They would stand there for hours, waiting for the doors to open, even in the dead of winter.

Bev VanLith, a regular volunteer who attended the same church as the Copelands, felt that one of the hardest parts of the job was seeing all of those cold, hungry faces peeking in through the frosted glass every morning, watching the other volunteers and her prepare the meal. The volunteers wanted to open the doors early to let them wait inside, but there just wasn't enough room for everyone. When they did open the doors, many people had to go through the food line, eat, and then leave right away so that others would have a chance to come inside to warm up and have their meal.

In addition to the increase in people, there was an increase in the services the people needed. Mary Jo's main focus was still to meet people's basic needs, serving as a safety net organization for those who could not get help through state or government-subsidized programs. Often people could not hang on to their jobs when they had lost their housing, and they were overwhelmed by having no place to put their families. Along with their housing and their jobs went their health coverage, so now in addition to being dragged through financial struggles, county bureaucracy, and emotional strain, people were finding their way to Mary Jo's doorstep, sick and exhausted, with their sick and exhausted children.

For Mary Jo this was unacceptable. No matter what these people had come out of, she believed they all deserved a chance for something better. She didn't make them fill out a mountain of forms and divulge their entire histories—she didn't have time for that—she just helped them. On a daily basis, Mary Jo's compassion brought mothers to tears who had been through months and months of frustration, being told "no" everywhere they went. Having someone finally say to them, "Yes, I will help you. Just tell me what you need" was almost more than they could believe.

Clearly, there was more need in the community than Mary Jo had resources for. She spent more than twice as much as her budget allowed for medical care and hotels, and the people were still coming. The building was full every single day, and there was never room for everybody. Sharing and Caring Hands needed more money, and she needed more space.

Mary Jo and Dick started talking to contractors about the possibility of expanding the building. Pushing out a wing all the way to the edge of their property would add 4,000 square feet, almost doubling the present amount of space. Having that much more space sounded like heaven to everybody. The dining room would be big enough so no one would have to wait in line outside anymore. The basement would be big enough so that everyone would be able to find the clothing they needed without swarming all over one another. Construction of a medical and dental clinic was also included in the plans. With the rising costs of prescriptions and other medical needs, getting the care they needed was the lowest thing on the priority list for most people. If Mary Jo could put in her own clinic and get volunteer nurses and dentists, she could effectively help a lot more people for a lot less money.

The problem, as usual, was still money. The cost estimate for this wonderful new plan was $450,000. True, the size of the building would double, but after only two years of being in the present facility, the amount of money needed to build it and run it would also double. As before, this was the time when Dick would start to get nervous.

"Honey, that's an awful lot of money," he said. "That's a bigger liability than we've ever had for anything!"

"Well, there's a lot more need!" said Mary Jo.

"But Mary, it's too soon. We just built two years ago!"

"What am I supposed to do, tell all those people 'I'm sorry, it's too soon for me to help you'?"

Once again, he couldn't argue. He had learned all too well by then that you just can't say no to Mary Jo. It wasn't as if she'd never made a mistake, but as far as helping the poor and serving God, she always did the right thing. Underneath Dick's apprehension about the numbers and the bottom line, he trusted her faith. He had no idea how they would ever raise that kind of money, especially when they were already so far over budget. But he knew she was right. It was the right thing to do. They went ahead with the construction plans.

Mary Jo's boundless spirit was present every day at Sharing and Caring Hands. Every volunteer, every donor, and every person in poverty felt that spirit. She had become not just a person that people met, but an experience they had. That experience was making miracles happen everyday. Not everyone recognized this, but for those who had been there, they knew it. For those who hadn't been there? Well, they were about to know it too.

For the people at Sharing and Caring Hands—the place where it was Christmas every day—Christmastime brought an undeniable miracle on 7th Street. People who generally spent the rest of the year preoccupied with their work, families, money, health conditions, and other daily activities would suddenly find their spirits awakened and feel a mighty urge to give.

During the Christmas season of 1989, Sharing and Caring Hands experienced the Holy Spirit as it never had before. Donations of food, clothing, toys, games, and electronics poured in, and volunteers came in droves. People who had never donated to Sharing and Caring Hands before, or donated to anyone before, were stopping in to drop things off. One man came in, checkbook in hand, and told Darliss that he was on his way home and had the sudden urge to turn the car around and come in to make a donation. He had remembered hearing about Mary Jo years before when she opened the Glenwood location, but he'd never been in, he said. Then he dropped a check for $10,000 on the front desk and left.

Word got back to one of the local news stations about all the activity at Sharing and Caring Hands, and a reporter visited the center. The day after the story aired, cash donations tripled. Mary Jo and Dick were amazed. Between the individual donations and foundation funds, they received enough money that holiday season not only to cover the overspent budget but also to cover the expansion cost and much of the operation costs for the following year. "Where there is a need, God will always provide the increase in resources to fill that need," Mary Jo said. "How else can you explain it?"

17

Late in 1990, Mary Jo received notice that she was among one of ten adults selected that year for the "Most Caring People in America" award from the National Caring Institute. The organization, based in Washington D.C., was founded in 1985 to honor and promote the values of caring, integrity, and public service. Inspired by the example of Mother Teresa, the Institute's philosophy is that the solution to most problems is found in the caring of one human being for another. The Caring Institute celebrates special individuals who, "in transcending self, devote their lives in service to the disadvantaged, the poor, the disabled and the dying. We honor those individuals who ennoble the human race with their long-standing commitments to caring."

The goal of the organization is to reinforce the message that success is defined by having a passionate concern for the welfare of others. The Institute's programs continually honor and promote a new standard of social responsibility and the concept that one person can, indeed, make a difference. The difference that Mary Jo made was brought to the Institute's attention by then-mayor of Minneapolis

Donald Fraser, who nominated her for the award.

Through the National Caring Awards program, each year the Institute pays tribute to the ten most caring men and women and five most caring young people in America. These select few are honored at a special series of events in Washington, D.C. because they have dedicated the better parts of their lives to helping others. By creating solutions for their communities, the power of their examples inspires a new standard of social responsibility. Their stories are highlighted at the National Caring Institute's Awards Ceremony. Every recipient receives a Caring Award bronze statuette designed by Mr. Frank Eliscu, the renowned sculptor who designed the Heisman trophy, the Presidential Medal of Freedom, and the Presidential Golden Eagle.

On December 3, 1990, Mary Jo and Dick were flown to Washington to celebrate the accomplishments of Sharing and Caring Hands and those of fourteen others at a two-day celebration, ending with a formal dinner and awards presentation.

Mary Jo was one of those people who just did not vacation very well. She wasn't comfortable having nothing to do. That was the reason that it had been twenty-five years since her last vacation, when Dick finally convinced her to take a break with him. She picked San Diego because she'd heard they had a great zoo. She would only agree to be gone for five days, but by day three she had seen the zoo and the ocean and gone to all the restaurants, stores, and parks that she wanted. She was ready to go home. She was not looking forward to the plane ride back, and she wanted to get it over with. They left early.

On her flight to Washington, she didn't have any children to supervise, and this trip was at least work-related instead of a vacation. Yet, Mary Jo still felt nauseous and anxious, white-knuckling the armrests on her seat the whole time. She concluded on that flight that if she were really meant to be in the air, then God would have given her wings. She would be perfectly happy reciting Hail Marys with both her feet on the ground from then on, thank you very much.

Upon their arrival in Washington, the honorees were housed at the Grand Mayflower Hotel. While Mary Jo could appreciate the beauty in the lavish decor, furnishings, and service at the place, she was uncomfortable in such a luxurious and unaccustomed setting. She did enjoy meeting all the warm and interesting people involved with the Institute, but she was used to being surrounded by people who needed something from her all day long, and these people wanted to honor her. She felt odd. She wondered how the children were doing at home and about Brian and Antonio and Charlotte and Al and Tom and June and Darliss and other volunteers and about all of the sore-footed souls that were wandering out there alone while Sharing and Caring Hands was closed and if the shipment of new shoes came in or not and if the food shelf was stocked and if the floor was clean.

Mary Jo was even more uncomfortable going to the formal dinner. In spite of all the talks and interviews she had given, she still felt apprehensive in a social setting, especially with so much money and power in the room. She could hardly sit at that table in that huge, ornate ballroom with all those dressed-up people sipping their lemon tea, expecting her to mingle and be conversational. She remembers looking around the room and thinking, "How did I get here? I'm just the foot washer!"

Just then the man sitting next to her introduced himself and struck up a conversation. He was another of the ten most caring people being honored that night. He was very warm and perfectly mannered and was wearing the finest suit that Mary Jo had ever seen. She'd never heard of him before, but she figured he must be wealthy. She figured right.

Ewing Kauffman was the founder of Marion Laboratories, chairman emeritus of Marion Merrell Dow Inc., and owner of the Kansas City Royals baseball team. Kauffman was receiving the Most Caring People award for organizing a foundation to which he contributed half of his wealth to fund programs to better the lives of children. Students Taught Awareness & Resistance (STAR) was his program to steer children away from the influences of drug and alcohol use and into opportunities for community involvement and education. All fifteen school districts in the Kansas City area embraced Kauffman's program, and more than 1,000 teachers and 130,000 students had benefited from it. He also created Project Choice, a program designed to encourage high-risk students to graduate from high school and go to college. Kauffman pays the tuition for the college or the vocational school of choice for individuals who complete the program. His philosophy was that "if you give children hope and something for the future, they will deliver. The children have to know that somebody is interested in them and cares about them." And furthermore, he said, "If you don't integrate your personal values into your business, then you're somewhat of a con artist. You're not living what you believe in."

Mary Jo and Ewing were on the same wavelength immediately. They spent most of the dinner trading anecdotes, and Ewing grew increasingly impressed the more he discovered about Mary Jo and what she had accomplished.

"Do you know Carl Pohlad?" he said suddenly.

"No," Mary Jo answered. "I mean, I know who he is . . . he has that baseball team." [Minnesota Twins]

"He's never given you any money?" Ewing asked her.

"No, I've never asked him."

"Mary Jo, you go over there and see him," he told her. "You tell him to give you some money. I'm his good friend, and I know he's got millions, so you just call up and tell his office Ewing sent you. With all the work you're doing for that city, he needs to give you some money."

Mary Jo laughed. She liked Ewing a lot. It was strange; she didn't even want to go to that dinner, but now she was actually enjoying herself. She didn't even realize at the time what an important contact she'd just made.

As she graciously accepted her award the next day, clearly Ewing Kauffman was not the only one who was impressed by Mary Jo

Copeland. The recipients of the Most Caring People award represented the best of the best in America, and out of the fifteen award winners that year, and the thirty award winners from prior years, Mary Jo was singled out to be included on an artistic poster entitled, "Essence of America." This featured her portrait alongside the likenesses of American figures such as Martin Luther King, John F. Kennedy, Helen Keller, and Mark Twain. Since then, nothing has been quite so humbling for her . . . except washing the feet of the poor.

18

Mary Jo arranged to make the trip to Washington without making much of a dent in her usual schedule. She would normally be at Sharing and Caring Hands until six or seven o'clock on Thursday evenings, but on the Thursday evening before the D.C. events, she took off a little early to catch the flight with Dick. On Fridays she usually had the day off to take care of things at home and spend time with the children. On Saturdays one of her children or the other regular volunteers opened Sharing and Caring Hands to supervise that day's visiting volunteer group serving the meal and giving out clothing, while Mary Jo would be out speaking at organizations and churches. On this Sunday they flew back from Washington in time for her to go to Mass, and then she went straight down to Sharing and Caring Hands to give the place its thorough weekly cleaning, right on schedule. She still lived her life exactly the same as she had for the past thirty years—on schedule, no matter what. Now that she had not just thirteen people to take care of, but also hundreds of people to take care of and all of their children, she held on even tighter to her framework of prayer and organization. Nothing would deter her from it—not a houseful of children, not an addiction to painkill-ers, not a day in jail, not a property upheaval, not even a national award.

The Copeland family pattern of rapid growth seemed destined to carry over to Sharing and Caring Hands. Just as with their family, every time a project on the building was finished, they were ready for a new one. With the last renovation only two years old (and completely paid for), the new and improved Sharing and Caring Hands opened with a total of 10,000 square feet, a bigger dining room, bigger kitchen, bigger clothing room, bigger waiting room, bigger everything. The facility now had a medical and dental clinic, more offices, more phones, and of course, more people. Just as at the last re-opening, people packed the place ten minutes after the doors opened.

Luckily, just like the last time, the re-opening also brought in more volunteers and other people willing to pitch in. The homeless were not the only ones drawn in by the compassion of Mary Jo Cope-land: The media had also become quite attracted to her activities. Every time she picked up a shovel for a groundbreaking, there were the cameras and reporters. This was just fine with Mary Jo. She needed all the sharing and caring hands she could get, and newspaper stories and television reports helped bring them in.

The publicity for the new wing started before it was even built. Along with public speaking, Mary Jo also developed a knack for hav-ing great timing with her projects. She hosted a groundbreaking cer-emony right in the middle of a political campaign, and just as ex-pected, it was well attended.

As Doug Grow put it in his June 19, 1990 *Star Tribune* article:

"The Photo Opportunity season is here. The arrival of the season means that parents who don't want their babies kissed by strangers should stay out of sight of politicians. It also means that homeless people who don't want their pictures taken shaking hands with candi-dates must stay hidden beneath bridges."

The article described Mary Jo's accomplishments, quoting her longtime friend and supporter, Father Bernard Reiser, "If you want to know how to live your life, here you go. You need only follow her example." In her own description of her work, Mary Jo said in the article, "I've prayed a lot. I've also worked my ass off. I've worked as hard as I've prayed."

The article noted the arrival of U.S. Senator Rudy Boschwitz, Democratic Senate candidate Paul Wellstone, and Republican candidate for the U.S. House of Representatives Jim Ramstad. With skeptical comments from a Sharing and Caring Hands client, the article took lighthearted pokes at the Senate competitors for bringing their political comments to the event, presumably for the television cameras, not the Sharing and Caring Hands regulars.

In fairness, it is part of the politician's job to show up at all kinds of functions like these. Taking flack for kissing babies is part of the job too, but there are a few who keep showing up whether the cameras are on or not. Jim Ramstad was one of them.

Ramstad first met Mary Jo at the Glenwood location, just after it opened. He had been invited to an event there and went down to serve a meal. As with thousands of others, witnessing Mary Jo's compassion and warmth and washing the feet of the poor had touched him deeply. Jim Ramstad was only a few years into his recovery from alcoholism at that time, and it was a big dose of reality for him to see so many people in a condition not too far away from where he had been at his worst—when he woke up in a jail cell in 1981. He had no idea how he got there, if he'd been possibly driving a car and killed someone. The last thing he had remembered was being at the bar.

He looked around the outreach center, recognizing the addiction and suffering of a lot of the crumpled, downtrodden people there, and it hit him that the only thing separating him from them was the sobriety medallion in his pocket and the grace of God. With Mary Jo doing everything she could to help these people, he decided that he could at least try to do the same. He sat down and started talking with a man whom he could tell was struggling with his addiction. "You're not alone," Jim assured the man, and then he shared his own story with him. Since then, he has continued to make part of his own recovery to help others with theirs. He visits Sharing and Caring Hands often, and on Thanksgiving and Christmas every year he brings his family in to spend the day, sharing in the spirit of serving those in need. He had grown quite close to Mary Jo by the time of her re-opening and continues to give his personal and professional support to her at every opportunity.

Along with politicians, clergy, and media, Mary Jo also drew in another person that year whose support would prove to be pivotal in the years that followed. Barbara Carlson had recently finished out her final term on the Minneapolis City Council. She did not have her next job lined up yet and was looking for a good way to spend her down time. Since Barbara had some friends who were volunteers at Sharing and Caring Hands, she decided to join the ranks.

A big heart and a strong drive to help others was not the only thing Mary Jo and Barbara had in common. Although they didn't know it then, in 1960 both women had been at St. Mary's Hospital together. During the time that Mary Jo worked there as a nursing assistant, Barbara was checked in for treatment of an "acute depressive reaction in an emotionally unstable personality." Barbara was twenty-one years old, distraught over a boyfriend, and failing all of her classes at the University of Minnesota. Her father decided that a stay in what she refers to as the "loony bin" was what her grade-point average needed. Her alcoholism was not diagnosed until years later.

With Mary Jo and Barbara each surviving a troubled childhood and difficult journeys, they became exceptionally strong women. Too strong, in fact, for them to be working under the same roof together.

Throughout her marriage to then-future Minnesota Governor Arne Carlson and her position on the city council, the outrageous antics of Barbara Carlson had become legendary. Whether sucking on pacifiers at council meetings, flashing her breasts at black-tie parties, or stabbing her husband with a ballpoint pen in a fit of anger, it was fairly safe to say that Barbara did exactly what Barbara wanted to do. Her behavior at Sharing and Caring Hands, albeit remarkably subdued by comparison, reflected her widely known reputation.

Barbara was on a "wonderful" new diet during the time she volunteered at Sharing and Caring Hands, which allowed her to eat as much as she wanted of whatever she wanted but just not swallow it. Many of the volunteers and the Copeland children remember that Barbara always carried a Styrofoam cup around with her into which she would spit all the food she chewed. That way, she reasoned, she could still have the taste of all the foods she loved without the calories. So there she'd be, giving out a bus token, spitting in a cup, giving a family new shoes and socks, spitting in a cup, joining in a prayer with Mary Jo, and spitting in a cup. Some of the others at Sharing and Caring Hands did not accept Barbara's bombastic behavior. Barbara and Charlotte did not get along at all. Their personalities were completely opposite. Barbara had a lot of energy and attacked whatever problem was in front of her. Charlotte was quiet, a people watcher, and she usually kept her opinions to herself until she was asked for them. Barbara didn't understand Charlotte's role as an advisor to Mary Jo. She didn't know that Charlotte had been with Mary Jo since the beginning, giving her insight to the people who came in for help and advice on how to deal with a lot of them.

Charlotte didn't understand what Barbara was doing either. Any volunteers who worked directly with the clients knew that if they asked for anything beyond food, clothes, showers, toiletries, a bus token or other minor things, then they needed to talk to Mary Jo. Not long after she started working at Sharing and Caring Hands, Barbara took it upon herself to make some of those decisions on her own. She operated on very good intentions and touched many families, but the thing she lacked was experience with Minneapolis' poor. Mary Jo made the decisions about people because she knew most of them. There were people who only needed one-time emergency assistance, but there were also those who repeatedly came back for help. For most of them, answering their needs was the right thing to do. They had taken a long time to fall as hard as they did, and they would need a long time to get back on their feet. But there were others who would keep asking for help that they didn't really need. What they needed was to learn how to help themselves, and that's what Mary Jo would do when she talked with them. Instead of just handing out bits of cash every time they asked, she handed out love and counsel on how to proceed productively in their lives. She would start by giving them half the money they needed to let them learn to take care of the rest on their own.

With Barbara not having any history with the clients, it was all the more reason to adhere to the established order of the place. But she did not. Barbara did things exactly the way that Barbara wanted to do things, and while most of the work she was doing was good, she clashed with a lot of the other volunteers.

After a number of complaints about Barbara, Mary Jo concluded that Barbara's independent decision making was counterproductive. With Barbara operating independently, something in the system was bound to break. In this case, that something was Barbara's ankle.

Barbara was walking through the dining room one day, after Antonio had just mopped the floor and warned her to stay off it. Barbara ignored him and continued walking wherever she wanted to, when she wanted to. One foot landed on a slippery spot and then the next . . . and down she went. She was in immediate and excruciating pain and perfectly furious about it. People came running to help, but all they could do was try to keep her leg elevated until the ambulance came. Barbara was furious at everyone trying to help, furious at the wet floor, and furious at the world. As she was being lifted into the ambulance, she howled out a colorful barrage of obscenities and threatened to sue. No one took this seriously until Mary Jo received a call from Barbara's attorney. Barbara was claiming that Mary Jo was at fault because the floor was wet.

After she calmed down and came to her senses, however, she decided not to pursue a lawsuit. When her anger subsided, she realized that suing Mary Jo Copeland would be foolish. It would only be taking away from the people she was helping. Barbara's broken ankle marked the end of her volunteering at Sharing and Caring Hands, but it was not the end of her support for the place.

At age forty-eight, Mary Jo was coping with media frenzies, broken ankles, threatened lawsuits, public speaking engagements, going to Mass at church every morning, and the daily routine at Sharing and Caring Hands. She and Dick also still had four teenagers at home, and they had two grandchildren by this time. Mary Jo continued to work hard with Brian Philbrick. He was making progress but slowly. He was going to his psychiatrist appointments on his own now and actually keeping most of them. Mary Jo's next goal was to get the man to a dentist. She taught him the importance of brushing his teeth every day, but almost thirty years of having no dental hygiene whatsoever had left his teeth in deplorable condition. His teeth were in as bad shape as his old boots had been in. He needed to see a dentist, and getting him to agree to that was about as easy as it had been to get him to shower, wear clean clothes, stay out of jail, and see a psychiatrist. To him, the dentist was worse than all of those things. Was he supposed to lie there while someone he didn't know dug around his mouth with sharp metal instruments? Forget that.

Mary Jo kept needling him until he finally agreed to go, and even then, just as with everything else, he fought it fiercely. He canceled his appointments for a month before he could bring himself to show up. When he finally did get there, he bolted once he heard the drill. She stopped making appointments for him and brought him into the dentist's office to sit there for twenty or thirty minutes, watching what went on and practicing getting in the dentist chair.

By the time he was finally ready to see the dentist, Mary Jo and Dick decided he was also ready to have a home of his own. The third apartment complex they moved him into was turning out not much better than the others. They took into account that Brian was going to have a hard time of it no matter what apartment they put him in. People weren't used to someone like him, and he still carried around a great deal of anxiety about other people. He would erupt over small things and would yell at anyone in his path. He also was still having flashbacks and would wake up screaming at all hours of the night. His landlord received one too many complaints from his neighbors and sent an eviction notice.

In the Camden area of North Minneapolis, there was a very small house for sale, smaller than the Newton house, but it had a little yard and a garage with a workshop in it. It was perfect for Brian. The place needed some work, but that's exactly the kind of thing he could keep himself busy with. He was happiest when he could just be by himself and tinker with gadgets and appliances. That's what his job at Sharing and Caring Hands had become—to fix things.

Brian never had the occasion to establish any kind of credit, so Mary Jo and Dick signed a contract themselves to get him into the house. He made his mortgage payments to the Copelands out of his disability checks, and it actually came out to be less than what he had been paying in rent. He had all the privacy he needed, and for the first time in his life, he had a sense of being in his own home. It wasn't just a place for him to be for the time being, he was buying it. It was his. Establishing a peaceful home was just one more step in establishing Brian's peace of mind.

Although Brian had made great strides of progress in the past few years, there were still many new volunteers and clients coming in every day who were intimidated by him. They didn't know how far he'd come, and they certainly didn't understand how it could be a *good* sign when he'd rant and rave because someone lined the garbage can with the wrong kind of bag. They didn't understand that while he'd indulge in one of his tirades over any little thing, he wouldn't yell at just anyone. He yelled at people he felt threatened by, but if he felt threatened by someone, this usually meant that he was starting to care about that person.

Antonio was one person who had a hard time understanding Brian when he first started working there. Antonio was not a person accustomed to taking hogwash from anyone, much less from this growling Philbrick fellow. Antonio didn't like him, and Brian didn't like Antonio. One day, when Antonio was helping Mary Jo mop the floor, Brian threw a rug out in the middle of where he was mopping. Antonio grumbled, narrowed his eyes, and mopped right over the rug. Well, that was the clearest invitation to a brawl that Brian had ever had . . . and at it they went. Not in the least bit fazed by the scene of these two grown men trying to kill each other, Mary Jo barked, "All right, both of you knock it off. You're messing up my floor." While they took a few more minutes to calm down, she just mopped around them.

The unruly behavior between Antonio and Brian continued until the next victim came along. Brian didn't have any serious problems with most volunteers. The groups of people who came in to serve the meals every day he left alone for the most part, but occasionally people came in who looked as if they might stick around for a while. Those were the ones who agitated Brian.

Mary Jo saw a young man in the waiting area one day who, much like Antonio, didn't look as though he belonged there. He didn't appear to be chronically homeless like many of the men and women who came in. There were no immediate signs of severe mental disorders or the telltale erratic behavior of the many addicts she'd met. He didn't have a large family in tow, nor was he a senior citizen having a hard time making ends meet. The only familiar thing Mary Jo saw was that he appeared to be in a great deal of pain, both physically and emotionally. His name was Brian also—Brian Weeber.

There had been a fire in Brian Weeber's apartment building. The fire department was called but not soon enough. Brian had to jump out of a window to save himself, and then he stood back and watched, with an injured back, as everything he owned disappeared inside the flaming building.

Brian did not have a full-time job or health insurance to see a doctor. He had been doing temp work with a cleaning company and a painting company before the fire, but now was in so much pain that he could barely move, let alone work. He had been estranged from his family for more than a decade, and he did not have many friends he could turn to who would help him. He had been independent and self-sufficient his whole life. He never thought something like this would happen to him. All in one night, he lost his home, everything he had, and his ability to support himself. He had nowhere to go.

Mary Jo got him a hotel room immediately. She gave him clothes and food and toiletries and some cash and made an appointment with a physical therapist. In the meantime, she sent him to the clinic down-stairs to get some pain medication and then up to the dining room to get some lunch. Not until the next day did he realize what had hap-pened. No one had ever been so kind to him. No one had given to him so unconditionally before. He couldn't believe it.

He went back to see Mary Jo the next day, and the following day, and the day after that. He just wanted to be around her. He wanted to find a way to pay her back, to thank her somehow. He started helping out with little things, here and there, and when his back felt better, he started working with the people on the loading dock, sorting the do-nations that came in. He had never been happier. Mary Jo was happy too, seeing him get better and seeing his spirit light up.

The only person who wasn't happy was Brian Philbrick. He didn't like this Brian Weeber business one little bit. The way he saw it, the place was only big enough for one Brian—and that was him.

One day during the first week that Brian Weeber was there, Mary Jo asked if he would help her by washing some of the walls down-stairs. While he was doing this, Brian Philbrick stormed down the stairs, throwing a fit because he thought Brian Weeber wasn't wash-ing the walls properly. Brian Philbrick yelled so loud that his voice was squeaking. Then he picked up a chair and threw it at his rival.

Now Brian Weeber knew how to behave like a rational person, but at that particular time, his life wasn't going so well. It hadn't been for a lot of years, in fact, and now that someone had come along to help him and care about him and show him how to get out of his rut, he was going to do anything Mary Jo asked of him, raging lunatics hurling chairs or not. Brian Weeber went back to his wall washing. Brian Philbrick accused him of trying to steal his job. Brian Weeber yelled back that he was stupid. Brian Philbrick yelled out that he was gonna get rid of him. Brian Weeber yelled back that he'd like to see him try—and they were on the floor punching each other.

Once informed about the two Brians fighting, Mary Jo rolled her eyes, finished her phone call, detoured through the lower level on her way to another emergency in the kitchen, paused only long enough to shout, "Honest to God, you boys are worse than my kids! Cut it out!" And they did.

Mary Jo's years of intense experience as a mother were paying off tenfold. The reaction from a lot of people witnessing two men fighting with a lifetime of anger and frustration and abuse behind their fists would be to back away and give them room or call the cops. The reaction from most mothers walking in on a brutal battle between their children would be to get between them, grab them by their arms, and send them to their rooms. Mary Jo was not just a mother to twelve any more; she was a mother to hundreds. She treated every person who walked into Sharing and Caring Hands the same way she treated her children—with the same love, the same discipline, and the same connection to them. She took responsibility for them when no one else would and tried to teach each of them to start taking responsibility for themselves. Some of them came to her ready to do that; some of them had a long way to go. Perhaps the most difficult part of her job was determining when and with whom to lay down the rules. With her own children, she had the benefit of experience with all of them. The challenge she had with the people at Sharing and Caring Hands was having to make a determination about them within the first fifteen minutes of meeting them. Because having this kind of discretion was never easy and she wasn't always right, she was starting to fall under plenty of scrutiny because of some of her judgments.

Rumors began to circulate among other local charities and public service departments that the money Mary Jo raised was being wasted on people who were taking advantage of her. To her, this accusation was just another demonstration of the difference in the approach she took in serving those in need. Most other agencies would put everyone who came to them for help through the same process for qualification, which usually would be determined only after an extremely involved succession of paperwork. Then the information they gave would be weighed against the situations of all the other applicants to determine the type and amount of aid. For instance, another who might have more children or a higher potential to get off welfare sooner could cancel out one mother's need for food stamps and rent help.

Mary Jo dealt with the same resource limitations, but rather than paying ten people to determine who needed what, and a board of people to determine who was hired to determine who needed what, she took the position that *all* of the people who came to her deserved and would receive decent clothes to wear, a place to bathe in privacy, and food to eat, no questions asked. Instead of paying out thousands in salaries, she put the money into things for the people and enlisted volunteers to help her provide for them. She operated on the understanding that the resources needed to fill people's basic necessities were *not* finite, they were infinite. There was no reason to waste time and money determining who gets food and how much—she just fed everybody. Mary Jo never had to turn away someone she wanted to help. There was always enough. There always had been.

As for the people with extended needs—money, transportation, a place to stay, medications—Mary Jo talked to each person herself. Were there people who tried to lie and take advantage of her compassion? Of course there were, and some of them succeeded, just as many people conned their way into the welfare system. The difference with Mary Jo was that she dealt with the people personally, and it was much harder for people to lie to her than it was to lie on paper to someone sitting behind a desk. If people intended to lie their way into Mary Jo Copeland's heart, they would have to do it while she was looking them in the eye, holding their hand, hugging their children, and saying a prayer for them. Those who were desperate enough to get away with that did not get away with it for very long. Certainly and inevitably the liars, cheats, and thieves would reveal themselves.

With this kind of personal attention in place, with her presence there daily, no person could go on deceiving her for years on end, as many did through county assistance. With Mary Jo, it was usually over in a matter of weeks, and the people she helped knew it. Just as the word on the street had spread to "go see Mary Jo" to get help with things no one else would help with, the word had spread to the people attempting dishonesty to target some other sucker. It was too tough to deceive her.

As the early 1990s continued, so did the recognition of Mary Jo's tremendous impact upon the city of Minneapolis. In 1991 she received the David W. Preus Leadership Award, which honors the presiding bishop-emeritus of the former American Lutheran Church. Previous recipients had been Preus, Richard R. Green, chancellor of New York City public schools, and Bishop Medardo Gomez of the Lutheran Church in El Salvador. She was also awarded the "Entrepreneur of the Year" by Merrill Lynch, Ernst and Young, Inc., and Gray, Plant, Mooty, Mooty & Bennett. And the Hennepin County Commissioners declared October 7, 1991, Mary Jo Copeland Day.

Although these awards were personal triumphs for Mary Jo, she was more grateful for the much-needed support that the recognition brought to contribute to the ever-growing expense of serving the poor.

The first year that Mary Jo had Sharing and Caring Hands open on 7th Street, she spent more than $50,000 paying for hotel rooms for people who had nowhere to go.

The second year that 7th Street was open she spent $100,000 on hotel rooms. By the end of 1990, the amount was up to $150,000; in 1991, $200,000. In 1992, the total was more than $300,000, on hotel rooms alone. Even Mary Jo balked after they added up that number.

"We can't keep this up, Dick," she said. "Those hotels and motels are sucking all the money. I could build my own hotel for what we're spending!" She paused for a moment. "Now that I think about it . . ."

"Uh-oh," said Dick.

"Maybe it's time we built that shelter we've been talking about," she suggested.

"Mary, you're not really gonna build a shelter. Come on. There's no way we can take on something like that."

"Why not?"

"There's no room! We've built as far as we can. We're at the edge of the property now with the expansion . . . you know that."

"But look at all that property next door, honey. It's just sitting there growing weeds. It's been sitting there this whole time getting weedier, and these people need a decent place to stay. There's no reason I shouldn't build there."

Dick sighed. He knew this was going to be a tough one.

19

Dick Copeland began hitting roadblocks for the property next to Sharing and Caring Hands the minute he started making phone calls about it. The first thing he found out was that the railroad owned the land. Glacier Park was the real estate company set up as a subsidiary of Burlington Northern Railroad for the specific purpose of getting rid of large plots of land bordering the tracks. Between the escalating taxes and environmental problems that kept cropping up, for the railroads to hold on to all the land became financially draining.

Many took advantage of this surge in availability of industrial property, including, as Dick soon learned, the block of land that Mary Jo was interested in. It already was under option by someone else. As far as Dick was concerned, that was final, but for Mary Jo and her ever-present optimism, this was no obstacle. "Find out who has the option," she said. She grew even more excited after Dick made a few calls and discovered that the current option holder was Project for Pride in Living, another nonprofit organization, that had plans to put in a detox center.

"It's PPL? Well, that's fantastic!" said Mary Jo, "We'll just call up Joe [Selvaggio] and see if he wants to go halves with us. There's five acres up there. They don't need that much space to sober people up!"

Dick actually agreed with her that time. It was a great idea, but it was one that would never come to fruition. PPL did not have the money to purchase the land. The group had been working for months, trying to get the zoning changed to allow their project, but when the time came to renew the option, funds were not available, and the option expired.

"So that means the land is available now, right?" she asked. "I'll just go get it myself then." If only it had been that easy.

Mary Jo was floored. She couldn't believe that Glacier Park wanted $1.5 million for a piece of property that had nothing on it but weeds. She knew there was no way she ever could raise that kind of money. That was twice as much as everything they had put into Sharing and Caring Hands—just for the land! They had to move fast if they were going to go after the property, and there just wasn't time to raise that kind of money.

Then a miracle happened. Dick Copeland, the man whose first answer to everything, no matter what the question, was "No, we can't afford it," said to Mary Jo, "Well . . . wait a minute now, honey. Let's look into this a little . . . "

"Dick, there's just no way! There's not enough time for me to speak in that many churches! People just don't have that kind of money."

"Some people do," said Dick. "Maybe it's time you called up your friend Ewing, Mary. Tell him you need to go see Carl."

Dick hired a lawyer to talk to Glacier Park and the land was reappraised at $1,050,000. Mary Jo tracked down the phone number for Ewing Kauffman's office in Kansas City, took a deep breath, and made the call, hoping he would at least remember her from Washington, D.C. She reached Ewing's secretary, explained what was going on, and asked if Ewing might be able to call Carl Pohlad's office for her.

Ewing's secretary called back a short time later to tell Mary Jo that she had an appointment with Pohlad the next day.

If Mary Jo had any doubts before about how she was going to proceed with this project, she certainly didn't now. She headed downtown to the Marquette Building and rode the elevator up to Carl Pohlad's office. She wondered about hundreds of folks over the years, who had stood in the very same spot, waiting nervously for their appointments with Mr. Carl Pohlad, owner of the Minnesota Twins, Marquette Banks, and several lucrative corporate investment ventures.

As Carl Pohlad was about to find out, Mary Jo Copeland was one visitor who was intimidated by nothing. She marched into his spacious, imposing office with her warm smile, dressed as she dressed every day—tennis shoes, a long denim skirt, and a denim shirt decorated with Donald Duck, Goofy, and other Disney characters.

"Good morning, Mrs. Copeland," Carl Pohlad said, rising from his desk and extending his hand. "I'm Mr. Pohlad. It's a pleasure to meet you."

"Hi, I'm Mary Jo," she said as she shook his hand, "and I'm not used to all this formality, so I'm just gonna call you Carl."

The initial reaction to Mary Jo Copeland was much the same with everyone she met. People were usually taken a bit off guard by her straightforwardness, but at the same time, they were put at ease by her warmth and genuine concern. Carl sat back and asked what he could do for her.

"There's a lot of need among the poor right now, Carl. I'm trying to help them." She told him the story about how she started building Sharing and Caring Hands and about all the kinds of people she helps. She told him the story of Brian. She described how much her operation had grown and also how much the problems had grown. Then she told him about the shelter she wanted to build.

"These families have nothing available to them anymore. The only options they have are motel rooms they can't afford or tiny, broken-down apartments, when they can find them. These conditions are unsafe, unstable, and not acceptable for children. They deserve something better. I want to give them a place to stay that's filled with love and color and dignity and peace. These children deserve a safe place, Carl. I need that land."

Carl Pohlad paused for a moment and then asked why they wouldn't just give her that land. Mary Jo laughed. "Yeah, I'd like that too, but they're not gonna."

"We'll see," said Carl. He told her he would make some calls to those railroad people and see what he could do.

Carl called those railroad people and talked to one person after another, but they wouldn't budge. They had lowered their price as far as they were going to. Mary Jo needed $300,000 up front to tie up the property before it slipped away. Carl Pohlad agreed to give Mary Jo $150,000 that day. He also gave her Irwin Jacobs' phone number. Jacobs was a Minneapolis entrepreneur who had built a fortune by buying and selling companies and holding on to a few of the best ones. "Remind Irwin that he owes me a favor," Pohlad told her.

Without stopping to revel in what she'd just accomplished, Mary Jo called and left a message for Irwin Jacobs. She also left a message for Burt McGlynn, chairman of McGlynn Bakeries. Mary Jo did not know McGlynn very well, but she did know that he had just sold part of his business to Pillsbury, so he had plenty of cash. McGlynn had already heard about the Mary Jo Copeland tornado, and he must have known better than to procrastinate when it came to helping her. He donated $50,000 right away. Excitedly, she called Jacobs again.

"He will get back to you, Mary Jo," Jacobs' secretary assured her.

Mary Jo was not very good at being patient. When there was work to do, she just did it. She didn't like having to wait for others to do their work before she could do hers. She didn't like spending that waiting time surrounded by people in need. The sooner she could do something about that, the better.

Before calling Irwin Jacobs a third time, Mary Jo waited a week. She was told again that he would get back to her. Mary Jo was getting annoyed with this Jacobs person.

She kept calling him, and she kept getting told that he was busy, he was out of town, he was in a meeting, he would get back to her. She thought, "Fine, if he wants to play this cat and mouse game, that's fine. I need that money." She just kept calling. She called him every week for three months. She and Rose, his secretary, were on a first-name basis now. "Good morning, Mary Jo," Rose would say each week. "How was your weekend? Great. Okay. Well, I'll tell him you called. Have a nice day."

All this wasted time was hard on Mary Jo. It took a lot to depress her by this point in her life, but her deadline was getting closer and closer. She was getting worried. She'd had enough.

"Rose, I've got to have that money or I'm gonna lose the land," Mary Jo finally pleaded.

She got a call back from Jacobs an hour later. He agreed to see her that Friday morning.

When she arrived at his office, she was stunned at finding herself in such huge, plush, marble-topped surroundings. All of the offices there were like that—so rich. She thought they were more like chambers than offices. And there was Mary Jo, right in the middle of it, dressed comfortably in jeans and a sweater. Friday was her day off. What else would she wear?

"Come in," she heard from a deep voice. She entered Jacobs' office slowly and sank into the chair across from him.

Mary Jo didn't know much about Irwin Jacobs before Carl Pohlad mentioned him. What she saw that day, from his presence and from everything surrounding him, was that this was a man who really liked his money. Her impression was that this was a man who was not going to part with his money very easily. She felt nothing but tension in the room, and she began to doubt that this meeting would be successful for her.

She started thinking that maybe this whole Jacobs thing wasn't such a good idea. Maybe Carl and Burt had some other friends who would understand more clearly that having all that wealth also meant having accountability. She knew from their demonstration that Carl and Burt were men who understood the bottom line—which was right in the Scriptures—that to whom much is given, much would be asked. She wasn't too sure about this Jacobs fellow, though. Maybe he didn't get that.

Putting her doubts aside, all she could do was what she had always done: speak from her heart. She'd made it into his office, and she at least had to give it a shot.

"There's an awful lot of need on my doorstep right now, Irwin. I'm seeing more and more of it every day. There is more anger and hurt and addiction and abuse inside people than ever before. These people are here through no fault of their own. Many of them have been born into their circumstances and dragged through neglect and abuse and sickness their whole lives. And I don't know how to fix the whole problem. I only know how to help the people who are in front of me right now . . . "

Irwin Jacobs did not say one word while she talked. When Mary Jo was finished, he opened his desk drawer. "How much do you need?"

Only a handful of people had succeeded in getting Irwin Jacobs to donate to their causes. He understood that he had a lot of accountability; he was just very particular about whom he was accountable to, usually only those people and organizations that were very close to his heart. Mary Jo certainly must have reached that part of him. Irwin Jacobs parted with $100,000 of his hard-earned fortune that day. And Mary Jo got her land.

20

By 1993, Mary Jo and Dick were close to living in a quiet and peaceful home. Most of the Copeland children were now grown up, moved out, in college, volunteering at Sharing and Caring Hands, working or married, and beginning to produce a collection of Copeland grandchildren.

With only Jeff, Matt, and Molly still living at home, you would think the place would have calmed down. No such luck. There was still much yelling, injuries, trying to sneak in and out of the house, and accidentally stepping on the gas rather than the brake and putting the car through the garage door. This wave of Copeland teenagers was perhaps a bit more daring than the earlier ones. For a time, they believed that they could get away with having wild parties while their parents were off on their Friday and Saturday night dates, but they eventually got caught. Mary Jo and Dick never once regretted having a large family, but they didn't realize that more than thirty-five years would pass before they'd have the house to themselves.

After thirty-two years of marriage, an emotional, physical, and financial struggle to raise twelve children to responsible adulthood, Mary Jo had moved past her childhood turmoil, rejection, and drug addiction. Then she honed her knack for plucking sad and lonely souls off the street, fending off bureaucrats with one hand tied behind her back, feeding, bathing, clothing, healing, and housing thousands of people as she developed a corporation with the kind of rapid growth, efficiency, and long-term stability that was the envy of many a CEO. Now was the time for Mary Jo Copeland to get busy.

Although she had the down payment money and a contract for the land, she still had to raise nearly $1 million to buy the land and more than $5 million to build the shelter. For a woman who bought everything in bulk, shopped on sale, and relied on donations and prayers to get what she needed fast and cheap or free, these multimillion dollar numbers could have been overwhelming. But this shelter was one thing where she refused to cut corners. She wanted this building to last. If she was really going to put the fifty to sixty families all under one roof that she was currently housing in hotels, the place would have to be energy-efficient, easy to maintain, and well designed to make the best use of limited space. Safety was another major concern. The building needed to be set up with a controlled entrance to give residents and Mary Jo the peace of mind in knowing that the only people in the building were the ones who were supposed to be there. She didn't want it looking stark and ugly either. She was very clear about that. She wanted a place with plenty of windows and light and warmth. She wanted to build a home.

After several meetings with designers and contractors, Cunningham Hamilton Quiter Architects presented Mary Jo and Dick with a plan for a 52,000-square-foot, 57-unit, 200-bed complex. One main lobby joined two wings. The 24-unit west wing was designed for larger families, with a bedroom for the parents and a second bedroom stacked with sturdy wooden bunk beds to accommodate up to ten children per unit. The east wing had thirty-two efficiency units for families with fewer children or infants and toddlers. Next to the security desk was an apartment for an on-site caretaker. Every apartment had its own bathroom and would be equipped with stove, microwave, refrigerator, sink, dining area, television, and a phone with voicemail.

Common areas included a community room for special meals and events and a children's playroom with a jungle gym and reading area, which featured a window wall to allow parents to keep an eye on their children while participating in adult programs. Also in the common areas were an outdoor playground and courtyard, free laundry facilities, a classroom for tutoring, a medical clinic for volunteer doctors, optometrists, or other professionals, and a resource room for parents to work from to make calls for jobs and housing.

"It's perfect," said Mary Jo.

"Five and a half million," said the project manager at Cunningham Hamilton Quiter. With the concrete plank ceilings and terrazzo floors and other materials Mary Jo wanted, that's as low the figure could go.

Mary Jo took a deep breath. "All right then," she said. "Let's do it."

And then she prayed.

Mary Jo started a fund-raising campaign such as the Twin Cities area had never seen. She called up every contact she had. She spent every Saturday and every Sunday, all day, speaking in churches. Most of them she had been to before, and all of them accepted her immediately, except for the handful of Catholics who still upheld the tenet of "no women" and "no laypeople" at the pulpit. She even added speaking engagements to her jam-packed schedule during the week. She spoke to every community group, business group, public and private club, social group and convention that she could find. She sent news releases to every radio station, TV station, and newspaper. She sent a newsletter to everyone who had donated to her. She wrote to every grant program and foundation that might conceivably be interested in helping her. If there were any spare dimes out there, Mary Jo was going to find them.

After every phone call, after every grant application, after every speech, Mary Jo prayed. And it was working. Checks were starting to come in. Hundreds and hundreds of checks were coming in. Huge checks were coming in. Just a few days before she passed away, Rose

Totino, the restaurateur and frozen pizza queen, donated $500,000 to Mary Jo.

Then the foundation money started coming in. The McKnight Foundation donated $300,000, the Bush Foundation added $200,000, and the General Mills and Cargill foundations gave $150,000 apiece. Loyal Burt McGlynn added another $450,000 to his previous gift. Mary's Place, to be named for the Blessed Mother, was on the way to reality.

Mary Jo did not slow down her campaign. There still was a very long way to go, and as she was soon to discover, money was not going to be the only obstacle.

21

After Mary Jo and Dick had spent about six months on meetings, planning, jumping through some major hoops and raising an unbelievable amount of money, the architects on the Mary's Place project came back with a problem that none of them could overcome. According to the city records, the property had an M-1 zoning, which meant that they would be allowed to build a residential property, as long as the residence was above the first floor. The Copelands submitted an application to the city for a building permit including the blueprints for Mary's Place, which showed all of the apartments situated on the second level. The city responded to the application by imposing a "conditional use" on the property. The property already was zoned for what they were planning, but the city now wanted to assess whether the zoning should stay that way. The building permit was not approved.

"This is ridiculous," Mary Jo said to Dick. She couldn't understand why, after all the work they'd done, the city was saying they couldn't build these people a home because of some regulation.

"You can't build anything without a permit," Dick explained.

"That's ridiculous! These children need a safe home, and I'm going to give it to them!"

Mary Jo was not familiar with the politics of city planners and officials, or how difficult it was for a nonprofit venture to develop property in a downtown area. No matter how they explained it, the architects couldn't get Mary Jo to understand that. Although Dick understood it, he knew how powerful his wife could be in her determination, but he also knew the city had the power to drag this zoning matter out long enough for them to lose their money and backing.

"Mary," he said to her as gently as he could, "we're not going to be able to do this, honey."

"Oh, Dick," said Mary Jo, calm as ever, her voice almost purring, "I'll get the zoning."

"Now listen, Mary," he said, "you've done a great thing here, but we've gone as far as we can. I'm not going to let you jeopardize what we've built here by trying to force this thing forward. Enough is enough."

Mary Jo just smiled. "You should know me better than that by now, honey. You're being silly."

And so the battle was on. Mary Jo had sailed through many more difficulties than some regulation stating what a piece of land ought to be used for. Those were just words. Mary Jo was dealing with people. She was going to build this shelter. It was the right thing to do. And the first thing to do, she decided, was to tell everyone that. Once again, she called her supporters. She called the TV and radio stations and newspapers. She announced to everyone that she was building a $6.5 million shelter, just as soon as the Minneapolis City Council agreed to let her get those mothers and children out from under bridges and from sleeping in the back seats of cars.

The mayor of Minneapolis, for one, was not pleased. The Minneapolis City Council members were not pleased. Mary Jo's phone was ringing off the hook. One of her callers was Jackie Cherryhomes, the City Council member whose ward Mary Jo's property was in. She wanted a meeting with Mary Jo immediately.

"What for?" said Mary Jo. "There's no reason for me to come down there." Cherryhomes told her that it would be in her best interest to come to her office and meet with her, which sounded to Mary Jo like nothing more than a power play.

"No," said Mary Jo. Even with the way the politicians flocked to her, Mary Jo was totally apolitical, and she refused to play those games. "I don't have time to come to your office right now, Jackie. I've got blistered feet in front of me that need my attention more than you do. If you want to see me so badly, you can come down to Sharing and Caring Hands, just like everyone else."

Things got pretty nasty after that. Cherryhomes was quoted in the papers as saying, "She's never going to build there. It's pointless for her to fight this." Mary Jo paid no attention. She proceeded with the fundraising, planning, and meeting with designers. "I *am* going to build there," Mary Jo told the reporters. "It will be a wonderful place for people to come together and share in what God has given them."

Dick was getting more and more nervous by the day. He was the one going to all the meetings and writing checks to architects and planners and lawyers, while listening to the City Council telling him every other day that the project wouldn't go forward.

"I'm glad you're so sure of the outcome of all this, Mary," he said one day while they were at the Monte Carlo Restaurant, their regular lunch spot. "Otherwise, I'd be really worried about all of this donor money that we're burning through with these architects."

"We've got to stay on schedule with this," Mary Jo replied. "I can't wait around and do nothing while the city messes around with all their meetings and whatnot. We need to be ready to go when it's time to build. So quit worrying and eat your lunch."

Soon after the blueprints were finalized, they submitted a complete proposal for consideration. Mary Jo never had a doubt in her mind that she would build this shelter, but nonetheless, she prayed harder than ever the night the council met to vote on the issue. Evidently, the city council members were just about the only people in Minneapolis that those prayers did not reach. Luckily, the media were among those that they did. In his May 7, 1993 column in the *Minneapolis Star Tribune*, Doug Grow wrote:

> Just as I was heading out the door, Mary Jo Copeland, director of Sharing and Caring Hands, called me back into her office. She grabbed my left hand. An associate grabbed my right hand. "Let us pray for the story you are going to write," she said, bowing her head.
>
> "But, but, but . . . " I said.
>
> "Dear Lord," Mary Jo said, "let your light shine on Doug as he writes . . . "
>
> So here I am, in front of my computer, seeking objectivity. But every time I begin to write, I sense Mary Jo looking over my shoulder, trying to shine a light on my screen.
>
> I have been compromised.

The columnist went on to say that even before Mary Jo prayed with him, he intended to report that the Minneapolis City Council's 6-0 decision to reject the proposed shelter was difficult to understand. Reasons he cited for his confusion over the decision were that the project would not cost taxpayers one dime, that the accumulation of upscale developments in the downtown area that *were* financed by taxpayers had made the need for this shelter even more necessary, and that the land Mary Jo intended to build on was sitting empty anyway. The article gave Mary Jo's angry reaction to the decision, and her response: It was time to pray. And to call her lawyer, Jim Erickson.

Doug Grow was not the only one questioning the council's decision to reject Mary Jo's proposal; many civic leaders and community members were shaking their heads. But the council's reasoning behind the decision never got any better, they just said it louder: It's not a good place for kids. It's too close to the railroad tracks. It's across the street from the garbage burner. We don't want that kind of "element" brought into that area. Blah, blah, blah. Mary Jo wasn't listening to any of it. She wasn't playing nice anymore either. She had no time left to be nice. Every day that went by was costing them money. She called her attorney.

"I think it would serve your interest to try and work with the city, Mary Jo," Jim Erickson advised her. He was still trying to play nice and make everyone happy.

"Why's that?" asked Mary Jo. Jackie Cherryhomes wanted to meet with her and discuss what her agenda would be now, was the message he relayed.

"My agenda is to serve God, Mr. Erickson. That's all. I don't know what your agenda is, but you're my attorney and I'm paying you to represent mine. I told you before, I don't have time for all this meeting mishmash. I have people to feed. You go meet with Jackie. Tell her we're suing," she said.

It was hard to believe this was once a tiny, terrified little girl who couldn't do anything but cry herself to sleep at night. Suing City Hall? "What is she *doing*?" people said, "Who does she think she is?" She understood that there were some people who had concerns about what she was doing and certainly about the way she was doing it, and she tried to answer those concerns the best way she could. But she also accepted now, in a way that she couldn't when she was growing up and when she was knocking herself out trying to please her parents and Dick's family and everyone else, that she was just different. She was not swayed by what was popular, she did not accept imposed limitations as a reason *not* to do what she knew was right, and she made a daily practice of putting her convictions into action. Not a lot of people did that.

She accepted that being different meant that there were just going to be people in her life who could not or would not understand her. They would never accept her. At Catholic Charities she was different, and they couldn't accept that. On Glenwood Avenue she was different, and her neighbors didn't want her there either. She knew that her current naysayers would discredit what she was trying to do, no matter how she did it, or how good her work was. Nothing she did would ever matter to them.

She was strong enough and smart enough not to let those people intimidate her anymore, but fending off the negativity and rejection was still hard on her. It always would be. Spending all day championing for the homeless would send her home exhausted every night. Dick saw that in her, and some of her children and others who were close to her saw it too.

She still fought on. She was different, all right. Other people stopped when they ran out of gas, but not Mary Jo Copeland. She just refueled and got right back on the road, no matter how tired, hurt, or sick of the whole thing she got. She got up every morning, went to church, and came out with her boxing gloves on. The thing her opponents continued to misunderstand was that her war wasn't even with them. Her war was with poverty. They were just getting in the way of her progress. Joe Soucheray said it best in his May 23, 1993 column in the *St. Paul Pioneer Press:*

> Look, it might be this simple: Mary Jo Copeland will win. These characters who populate City Hall in Minneapolis have never been up against anybody like her. They think they have, but they haven't. They do not have a clue what lies in store for them. . . .
>
> . . . Along came Mary Jo, a kindred spiritual descendant, the same grit and ferocity of conviction shared by angry baseball managers, theatrical courtroom attorneys, method actors. Only she isn't acting. The woman works at it, Sharing and Caring Hands, her business of caring for the poor, and now she is taking

on Minneapolis. I actually feel a little sorry for these politicians who think they can quiet this human storm with language of codes and ordinances and zoning.

Are you kidding? Copeland will have these people for lunch. She will let a few lawyers of her own attach themselves for the ride, but there is no mistaking that she will win.

Now, if you have not heard, Copeland wants to build a beautiful new residence for poor people in downtown Minneapolis. She intends to do this privately. This is such novel thinking that politicians should be washing Copeland's feet, the way she has literally washed the feet of the poor. Possibly the concept is so novel to lifetime bureaucrats that they are confused by having been left out of the process.

Instead, the Minneapolis City Council appears to be politically paralyzed by the fear of doing something "inappropriate."

That is one of the words that is undoing America, incidentally. It absolves people, they think, from making hard and fast decisions about right and wrong.

Well, perhaps Mary Jo should look for "a more appropriate place," the politicians say.

Oh, that will really stop Copeland, all right, knock her back on her heels. I am sure she is extremely worried. This mother of 12 started taking care of the poor out of a storefront on Glenwood Avenue. When the Target Center got built, she lost the store. She then discovered, providentially, her current location, a former insurance office on North 7th Street. It was sturdy brick with a dry roof. Privately, mind you, she operates a more efficient outreach to the poor than the governments of the world have been able to accomplish. She feeds people, clothes them, bathes them, gets them back on their feet. The people who know her best are comfortable with the idea that she had no knowledge of political correctness.

The poor are not Mary Jo Copeland's cotillion cause. The poor are a people.

Look, it's folly to try and stop her. She owns the land on which she intends to build her new residence. The politicians say the land is near railroad tracks. So what? Poor people sleep near railroad tracks all the time. The city says, no, that property is zoned industrial. So what? The people Mary Jo Copeland caters to are not exactly coming off Rodeo Drive in Beverly Hills. A smokestack is not going to bother them.

See, that's the point, the proof. Copeland could give a good hoot about meeting some vague collective idea of what constitutes propriety. She doesn't have time for that kind of posturing and preening. There are poor people to tend. Poor people are her business, in the best and most efficient sense of the word.

Besides, you would think it would go without saying, Mary Jo Copeland is *connected*.

The one thing boggling everyone's mind in all this was that the city council seemed to have no substantial argument against granting the zoning variance. Everyone knew what Mary Jo was fighting so hard for. But why was the city fighting her? What could they have to gain by not giving her the zoning she needed?

After going to meetings and being in the fight for almost a year, Dick began to realize that the question was more about what the city had to lose. Mary Jo had been wrong in thinking that the land had just been sitting there growing weeds. It hadn't. The city had plans for that land long before Mary Jo Copeland came along. It wasn't just her land involved in the plans either; it was the corner down the block where a defunct auto repair shop sat, and the property across from hers. There were plans to develop the whole area.

Dick was discovering that all this political chicanery wasn't about the city council being stubborn. There had been promises made to Hillcrest Development for plans with that land the whole time. Having PPL tie up the biggest chunk of the target property in an option that it would most likely never be able to complete was a great way for the development company to buy some time for the land prices to drop, which they did. Sharing and Caring Hands had scooped up the property at two-thirds of the purchase price that PPL had optioned, sabotaging those development plans.

Now Dick and Mary Jo understood where all that city opposition was coming from. The city council was never going to give Mary Jo the zoning for her building. There was too much at stake.

It would seem that this would be the end of the line for this fight. Building without a permit was illegal, and the city wasn't going to grant one. Period. But Mary Jo Copeland wasn't finished yet.

"You know what, Dick?" she said. "I'm tired of being toyed with. I've got no more money or energy to waste on this thing. There are people out here who need my help. I'm putting an end to this right now."

Mary Jo did not call the lawyers or the city council. Instead, she called a press conference. And when Mary Jo Copeland called a press conference, no reporter missed it.

Within the hour, reporters from the local TV and radio stations and the newspapers packed Sharing and Caring Hands, and to everyone's surprise, along came Barbara Carlson.

Since the end of her tenure on the city council, some of Barbara's friends encouraged her to take her outrageousness into the media. It just so happened that KSTP radio was looking for a cutting-edge "female Rush Limbaugh" or "hormonal Howard Stern," in Barbara's words. There could be no one else for this job but Barbara Carlson.

Her morning talk show was a hit, with her acting as harassing host to everyone from her ex-husband, the governor, to an interesting array of strippers. Barbara had found her niche, and she was a smash.

One of her favorite things to do was to take her show on location. She had broadcast live from her hot tub on several occasions. The day that Mary Jo called her press conference, Barbara decided was a perfect opportunity for her to do some good in the community and wreak havoc with her former city council colleagues at the same time. She brought her entire crew and equipment to broadcast live from Sharing and Caring Hands.

"Good morning, everyone, this is Barbara Carlson, live from Sharing and Caring Hands today, where Mary Jo Copeland has been helping the poor for nine years now," she explained. "She's been taking these people off the streets for us. She's putting food in their mouths, so they don't have to dig out our leftovers from the garbage bins. She's been saving us tax dollars and making it safer for all of us for years, and how are we repaying her? Trying to stop her from giving our children and families a safe place to stay. Why on earth are we fighting this good woman? Here are the phone numbers for your city council members. It's time you all gave them a call to remind them what their jobs are."

The staff at Sharing and Caring Hands all agreed; this was a much more effective way for Barbara to volunteer. Every member of the city council was flooded with calls that day. Barbara kept up her crusade all morning. Meanwhile, reporter after reporter was interviewing Mary Jo. If there was anyone in Minnesota who didn't hear about Mary Jo Copeland that day, it was because they didn't own a television or a radio, didn't read the newspaper, or never left their home.

The result? There were many people whose spirits woke up that day, including, finally, Minneapolis City Council members. On May 28, 1993, in the *Minneapolis Star Tribune*, Doug Grow wrote of the epiphany experienced by council member Walt Dziedzic. Aside from the 150 calls he received from outraged voters the day that Barbara

Carlson took the issue to the airwaves and the leftover bruises from the last time the council was sued, Dziedzic said the reason he suddenly felt compelled to approve the proposal "came from a higher source." Dziedzic had been at Mass the Sunday before and hadn't been paying much attention until the guest priest started talking about Christ being a beggar. Dziedzic was quoted in the article, "This shifts my mind out of neutral. I say to myself, 'This guy is giving a helluva sermon.' I start thinking about poor people. I grew up poor. My dad died when I was two. I'm thinking about that and I say to myself, 'Mary Jo's got to have that shelter.' See what I mean? This is from a higher source."

Dziedzic shared his experience with his fellow council members and then convinced each of them to let Mary Jo do the work she needs to do. Mary Jo's joyful reaction was noted in the article, but then she said she needed to pray for the $6 million to build the shelter. She was quoted, "Before Mass I have been saying, 'Harden not your hearts if you should hear His voice today.' What I mean by that is that we have to get the rich people off their duffs and get them giving us the money to get this thing done."

Mary Jo continued working and praying harder than ever, day after day. She continued getting increased community support and recognition. During the course of this battle, Mary Jo was awarded an Honorary Degree of Doctorate of Humane Letters from Macalaster College in 1993. In 1994 she received the annual award in Humility from the Positive Thinking Foundation, the Service Above Self award from the Minneapolis Rotary Club, and the Angelus Award from Holy Angels Academy. In May 1995, Mary Jo was given the Pax Christi Award from St. John's University for living the life that Jesus taught. She opened the shelter the same month.

By the time Mary's Place was up and running, the total cost of the project had escalated to $7 million. For a project of this scope, an extra $500,000 was not an outrageous overrun, but putting that number in terms of how many people Mary Jo could have fed with that money—that was staggering. Who knows how many dollars could have been saved without the time and expense the zoning fight took? But then again, how much exposure would the project have had without such an exciting cause for the media to champion? By the time the Christmas receipts were counted, that $7 million was almost paid.

22

Every Thursday evening at five o'clock, the end of Mary Jo's work week for Sharing and Caring Hands, she met with all of the residents of Mary's Place. It was a time for her to re-group, touch base with everyone, go over the rules, remind everyone how much she loved them and pass out hugs, candy, and dollars to all the children. She still spent the majority of her day in the main build-ing, tending to the individual needs of the people coming in, with her attention being pulled in a thousand directions all day long. But she spent an hour each morning and every Thursday evening at Mary's Place to keep herself regularly available to the people living there. A host of volunteers ran the place and tended to the residents, but Mary Jo believed it was important to stay connected to each family per-sonally.

The rest of her schedule remained unchanged—up at 3:45 in the morning and in bed by 8:00 at night. In the morning she would have breakfast, go to church and pray for two hours, attend Mass, arrive at Sharing and Caring Hands by 7:45, spend a half-hour pedaling her exercise bike, then get the morning meal going in the kitchen, check the residents, then back to the main building to open the front doors by ten o'clock for the three hundred to four hundred people who would be waiting. Mary Jo stood at the front door to give a personal greeting—a hug, a handshake, a smile, a "good morning"—to every person who came in. The people then dispersed either to the food line for breakfast, the clothing line, the groceries line, the shower line, or the "I need to talk to Mary Jo" line, which continued to grow throughout the morning and kept her occupied nonstop until noon, when she would go out into the dining room to greet the lunch crowd and say a prayer. While volunteers were serving the noon meal, Dick came to pick her up and take their lunch break. Together, in the "Mary Jo and Dick booth" at the nearby Monte Carlo Restaurant, they opened and sorted the daily Sharing and Caring Hands mail over their sliced apples and oranges and sandwiches. By 1:30 P.M. she was back at it, pausing only to pray privately before tackling the sea of poor and needy that backed up while she was gone. She would continue passing out hugs, prayers, and assistance until five or six o'clock. Once at home she would make dinner, make and return phone calls, do the laundry and other household chores, then get ready for bed, lay out her clothes for the next day, pray, and turn in for the night. Once in a while she could get through all that and have a little time left to relax in front of the TV with Dick but not very often, and never on Thursday nights when the regular weekly meetings would eat up that window of free time. When she has a late meeting, such as various city council meetings, sometimes lasting until midnight, she sacrifices sleep.

One Thursday in November 1995, after an especially excruciating week and a long meeting at Mary's Place, Mary Jo had to speak at the National Youth Conference at the Minneapolis Auditorium. There was no time to go home and make dinner, so she and Dick went back to the Monte Carlo to eat. She wasn't scheduled to speak until nine o'clock, and she never stayed up that late, so she was struggling.

"Dick, it's so late," she said. "I'm exhausted. I don't know how I'm gonna get through this talk tonight."

They arrived at an auditorium filled with more than 10,000 people, mostly junior high and high school youth. Mary Jo had never spoken to 10,000 people in her life. She had never even spoken to 5,000 people in one sitting. A huge projection screen and a sophisticated sound system were in place.

Dick gave her a kiss and some reassurance, then took a spot in the front near some of the Copeland children who also were there for support. Before Mary Jo was to speak, she met Archbishop Harry J. Flynn, who recently replaced the retiring Archbishop John R. Roach in the archdiocese. Flynn was just about to leave but decided to stay when he found out that Mary Jo was going to speak. Months earlier, Mary Jo had started a correspondence with him to introduce herself and her work. When Flynn visited Sharing and Caring Hands, he called the place remarkable. Mary Jo did mention to him then that a large part of the support for the place came from the talks that she gave in area churches. Archbishop Flynn had traveled extensively. He'd met Mother Teresa on a few occasions, he'd been to outreach operations all over the world, and he considered himself to be quite progressive. Although he was impressed with Mary Jo, he still opposed lay people speaking at the Catholic altar, as Archbishop Roach had before him. But he had never heard Mary Jo speak before.

When Mary Jo stepped out on that stage that night, the applause for her and the noise and energy in the room was incredible. She had never experienced such an overwhelming ovation. Mary Jo walked into the conference completely unrehearsed, exhausted, overcome by the size of the crowd. She spoke from her heart, as she always did, and focused on inspiring the youthful crowd. Dick, who accompanied her on speaking engagements, always was impressed at what a good job she did. But that night, he was more impressed than he'd ever been. She never once stumbled, and she covered everything flawlessly. The applause thundered.

After she finished, several people came up to Dick to tell him that it was the most powerful speech they'd ever heard. Dick saw Archbishop Flynn shaking his head in amazement. The Archbishop turned to the two nuns he was sitting with, saying, "That woman can certainly speak in my church any day."

What kind of speaker gets a reaction like that? Here is a transcription of the speech she gave that night:

> Thanks a lot for inviting me here tonight. You know, I came in here tonight, and I really felt the presence of God. I felt the peace. I felt that so many people here tonight love Jesus Christ, so much. You are our present and future voices of Jesus Christ. Each one of you here tonight are the movers and the shakers and are gonna bring the message of God to this world.
>
> Every day of my life, I work with the homeless, people in poverty, the poor, the lost, the broken. Those that live within anger, fear, loneliness—many of them have alienation from family . . . all of them born into a set of circumstances they didn't ask to be in. Every one of them, waiting for the good news of Jesus Christ to be brought to them.
>
> A few years ago I met a man on the street. I will never forget, he had a knit hat that came down over his eyes, he wore dirty, raggedy clothes, he had on big black boots, oh, and he carried a big potato sack. And in that potato sack, everything he owned clanked and clanked. Oh, he was so angry, you'd go near him and he'd say, "Get away from me, get away from me!" I knew he must have had bad feet, so I convinced him to sit down and soak his feet one afternoon, and he didn't even want me to go near him, he was so angry. People that live outside get very angry and very upset because they've been hurt. And so I knelt down and started to yank off his black boots, and then his wet

socks. Oh my God, I have never seen such sores in all of my life. I looked up at him and said, "How did your feet get so bad?" and he said, "Mary Jo, I live outside, and I try to soak them in the river every single day but they don't get any better."

And then his story unfolded. He said, "Every time I close my eyes at night, I picture my dad and my brother beating my head against the bumper of a car, takin' a billy club to my face, sayin', 'I'm gonna beat you, boy.'" He said, "You know, when I was fifteen years old, they tried to drown me, they tried to suffocate me, and I slept in my own urine for five days at a crack because they handcuffed me to beat me up and I couldn't crawl to the bathroom. I never had a bike; I never had a ball. I never smelled a homemade cookie. And I never ever had anyone say 'I love you.' Why me, Mary? Why me?"

"When I was fifteen, I left home," Brian told me. "I bought a gun. I kept rocks in both my pockets and a knife. I've been living in the woods. I've been living under bridges. I've been living in doorways. I've been arrested in every state of the union for being a vagrant, for being a trespasser, for being a bum."

I looked at him and I said, "I don't know everything you've been through, Brian, but I know God loves you and I love you and I'll help you." He said, "You can't help me, I'm an animal, Mary."

But I brought him inside my office, and it took about four months, and then I gave him a broom and I told him to sweep. He did it at night because he couldn't be around the volunteers in the day, he was too angry. They'd all leave. Then I taught him how to turn a key in a door. How to get dressed. I took him in to a trauma specialist. I brought him in to the dentist to get his teeth fixed. I taught him how to drive and got him a house to live in, and gave him the dignity the almighty God intended him to have. He's still got a long way to go, but he's doing it. He came in to see me one day and said, "Thank you, Mary, for saving my life." And I said, "Praise God, Brian. God works through people. He doesn't just work through me. Blessed are you, you are the merciful. Blessed are you, you are the peacemaker. We are all channels of God's peace, and instruments of his love, not just me."

A little girl came in to see me, little Teresa, thirteen years old, she said to me, "Mary Jo, I want to die. I'm dirty. My mother prostituted me out, sold my body for drugs." She said, "I'm not like the other children."

For six months, we counseled her. I told her that God loved her, over and over. I told her to forget about what her mother did, and forgive her. I told her how to become better instead of bitter and told her how to put energy into positive things. She came in one day after school and said, 'Mary Jo, I don't want to die anymore. I want to live.'

Love and compassion are what this little girl had, and this little girl is going to make this world better because she's in it. Because love and compassion are the secrets to our world's peace. People are starved for it. Little children come up to me, these people every day, they just want to be touched. They want to be loved. And I touch them and hug them and they don't let me go, and I always ask myself one question . . . how long has it been since one of these dear people has been touched, or even acknowledged? How long?

What you do to the least of mine, you do unto me.

224

My story is no different that Brian's and Teresa's. My dad beat up my mother every time he had a chance to punch her. She had black and blue eyes. Black and blue ribs. I remember shivering in the corner of my room like a little mouse, with my self-esteem no bigger than this, saying, "Please Mom, please Dad, don't fight anymore." The children at school made fun of me because I didn't take a bath, I stunk. My mother didn't clean the house. And I remember after my dad telling me for all those years, "you'll never amount to a hill of beans, Mary Jo," I began to believe that. If someone hadn't reached for me, I wouldn't be reaching to you tonight, nor to God's world at all. Where there is light, there's hope, and that hope comes through each and every one of you here tonight . . . when you reach out, and touch someone with the love of Jesus Christ.

John Powell said, "Our lives are shaped by those who love us, and by those who refuse to love us." Think about it. Saint Theresa said, "It's not great deeds that matter, it's great love." What is success tonight for all of us? Each one of us? To love one another, as I have loved you. God did not ask us to love one another, he came to command us to love one another. We live in a Good Friday world, and every one we meet on our journey is waiting to have the Easter joy brought to them, and you're going to bring that joy to them. What is God calling each one of you to do tonight? Maybe he's asking you to share your time. Maybe he's asking you to give up an unhealthy relationship. Maybe to visit someone in a nursing home. Maybe share your pencil, or even share your smile. Your smile and outstretched arm can be the beginning of a miracle in the unspoken need of a heart. Kindness is a conversion, don't ever forget that. If you see somebody who needs to be helped, help them. If you see something that needs to be done, do it. If you see something that needs to be changed, go change it. Each one of you must be bread, broken, and given . . . wine poured and shared. We must not be reservoirs that store up; we must be vessels that pour out, continually giving to the world.

When Jesus Christ came to this world, he came to serve, not to be served. Can we do less? To each one of us tonight, much has been given, and much will be asked. Great leaders are great servants. Serve your God, serve your family, and serve your community, and you will truly be great leaders, serving one another. And remember something, you are always responsible for the effort, not the outcome. One hundred percent into effort, and the outcome is in God's hands. So tonight, be beacons with your light shining with the love of Jesus. Be channels of his peace, and instruments of his love, all the days of your lives. And always be his hands, his heart, his feet, and his mouth. And let other people see Jesus Christ in your eyes.

You know, I didn't share something in the beginning, I'm the mother of twelve children *(thundering applause)*. Might I say that after you raise twelve children, what I'm doing is a cakewalk, believe me. The oldest one is Therese, and Molly's the youngest, and during the years of raising those children, I taught them how to make the world better because they're in it. But the most important lesson you learn in this life is how to love Jesus Christ. You can't learn anything better. And you will never fulfill the Scriptures you read until you live them. And we are all called from worship into service. Today, this day, be beacons with your light shining with the love of Jesus, channels of his peace, and instruments of his love. And when you wake up in the morning, just take Jesus by the hand, first thing when you open your eyes, and say, "Jesus, help others to meet you when they meet me," and you won't have a problem. I want you to pray in your heart, just for a moment, I'm gonna end with a prayer. Ask God where he wants you to bring the kingdom to the world, and the world back to the kingdom. And when others meet you, always let them meet Jesus, and his Blessed Mother. Lord, make me an instrument of your peace. Where there is hatred, let me love. Where there is injury, let me pardon. Where there is doubt, let me have faith. Where there is despair, let me hope. Where there is darkness, let me bring light. Where there is sadness, let me bring joy. Grant me that I not seek so much to be consoled as to console. To be understood as to understand. For it is in giving that we all receive. Pardoning that we are pardoned. And it is in dying that we are born into eternal life. In this the name of Jesus, I pray that we pray.

In the evening of this life, each one of us will be judged on only one little thing: Love, love, love. Until it hurts. And the only thing you will take with you when you leave this world is what you give away. Wherever you go back to, be sharing and caring hands, to everybody you meet. Hug your parents, hug your teachers, and always remember that God showed you the way, and He'll always be with you until the end of time. I am the handmaid of the Lord, do with me what thou will. Amen.

23

The condition of some of the people coming in to see Mary Jo was growing more heartrending. It wasn't just the wandering souls with bad feet any more. Women were coming in who didn't even have a dollar for the bus and had been walking for days in old shoes with broken straps and worn soles. Their stockingless feet were blistered, bleeding, infected, and frostbitten. Their children's feet were in the same condition. Mary Jo remembers several children who would scream in pain at the slightest touch when she tried to tend their little feet. They wore flimsy clothes, some of the mothers had no diapers for their babies, and most of them had no hope left anymore.

The conditions for the vagrants and others who did choose to live outside were getting worse too. Volunteers June and Darliss will never forget when their friend Zone was missing. They were worried for more than a week when he hadn't come in to Sharing and Caring Hands. The police finally came and said that they'd found him near a dumpster behind a White Castle. He'd been robbed, beaten, and stabbed to death. A witness had helped lead police to Zone's assailant and reported that the two men were fighting over a spot to sleep. A sweet, gentle friend was gone.

Darliss arranged a memorial that Zone's friends from Sharing and Caring Hands and from the Yukon Bar attended. His real name was Ron Stickler. He'd been married with three children and battled alcoholism his whole life. Despite his miserable circumstances, Zone had touched his friends' lives with the same kindness that Mary Jo had shown to him. His name, "Zone," is one of a few that survived the sealing up of the "hole in the wall," the bridge under which Brian Philbrick and many others living on the street sought shelter. It remains inscribed in the wood along the border of where the hole used to be.

Additionally disturbing were the growing numbers and changing faces of those near poverty. They were not always completely destitute. Some were doing temporary work but living out of their cars or staying a few nights here and there with friends. Mary Jo was starting to see more situations where the mother and father were together, with stable incomes, but not means enough to support a large family. After years of struggling financially, they would lose their housing because of repeated delinquent rent payments or more often because their building was being condemned. There was very little new low-income housing being built, and existing buildings were being torn down. Because of a 1995 legal settlement known as the Hollman case, more than 700 low-income units in Minneapolis were demolished. The settlement called for 778 replacement units to be developed across the metro area, but this program would take years to get up and running. In the interim, lower-income families looking for an affordable apartment in the Twin Cities found that was nearly impossible. Real estate and rental rates began soaring in 1996, and families that lost their housing were faced with rent increases of $300 or $400 more per month than what they had been paying. Even if they could have found a way to afford it, most landlords now had occupancy restrictions and would not allow more than two people per bedroom. Parents with more than four children were out of luck. Parents with fewer than four children were out of luck too; if there was an abundance of applicants, landlords gave the apartments to the people who would have the least impact on the building. This generally did not include families with children. Lower-income families had nowhere to go.

This was the situation when Mary's Place opened. It was intended as a transitional home for families to stay for two or three months, allowing them time to look for a decent place or a decent job, rather than jumping at the first thing they found out of desperation. While staying at Mary's Place, they didn't have to worry about the costs of rent and utilities and other daily living expenses; everything they needed was provided for them. This took the immediate financial burden off people so they could finally have time to re-establish themselves. Those who were sick had access to a doctor on-site. There were employment and housing referral workers on-site. There were tutoring and activity programs for the children. Mary Jo also helped residents pay for damage deposits when they did find a place to move into and would help get them set up with dishes, linens, furniture—things they needed to get back on their feet and make a home. The entire facility was set up as a place for parents to rest their spirits and be free from worry about how they would pay for necessities. It was a place for them to be rejuvenated. It was a home.

Families filled all fifty-six apartments within the first week Mary's Place opened. When homeless families kept coming and coming, Mary Jo put them in hotel rooms. The total hotel expenses were significantly less that year, as expected, but the need at Mary's Place kept growing.

Meanwhile, at the Sharing and Caring Hands building next door, a more immediate problem was at hand. The place had become overrun with people—again. Between the Mary's Place residents who were there regularly and the general increase in the population of people in need, everyone was tripping over one another. The volunteers in the kitchen were practically cooking on top of one another, there were never enough seats for all the people in the waiting area, and people were having to line up all the way outside of the building again. It was time to expand.

Being trapped within property lines prevented any further additions to the building, so the only option to squeeze in more space was to use a triangle-shaped lot across the street. Demolishing the old, rundown building there would provide needed land to expand.

When Mary Jo and Dick first contacted the owner of the land, he told them that the land was not for sale. Dick didn't want to play around this time. That piece of land was the only property left nearby, and they needed it. Dick also knew that the man had owned the property for years and had put very little into improving it.

"Look," Dick told him, "I'll offer you what you want for it. How much will it take?"

Suddenly the land was for sale. The owner said he would sell for $280,000. That was a steep price for less than half an acre, but it wasn't much more than the appraised value. They paid it. They needed that land.

As soon as the sale of the land went through, there was City Hall again, refusing permission to build there. So, once again, Dick was dragged into meetings. This time around, city council members pulled out an old law that said a charity could not be built within 600 feet of another charity. According to the city's records, another charity had applied to put in a food shelf next to the gas station across 7th Street, which fell within 600 feet of the newly purchased property.

"What are you talking about?" said Dick, "There's no charity there. There's nothing there!"

"Well, it's on the books," city officials told Dick. "They've applied. It's going to be there."

"Why would they do that? There's no point to it," said Dick.

"It doesn't matter if there's a point or not. It's on the books. Rules are rules," he was told. On a map Dick was shown where the street lines and the 600 feet were. "We can't allow you to build there. Sorry."

Looking closer at the documentation they showed him, Dick saw that the other application had indeed been filed long before his was. And he saw that their new land was, indeed, within 600 feet of the proposed food shelf. What he also saw was that the proposed food shelf was within 600 feet of the building they were already in!

"All right," Dick said. "If your law says that charities can't go up within 600 feet of each other, then this proposed food shelf is illegal because it's within 600 feet of *us*." That was the end of that road-block.

Dick remembers that various city officials went through some other maneuvers to try to stop them from building, but finally he reminded them of how much it had cost the last time they wanted to fight. It had only been two years before, and no one on the council had a memory that short. They backed down and gave Sharing and Caring Hands a permit to build.

When designing the new Sharing and Caring Hands building, Mary Jo and Dick had to think much bigger. They needed space, efficiency, and storage. At 27,000 square feet, the new building would almost triple the size of the old one. Two loading docks would accommodate the truckloads of food and clothing that came in every day. At the front entrance was an oversized, sheltered ramp separated by a railing, just like the line for an amusement park ride. No one would have to line up outdoors again.

The dining room was large enough to seat approximately 350 people, and when there were more people than that at one meal, (they were now serving three times a day), those who went through the line first would be finished in plenty of time for others to have a seat. There was a restaurant-sized kitchen with stainless steel counter space, a walk-in refrigerator and industrial appliances, and plenty of room for volunteers to work.

There was a service window and a large waiting room at the opposite end of the dining room from where the food was served. There people would line up, and volunteer attendants behind the window would assign services. It would serve as a pre-screening process for Mary Jo. Although she still wanted to greet everyone personally as they entered in the mornings and talk with those who needed help with shelter or other assistance, so many people were coming in now that there simply wasn't time for her to hand out every pair of new shoes and every bus token herself. She still washed ten to twenty people's feet each day.

Behind the service window were two desks, where all incoming and outgoing information was handled. A sophisticated computer system now tracked who was helped and when. There was a large stockroom dedicated for new shoes, a waiting area, four offices, two large conference rooms for visiting volunteer groups and board meetings, and one of Mary Jo's most novel ideas yet—two interview rooms where the county's social service employees could work. People who qualified for public assistance could now be taken care of right there instead of being shuffled all over the city. County workers would bring in their laptop computers with records on everyone currently on public assistance, and they also would be able to determine whether new families would qualify. Those who did not qualify could go to Mary's Place.

Downstairs everything that came in through the loading dock went to the walk-in freezers, refrigerators, the stockroom for food to be cooked, the stockroom for food to be given out at the food shelf, the stockroom for household items, or the free clothing room. Imagine a department store receiving warehouse, plus the locker room and showers of a health club, then add on a clinic of medical and dental exam rooms—all of this was included in the first level of the new Sharing and Caring Hands building.

And just in case all this space someday would not be enough, Mary Jo applied one last bit of vision to the project. Since no more land was available to expand the building outward, she asked the architects to design it so floors could be added in the future.

The total cost for this project would be $5 million in order to have it completed in 1997. Mary Jo prayed and rallied again for financial support. That special ability she had to inspire people's giving spirits drew in enough contributions during the 1996 holiday season to pay for the new building as well as much of the budget for the coming year.

As soon as the new building was up and running, there was the matter of what to do with the old building. It was not a mystery for very long. The first summer that Mary's Place was open, young children and teenagers were running everywhere, all day long. Some of them helped volunteer, but the majority of them did not have enough to do. Mary Jo rarely had her own twelve children in the house at the same time when they were growing up, unless they were asleep. Having 150 children, most of whom were coming from situations with no structure whatsoever and many with significant behavioral problems, all living under the same roof with too much idle time, was a handwritten invitation to disaster. She wanted to give them more structure and activities, particularly during the summer months.

The upper level of the old Sharing and Caring building was remodeled into a children's activity center. The entire floor was sectioned into brightly painted half walls, separating different play areas. There were two yard-sized play structures to climb on and slide down and a playhouse complete with table and chairs for tea parties. Activity centers, well stocked with toys and games, were set up for different age groups. There was a table for computers and video games and even a puppet theater. A separate TV room provided space for watching movies or children's programming or for those who needed to pull up a mat and take a nap. Included also were an office for day care volunteers, a small lunchroom for the children, and kid-sized cupboards, shelves, drinking fountains, and bathrooms. Giant, plush stuffed animals and tiny, soft stuffed animals perched throughout the place. Mary Jo also kept a supply of every Beanie Baby imaginable to give out to the children.

The lower level of the former Sharing and Caring building was renovated into a teen center. Outside were basketball courts and a playground. Inside was a gym with workout equipment, weights, and a boxing ring. They put in pinball machines and arcade games, computers, TVs with Sega games, an air hockey table, a pool table, and dartboards. They put in a movie room with a big-screen TV and surround sound. A snack room was stocked with pop and goodies, and conference rooms provided places for boys' and girls' clubs to meet or a quiet place to study. In the middle was an office for a teen center supervisor, and Mary Jo had the perfect person in mind for the job. Robbie Wills, her son Mark's best friend since childhood, had been involved in a serious car accident when he was nineteen, which left him paralyzed. He had just graduated from high school. Having grown from being the one that everyone wanted to pick on in grade school to being very popular in high school, in one night he went from an active, happy life to being a big inconvenience to everyone, at least in his eyes. That was the hardest part for him. But he had a lot of support and worked hard at becoming stronger, wheelchair or no wheelchair. He got back into weightlifting with Mark and eventually won several championships across the country and internationally.

Mary Jo decided that someone with that kind of drive was someone she needed on her team to inspire those children. "Remember when I told you that God had a special plan for you, Robbie?" she said. "I know you've got a steady job with the security company, but you were meant to do a bigger thing with your life. These children need you." Just as with everyone else who knew her, Robbie couldn't say no to Mary Jo.

The renamed building, Mary My Hope, opened by the beginning of summer in 1998. Mary Jo didn't have a year to do the fund raising this time, so she and Dick took out a loan for the $500,000 in renovations and made payments out of the operating budget.

The children's reaction to the place was incredible. Children had long been Mary Jo's weak spot, and she spared no expense when it came to making them happy. Seeing their faces when they entered the Mary My Hope building for the first time was worth twenty times what it cost. It was Disneyland. Most of those children had never even seen some of those things that other children take for granted, and none of them ever imagined they would have such a great place as part of where they lived, three hot meals a day, nice, new clothes like other children. And they really never thought they'd ever have so many people in their lives volunteering to hug them, play with them, help them with homework, and listen to their problems. There was no time for them to feel sad about being poor at this place. There was too much fun to have.

At age fifty-three, Mary Jo Copeland was not stopping. The winter after Mary My Hope opened, Sharing and Caring Hands' hotel expenditures were back where they were before Mary's Place was built. Despite widespread prosperity, tightening welfare policies and escalating housing costs led to more and more demand at Sharing and Caring Hands.

Now more than ever, the people coming to see Mary Jo were coming from places like Chicago, Detroit, Omaha, New York, and Gary, Indiana. People would pack up their children and everything they had to head to a place they had never been, where they had no job and no place to live. It was unimaginable, but so were the conditions that they were leaving. They were leaving violent relationships. They were trying to break their children free from the cycle of ghetto violence, poverty, drugs, and gangs. There were outreach centers in their own towns, of course, but none that were run with the kind of love and compassion and generosity and structure of Sharing and Caring Hands.

Some people came to find work because they'd heard the job market was better in Minnesota. That was true, but what they didn't find out until they got there was that the housing situation was worse. Affordable housing was growing more scarce by the day, disappearing altogether in many areas that had been acquired by developers.

As a result, residents at Mary's Place were taking longer to find a place to live. It was intended for stays of one to two months, but in reality, especially for the larger families, even when they found jobs, they were staying five or six or more months. The number of families that needed Mary's Place kept increasing, and the charges for the hotel rooms Mary Jo utilized meanwhile were getting higher and higher. More rooms were needed at Mary's Place.

Again, though faced with lack of space and a lack of money, Mary Jo, determined as ever, called the architects to look at the land remaining around Mary's Place. She made sure they kept looking until they came up with a way to use the space for an addition. They came up with a plan to add an angled wing at each end of the building to add thirty-six new family-sized units.

The cost of the addition would come to about $6 million. That was a bit more than the bank was comfortable loaning, especially since the balance on the $500,000 Mary My Hope renovation still was outstanding.

Mary Jo started her fundraising rounds again, going forward with the construction plans on nothing but faith. "We have to move forward with this right now!" Mary Jo insisted to Dick. "How else will we begin building next summer?" In May 1999, the plans were finished, but she had yet to raise one dime for the project. Two months later, she had raised $1.6 million and had another $500,000 pledged. Groundbreaking took place in July 1999.

Mary Jo's pace still made Dick a bit nervous, but he had seen her in action long enough to know that her hard work and faith would pay off. Inevitably, someone would come down for a tour of the place who would rally friends to make donations. This had happened over and over, and that's what happened this time too. When the $1.6 million came in from donors for the project, the bank was willing to loan another $3,325,000. For the remainder, Mary Jo and Dick convinced past donors to pledge assets to back an additional loan. With the backing of Burt McGlynn, as well as Bernie Hofschulte, owner of Bernco, a window company, and Tom Lowe, owner of Lyman Lumber, the bank approved a loan for the remainder of the building costs.

Arranging the loan this way made Dick a lot less nervous. The reason that secured loans worked so well for Sharing and Caring Hands was that they knew they would never have to touch any of the backers' money. Every year at Christmastime donations surged, much of which went towards capital projects. In recent years, surpluses had averaged between $800,000 to $1.2 million. Thankfully, every year the surplus was increasing. People now were donating stock and anonymous gifts as large as $100,000.

Both wings of the Mary's Place addition were completed and all thirty-six of the new units were occupied with families by the fall of 2000. Not including the families Mary Jo still put up in hotel rooms, she was now housing more than five hundred people. "It's the power of prayer," Mary Jo reiterated. "There is no other way to explain it. There is no way I could have done all this myself. I'm just one woman."

The tiny storefront outreach Mary Jo started has become the largest independently funded charity in the state. In the spring of 2000, Dick Copeland retired from his position at Rainbow Foods to meet the increasing demands of his general manager's duties at Sharing and Caring Hands. He is one of only fourteen paid employees. The greater part of the organization is supported by thousands of volunteers each month, more than fifty community service and church groups, as well as hundreds of businesses and individuals donating goods and financial support. The Sharing and Caring Hands volunteer board of directors, consisting of Mary Jo and Dick and six other board members with backgrounds in business, social, and spiritual leadership, meets quarterly to guide the growth and future of the organization.

One eventual mission of the board is to ensure the organization's stability and continued success should Mary Jo retire or become incapacitated in some way. This is hardly a concern today, since Mary Jo, who is now sixty years old, has taken no sick days in eighteen years. But some day, the board will have the task of finding someone to take over the leadership of this extraordinary mission she has built. One or more of the Copeland children would be likely candidates. Most of them have been involved at Sharing and Caring Hands at different times and in various capacities, but only a few are presently involved. The others have followed their own paths, concentrating on careers and raising their families, staying out of the public eye and stress at Sharing and Caring Hands. As for herself, Mary Jo faces the future with her unwavering faith; she is certain that just as God provided the resources upon which this mission was built, he will continue to provide what is necessary for it to go on.

With God's love guiding her life, recognitions for her work continued coming. In 1996, Mary Jo won the WCCO Radio Distinguished Good Neighbor Award, the 26th Annual Women in Business Career Achievement Award and the Norman Vincent Peale Unsung Hero Award. In 1997, she received the Toastmaster International Award in Communication and Leadership, the Dr. Martin Luther King Jr. Award for Outstanding Community Service, and Governor Arne Carlson declared February 15 as Mary Jo Copeland Day in the state of Minnesota. In 1998 she received the John A. Ryan Award from the University of St. Thomas. Honors in 1999 included the Mercela Trujillo Award for service to the Latino Community and the Caritas Award for Protection of Women. She was named the Person of the Week on ABC's *Nightly News* with Peter Jennings, featured on Tom Brokaw's *America Close-Up*, and was a featured speaker at the 2001 National Prayer Breakfast in Washington, D.C.

Mary Jo displays these and all of her previous recognitions on her office wall as a daily reminder of just how much one woman *can* do. She keeps a collection of the articles about her work that have appeared in *The New York Times Magazine, Good Housekeeping, Parade, Reader's Digest,* and *People* magazines, plus national religious publications, the *Minneapolis Star Tribune, St. Paul Pioneer Press* and other local newspapers. Between new building construction and the services she provides, Mary Jo has raised more than $50 million for the poor and homeless in the past seventeen years. Without one dime of public money, she runs her organization with only 7 per-cent of her total budget being spent for administrative costs and fundraising, and 93 percent going directly to the needs of the people, a percentage nearly unheard of with other charities of this scope. In 1999, then-Texas Governor and future President George W. Bush visited Mary Jo at Sharing and Caring Hands. On July 6, 2000, he singled her out in his acceptance speech televised nationally at the Republican National Convention when he said:

"I think of Mary Jo Copeland, whose ministry called Sharing and Caring Hands serves 1,000 meals [a day] in Minneapolis, Minnesota. Each day, Mary Jo washes the feet of the homeless, then sends them off with new socks and shoes. 'Look after your feet,' she tells them. 'They must carry you a long way in this world, and then all the way to God.' Government cannot do this work. It can feed the body, but it cannot reach the soul. Yet government can take the side of these groups, helping the helper, encouraging the inspired."

Mary Jo Copeland has healed the hearts and helped the lives of thousands of people. The little girl who wouldn't amount to a hill of beans has become an American hero. And her work isn't finished.

Epilogue

The first edition of *Great Love* was published in 2003, shortly before the United States went into a housing and economic free fall. Banks imploded, both here and around the globe. Many people lost jobs; the unemployment rate soared. The revelation and subsequent downfall of corporate criminals like Bernie Madoff, and, locally, of Tom Petters made an already shaky economy even worse; many investors and their families lost everything as a result of these dubious business schemes. The War on Terror was underway, and casualties were coming home at a rate that an entire generation had never imagined.

Despite these drastic social and economic challenges of the past ten years, Mary Jo Copeland has forged on with her work at Sharing and Caring Hands and Mary's Place. With so many people out of work, the needs at the outreach center multiplied to new levels. When the financial portfolios of would-be donors came crashing down, raising funds became even more difficult. But Mary Jo did not give up. She did not give in. She continued praying and giving and caring for the poor.

Mary Jo has raised an estimated total of more than $100 million for her organizations over the past thirty years. Sharing and Caring Hands now serves more than 240,000 meals each year. It provides more than 10,000 showers each year to people with no other access to bathing facilities. In 2012, Sharing and Caring Hands provided free eye exams and glasses for more than 600 people, half of them children. More than 375,000 pounds of food each year are distributed to those in need. Mary's Place transitional shelter now houses more than 500 people (a recent count was 436 children and 140 adults) in its 92 family apartments. In 2012,

Sharing and Caring Hands also paid for 19,033 nights of shelter for people in area hotels and shelters.

Also in 2012, Mary Jo successfully fought off another attempt by local developers to eject her from her property. North First Ventures proposed a plan for a new NFL stadium that would occupy the Farmers Market site. This would include Sharing and Caring Hands, Mary My Hope and Mary's Place campus. Mary Jo was ready this time; she would not be evicted again. On Sunday, January 22, 2012, Joe Soucheray wrote in the St. Paul *Pioneer Press*, "The players took a look at the Farmers Market site and encountered Mary Jo Copeland in full fury and quickly came up with a grading problem, real or imagined, that would be a greater obstacle than taking on Copeland and her institution, Sharing and Caring Hands." Developers and city planners moved on to another location for the stadium.

Early in 2003, the $60 million dollar Gift of Mary Children's Home project was in full swing, but as time wore on and the economy sank lower and lower, it became evident that it would not be possible to raise adequate funding to bring the project to conclusion. Although this was a disappointment, just as she had always done before, Mary Jo turned an adverse situation into an opportunity. She will sell the 40 acres of land in Eagan, Minnesota, where she had hoped to build Gift of Mary Children's Home; the proceeds will be used add more apartment units to Mary's Place.

While these events and statistics are nothing short of miracles in these troubled times, for Mary Jo the real miracle started thirty years ago with the very first homeless man that she met and made a connection with while working at Catholic Charities. It is this same connection she makes today—one person at a time.

Melisa and Kevin Demers met and married when they were quite young. Kevin's family believed that 18 was far too young for a girl to be a wife and mother, and Melisa's family doubted that Kevin had the maturity to be an effective father. Either way, a baby was coming, so the two of them stuck together and hoped for the best. Several years later they had five children and a life filled with love.

They lived in Fergus Falls, Minnesota, a very small town about 180 miles northwest of the Twin Cities. Their children were each born about two years apart, and after their fifth child was born, they were really struggling financially. Melisa stayed home to care for the children while Kevin worked full time in a furniture factory. There was a salary cap for factory workers at the time, so no matter how hard Kevin worked, he would not make more than $9.80 per hour. It was not enough for a family of seven to make ends meet. They were almost at the end of their rope in 2005 when they got a call from long-time friends who had moved to Texas. Their friends told them there was really good work on the oil rigs down there. The lure of making real money for the first time weighed heavily on them. After a few more months of struggling to pay rent and buy food and formula for the baby, they decided to pack up and try for a more prosperous life in Texas.

They packed everything they owned into a U-Haul trailer, packed the kids into their minivan and drove through the night to Texas, excited about their prospects and new life.

The night they arrived, their dreams came to an abrupt halt. The friends they had pinned all their hopes on, whom they had known for twenty years and considered to be like siblings, had lied about their connections to oil rig work.

"They were making plenty of money, all right," Melisa remembers, "but it was on crystal meth, not oil."

Kevin and Melisa knew right away that they could not have their children in that situation. The kids were ages 10, 8, 5, 3 and almost 1. Their three-year-old, Jacob, was having a lot of issues at that time. He couldn't walk or talk and didn't eat very well. He was extremely hyperactive, but he didn't communicate at all. He'd just grunt. The doctors in Fergus Falls said it was because Melisa didn't know how to raise a boy. The other four children were girls, so they told her it was simply her lack of experience with boys.

When Jacob started having seizures, the doctors took two weeks before they were convinced it was more than just a "temper tantrum" and prescribed him some medication.

Now they were stuck down in Texas, their youngest still in diapers, behavior issues with Jacob, three older girls who were hungry, and no one to turn to. Kevin spent every day looking for any kind of work, but came back with nothing. After three days they could no longer afford the hotel, so they had to move to another hotel in a very bad area. They tried to get welfare help, but because they were not Texas residents, they did not qualify for any services or assistance there.

"We really thought things couldn't get any worse at that point," said Melisa. All seven of them were stuck in a tiny motel in a bad part of town, Jacob's medicine was running out, they had no food, they were running out of diapers for the baby and Kevin still couldn't find any work.

"Then our so-called friends who got us into this mess in the first place stole our trailer." Everything the family owned was in it. Everything. Furniture, washer, dryer, clothes, photos—everything was gone.

They finally called Kevin's mother and admitted, "We screwed up. We never should have come here. We need help to get home." Kevin's mother sent them $600.

Home to them was Fergus Falls. The $600 ran out when they got to St. Paul. All they had was their vehicle, the clothes on their backs, and the diaper bag they had with them in the hotel when their trailer was stolen.

They stayed with Kevin's mother for a couple of days, but she was getting on in years and there were seven of them crammed into her little place. It wasn't a permanent solution. They went to the welfare office in Minneapolis and explained what had happened and asked for help.

"They told us that, because we voluntarily moved to Texas, we lost our Minnesota residency," Melisa said. "According to them, we were not Minnesota residents. We were not Texas residents. We were nobody. We were gone for two weeks, and we lost everything."

They spent a couple more days trying to figure out what to do, what their options were. It was September now; the kids should have been back in school. Jacob was all out of medicine and his behavior started deteriorating. "We went to a shelter but they wouldn't let us stay because Jacob has a disability and also because Kevin was with us," said Melisa. "If you are married and the kids are all yours together, you can't get help. If I had been a single mom with five kids, there would be no problem. Because we were a family, there was no help for us."

They went back to the state welfare office to try to make someone there understand that they had lived in Minnesota all their lives; they had only been gone for two weeks, and they felt they shouldn't lose their residency because of two weeks. The instructions they got that time were to fill out a form with their address and phone number, and after thirty days they would qualify to get some help.

Address? Phone number? They were living in their mini-van! Thirty days? What were they supposed to feed their children for thirty days?

Kevin and Melisa were devastated. It was the end of the line for their family; there were no options left. As this hard reality became clear, they lost all hope. There was no other option but to split up. They couldn't take care of the kids anymore. They would have to turn them all over to the county.

They both agreed to explain everything to the kids. They would not abandon them in a strange place with strange people without explaining what was happening and how much they loved them all.

"That was the hardest day of my life, the hardest thing I've ever had to do," Melisa remembers with tears in her eyes. "But we knew how the system worked. With five of them, there was no way they would be kept together. I wasn't going to just drop them into that situation without their knowing. We had to tell them."

After that, there was nothing but emptiness. That was it. For Kevin and Melisa, losing the kids was losing everything. Their future was nothing. Melisa had lost the will to live. She felt certain that she would die of a broken heart and that Kevin would probably drink himself to death.

On their way down to the Hennepin County foster care program to drop off the kids, all seven of them in tears, something made them turn the car around. "I can't explain it," said Melisa. "God must have done it. I don't have any other explanation."

Someone in the waiting area at the welfare office had mentioned Mary Jo Copeland to them. They considered going to see her, talked about it, but decided it would be the same answer they got everywhere else. But now for some reason, they suddenly felt compelled to go to see her. They turned the car around.

When they arrived at Sharing and Caring Hands, the center wasn't open yet. All the people were lined up inside the ramp. People were packed in so tightly that they could barely move. The kids were all terrified.

"Up until that point, we were real country bumpkins," Melisa said. "We had never spent time in the city and had never seen so many people in one place before." It seemed there were more people in the building that day than in all of Fergus Falls. Kevin and Melisa tried to shield the frightened children from the others and exchanged a knowing glance with each other. They knew they would never get help. There were so many people in line ahead of them, there was just no way.

Then the doors opened, and everyone filed into the dining area. Kevin and Melisa just stood there in line, broken and hopeless, their children crying. Suddenly, one of the volunteers walked up to them and said, "What do you need?"

Melisa couldn't say anything, she just cried. Kevin told the volunteer that they were hoping to talk to Mary Jo to see if she could help them.

The volunteer turned around and called to Mary Jo on the other side of the room, "Mary Jo, we have a family here who needs you." He brought the whole family up to the front of the line and had them all sit down behind the half-wall where Mary Jo was washing feet. The children calmed down once they were away from all the other people. The whole family sat there watching Mary Jo, completely bewildered. When she was finished with the feet, Mary Jo told the Demers family to come with her. They followed her back into the office area.

Melisa said she will never forget what happened next. "Mary Jo turned and looked me in the eye, and it was like she already knew why we were there. She just knew. I was about to explain our situation, but Mary Jo stopped me and said, 'Don't say anything. God brought you to me for a reason. You are where you are supposed to be. Everything is going to be okay now.'"

Melisa started sobbing. Kevin was a little tearful too. Mary Jo gave them some Target gift cards and gave them some food and said, "Go buy your kids some warm clothes and get them something to eat. Then come back here and see me in two hours, okay?"

They still weren't sure what was going to happen, but they did what Mary Jo told them to. When they got back, Mary Jo had an apartment at Mary's Place ready for them to move in—just like that. Kevin felt a huge weight lift off of him. Assuming the apartment was just for Melisa and the kids, he was so relieved that they would finally be safe and warm. Mary Jo set him straight. "You aren't going anywhere," she said to Kevin, "You are a family and you will all stay here as a family."

Melisa was so stunned that she burst into tears again, realizing what was happening—they had a place to live. They weren't going to lose the kids. They were fed. They had clothes. Some one came the next day and got the kids enrolled in school, and Mary Jo gave them school supplies. They got Jacob into the medical clinic and although it was evening, the volunteer nurse spent three hours on the phone with pharmacies and doctors to get medicine for him that same evening. He was evaluated at Children's Hospital and diagnosed with severe autism, epilepsy and ADHD. Mary Jo was the first person to acknowledge that Jacob had real medical problems, not bad parents. She brought in special help for Jacob until they could get him into a kindergarten that supported special needs kids. Then she arranged transportation to get him there.

After one month of staying at Mary's Place, Kevin was offered a full-time job with full medical benefits at Viking Tool and Electric. He had to start out working nights, but they were happy with this opportunity for a solid paycheck. Mary Jo gave him a bus card to get to and from work so Melisa and the kids would have the van available.

From the day they met Mary Jo, Kevin and Melisa felt nothing but compassion and support. No matter what problems came up, they found support and solutions from the nuns and volunteers at Mary's Place. "We were never once made to feel ashamed," they said. "I mean, let's face it, we got ourselves into this. We were young and made the bad decision to move to Texas with no resources." But staying at Mary's Place was the opposite of what they had experienced in the past. No one there made them feel like bad parents. No one turned a blind eye to their real needs.

"That's the biggest difference with Mary Jo," said Kevin, "she really understands what needs to be done right away, and she does it. She delivers." After Kevin started working, his number one priority was to pay back Mary Jo in some way. Although Mary Jo was touched by this gesture, she told him, "Now is not the time for that. Now is the time for you to save your money. When it's time for you to go, you will need that savings. I don't want you struggling when you leave here."

About four months after they arrived at Sharing and Caring Hands, Kevin and Melisa found a new home that they could now afford to rent for their family. They had arrived broken and hopeless, and four months later were revived, thriving and full of love and gratitude.

"We were a little nervous when it came time to leave," said Melisa. "After what we came from, we were still afraid of everything slipping away again."

Their confidence was shaken, but Mary Jo understood that, too, and she knew how to take care of it. They came to her with nothing but the clothes on their back and a broken-down van, but they would not leave that way.

On moving day, Mary Jo paid the rental deposit on their new home. She arranged delivery of beds and tables and a sofa and chairs. She sent them with bedding and towels and dishes and pots and pans and silverware, all the things they needed to set up a home. Kevin and Melisa were in tears again. "All these things you don't even think about," Kevin said, "you don't think about them until they are gone. When it's all gone and you don't even have a fork? These gifts— you just can't measure how much they mean."

The only challenge still facing them was that their van was on its last legs. They had it fixed several times after breaking down while living at Mary's Place, but there weren't many miles left in the vehicle that had served as their home for many weeks. Mary Jo knew that losing transportation could devastate them all over again.

Where there is a need, God will fill it. Someone donated a car to Sharing and Caring Hands that week. This became Kevin and Melisa's new car.

The last thing Mary Jo gave them on moving day was perhaps the greatest gift of all. She told them, "Go on out now and succeed in your life. If you focus on the love you have, you will get past the bumps that will come. If the bumps get too big, I will always be here for you. Always."

That made such a difference to them. Just knowing they never had to be desperate and alone again, knowing someone cared made all the difference.

Money was tight for them; they knew it would be with seven people on one income. They struggled, and they knew they weren't going to have expensive clothes or the newest electronics on the market, or the best of anything else, but they were so grateful for everything, every moment that they did have.

Kevin and Melisa moved the family into their new home in February of 2006. Kevin thrived in his job with Viking Drill and Tool and still works there today. When Melisa had become pregnant with their first child during her senior year of high school, she had to drop out a few months before graduation. With the family stabilized nearly fifteen years later, Melisa went back to school and earned her GED. Then she earned an associate's degree in administration of criminal justice. Then she earned her bachelor's degree in organization and security management. In November of 2012, Melisa graduated with a master's degree in administration of justice and security. Shortly after graduation, Melisa landed a position with Allied Barton Security. The Demers are now a two-income family.

Their oldest daughter, Katlynn, graduated high school in 2012, four months early and at the top of her class. She is now a college freshman. The next oldest, Kyrsten, is a high school sophomore working a twelfth-grade curriculum. She will also graduate early. The next oldest, thirteen-year-old Jourdan, has been diagnosed with autism, but she is extremely high functioning, on the opposite end of the spectrum from her younger brother, Jacob. They are both exceptionally bright in certain areas and are flourishing now that they are getting the support services that they need. The youngest, Rylie, is happily zooming through elementary school.

Melisa thinks back on the family when they first arrived on Mary Jo's doorstep with tears in her eyes. "When I think of who my kids might have become if they had to go through foster care—

it's overwhelming. The girls, they'd probably be on the street, not succeeding in school. And Jacob? He would have been institutionalized for sure. He was 24/7 hands-on care. No foster home would have taken him."

She credits Mary Jo with all that they have overcome. "We have five well-adjusted, giving, super kids and none of it would be possible without Mary Jo. Every time we see her we thank her, but she always says, 'I didn't do anything, God did it.' But really," Melisa goes on, "if it hadn't been for her—she literally saved the family. She saved seven people."

Along with helping many families like the Demers that were struggling to secure employment and housing in the mid-2000's, Mary Jo also saw a new trend in Minnesota: homelessness stemming from across the globe. As the last of the Hmong refugee camps in Thailand were shut down, a new wave of Hmong immigrants began arriving in the Twin Cities. With the language barrier and limited job skills, immigrants had no hope of earning enough to afford rent, especially for large Hmong families with more than ten members, including grandparents. In the spring of 2006, Hmong families occupied more than half of the 92 units at Mary's Place.

"They are very grateful people, very humble people," Mary Jo says. They are hard-working and committed to working with interpreters and job training to get on their feet. After living most of their lives in refugee camps, it was going to take time.

In addition to the Hmong refugees, yet another wave of immigrants began arriving in the Twin Cities from war-torn Somalia. Although Somali refugees began appearing in Minnesota in 1993, the steady escalation and intensity of violence in Somalia the past twenty years has driven much of the population out of the region. Today, Minnesota has the largest Somali population in the U.S.

In the summer of 2012, Diamond and her two children were among the approximately sixty Somali families living at Mary's Place. Diamond was born in Somalia but moved to Kenya when she was two years old, so Kenya was really all she knew. Shortly after arriving in Kenya, Diamond's mother abandoned her, and she lived with her aunt's family. She never knew her father. Because she was born Somali, her aunt never considered Diamond to be part of the family. She was neither cared for nor fed. Her aunt did not allow her to go to school. She worked in the house and that was her life.

When she was ten years old, Diamond ran away from her aunt's house. She went to the United Nations for help. They sent her to live with a family in Nairobi. It was a safe home for her, but after two months, the husband died of cancer. The wife found work in Uganda, but Diamond was afraid to go. "I know Kenya," she said, "I don't know anything else but Kenya. If I am going to die somewhere, let me die in Kenya."

The UN placed Diamond with another family in Nairobi. They were a kind family and took good care of her for three years. When the husband's work contract expired, the family had to move back to Germany. But Diamond didn't want to go. There were stories about people traveling who were attacked. They would be cut open, and their organs stolen to sell. She was too afraid.

She went back to the UN for help again, but this time she learned that she couldn't get any more help. She pleaded with them, "I'm from Kenya. I belong to Kenya. I don't know Germany; I don't want to go anywhere else. Let me die in Kenya." The UN turned her away.

She was thirteen years old, and with no other choice she returned to her aunt to beg for help. Her aunt allowed her back to the house on the condition that Diamond get married to the man her aunt chose for her. There was no other place for her to go, no options, so Diamond was married. But her aunt did not give her a wedding. There was no ceremony. She was given a painful female circumcision and then told to go with this man. "I go inside the room right after they cut me, and I went in the bed, and I was a small girl you know, and the man, he just come in and use me. It was so awful. I felt numb, like a dead person."

Diamond soon became pregnant, and one month after giving birth, the baby was taken away. "I don't even feel like I had a baby. I was so young. But awhile later I got another baby, and they take that one away too."

Her life was too hard. She took care of the family; she did the cooking and the washing. She was like a servant girl and they abused her. "I was like dirt," she said.

She ran away again. She was sixteen. During the next couple of years she found work in a cafeteria, in a small market shop and in a clothing manufacturing company. She stayed in different places, sometimes outside, sometimes with friends she met. She had a boyfriend for a while, but she was never stable. She often ran out of money and was never sure where she would sleep. When she discovered she was pregnant, her boyfriend left.

She was alone when the baby came. She used some cut-up cloth to wrap the baby girl in because she had no baby clothes. She left town with her baby daughter, not knowing where she would go. She only knew that she had to leave because of the shame she would bring on her aunt's family, having no father for her baby.

She walked for days or weeks maybe. When she got to the other side of Nairobi, she happened to meet a man whom she knew. She told him about her problems, all she'd been through and now having a baby and no money. He invited her to join him, along with three men he was with, for something to eat. She ate with them and then they showed her a place she could sleep for the night, so she lay down with her baby near her in a bag. Some time later she woke up to find one of the men lying next to her.

"He wanted to use me but I begged him, no please, I can't. I have my baby here with me." The man that knew her heard what was going on and came to stop it, but the other one had a long knife and fought him. Then the three other men came back to her. She begged again, "Please don't hurt me, don't kill me! I have my baby here. Do whatever you want, but please don't kill me." All three of them raped her.

"I wanted to go after that, but they said no, I had to stay. I was with them one more night, and it was the same thing. Then one more night, and again, the same thing. Three or four nights they used me. Then they just go their way and I go mine."

The police caught Diamond trying to cross a river bridge without a passport and took her to jail. This was all right with Diamond; at least she would have a place to sleep. Her daughter had become bright red all over her body, red rings covering her. They hadn't had a bath in weeks.

She met the wife of one of the soldiers in jail and told her all that had happened to her. The wife convinced her husband to help Diamond. Since she couldn't get on a bus without a passport, they drove her to town themselves. They paid for her hotel for the night, and the next day she would go back to the UN.

She discovered the next morning that all the people at the UN who had helped her when she was young were gone now. No one knew her, and because she was 18, she couldn't get any more help. She went outside of the UN building and sat down across the street underneath a giant tree. She didn't have a blanket. She didn't have any food. It was so cold that she could see her breath in the air. She lay down on the ground, cuddling her baby close, and looking up through the branches and leaves of the tree she thought, *God gave us this tree to keep us from the rain.*

In the morning, some women came out of a nearby church and brought some bread and milk. She told them what happened to her, and every day the women came back with food and tea. They invited Diamond to come inside the church to wash her clothes. That Sunday the church collected money and clothes for Diamond and her daughter. At night, when they slept outside there would sometimes be Americans coming down the street, laughing and drunk after the clubs closed. They would see Diamond and her baby there and wake her to give her money. The Kenyan police would also give her money occasionally. She saved all of it, spent nothing. She ate only what the church gave her.

After about a month, she had almost three hundred dollars saved. She thought, *I am rich!* She went back to the shop she worked in before, and the old man who ran the shop remembered her. He gave her a room to stay in, and she worked in his shop for over a year. She had four hundred dollars saved. She decided soon after, *I do not want to die in Kenya.*

She decided to try to get to America and went back to the UN for help. Again, she could get no help. She learned that her case was closed. She traveled north towards another UN office near the border, west of Sudan. When she arrived, the office was closed for the New Year's holiday. Outside a police station across the street, she spread out some blankets and cuddled up with her daughter, who was now two years old. In the days that followed, she got help again from a nearby church. Some of the policemen helped her and gave her money and food, and they let Diamond and her daughter sleep inside the station doors at night.

She became involved in a relationship with one of the policemen who had befriended her, and soon became pregnant again.

"I did not tell anyone he was the father because they don't allow refugees and Kenyan police to have a relationship. If I told, they can take away his job, and after that he can kill me. I just keep quiet, I don't tell that I'm pregnant to anyone."

Since Diamond still had all the money she saved from living outside, she thought maybe she would have luck to get a passport and go to America soon. It was around this time that she was attacked by a group of Somalis. She was stabbed nearly twenty times on her arms and chest and back.

"They saw me going into the church for help every day and that's why they stab me, because they don't allow a Somali to go to church. Even though I live in Kenya all my life, I was born Somali and they think I am going against Muslim, so they stab me. There is no protection for someone like me who has no family. Anyone can do anything to you when you have no family."

Some bystanders found her after the attack and took her to a hospital. Her wounds were treated, but as a refugee, she did not have access to medicine, so she was released. She had her daughter and was pregnant, and she was so tired. The weather was good. She looked up to the sky and thought; *God has given us a clear night with no rain.* She lay down with her daughter and slept outside.

Later that night, she woke when a man came by and took her bag. She sat up and shouted, "Hey, man, there's nothing in there. That bag has my daughter's clothes!" He slowly came back and handed the bag to her. He sat down and asked her what she was doing there. She told him everything.

"I have my girl here and I'm pregnant and I'm looking for the UN. I am very hungry, and the knife wound on my chest is infected now. I have no medicine. We have no food. My daughter is breastfeeding on me while I'm pregnant because I have nothing else to feed her."

The man left then and came back with food and they ate. He convinced her to come with him to stay in a camp until morning. She didn't trust anyone then, but he said, "Diamond, if you stay here, some other fool is going to come along and take your bag."

She followed him to a camp near the river where there were all kinds of people who slept outside. There were a hundred people or more in tents everywhere. They didn't like strangers. They would not let her stay until they heard her story, so she told them everything.

They let Diamond and her daughter stay. Everybody in the camp collected what money they could and gave it to her. They took her to a healer who gave her medicinal tea for her infection. Everyone in the camp prayed for her and took care of her.

By the time Diamond was finally given a passport by the UN, her son was a year old and her daughter was four. The UN arranged passage for Diamond and her daughter and son from Kenya to New York, and then to Minnesota. She doesn't know why she landed in Minnesota. She said; "The UN decides where you go."

She came to Minnesota with her two children and nothing else. She received some help from Lutheran Social Services, and stayed the first month in subsidized housing, but it was a constant struggle to pay the rent. Every month it was either buy food, or pay the rent. She couldn't do both. Soon she would lose her apartment because she was expected to sign a lease for six months, and she didn't have the money for it. That's when she heard about Mary's Place.

From the minute Mary Jo laid eyes on Diamond and her children, they had a home in her heart forever. After all these years working with people in poverty, Mary Jo could recognize human suffering like no one else. Mary's Place became Diamond's home that day.

Diamond had never experienced such love in her life; she didn't understand it. All she understood were the rules she was presented with when she moved into Mary's Place. If she broke the rules, she would be kicked out. You have to sign the rules when you move in, and if you break them, you are out. The rules require residents to keep their units clean and their children supervised at all times. There is a nightly curfew except for those who work late. In general, residents must demonstrate respect for the building and for one another at all times.

"When I first came here, all I could think about was those rules I signed. I did not want any mistakes because, tomorrow if they kick me from Mary's Place, I have nowhere to go. I have no relatives. I have no friends. I don't have a job. I did not sleep; I was so worried all the time about making a mistake. I don't sleep nighttime or daytime; all I do is think about my problems. I'm so glad my kids are safe here, but all I can think is, why God? Why did I do all these things in my life and why did people do bad things to me? Where are my kids, God? My babies that were taken away, where are they? I think over everything again and again, and I HATE my life."

Nalee Lor, Diamond's case worker at Mary's Place, saw how she was struggling, saw the blank look in her eyes and the lifetime of sadness she'd endured. Diamond slowly began opening up to her.

"I'm so worried about making a mistake here," she told Nalee. "The other Somalis, if they get kicked out, they have a community, they have somewhere to go. For me, I have no tribe. No Somali will help me because I come from no one. I am nothing."

Later that day, Mary Jo sat down with Diamond at Mary's Place. "Diamond, you have freedom here," Mary Jo told her. "You have a family now, you belong here, so never worry. Never think I don't love you. You will stay here as long as you need to."

For the first time in her life, Diamond experienced what it felt like to have hope. Her spirit woke up that day. She continued counseling with Nalee, working past her deep emotional scars. She began studying, working on her English and writing. She learned how to use a computer to navigate the Internet. She got a job working at a Montessori childcare center.

"Mary, she's so busy with all these people every day, but every day she call me and she say, 'Diamond, how is your life today?' One day Mary call me and said 'Let's go out to lunch today.' I never went out to lunch in my whole life before. When we got back, there was a car here, a 2005 Chrysler. The whole staff was here and they say, 'Diamond, this is your car!'"

"I didn't know how to drive, but Mary, you know what she did? She paid all that money for my driving lessons. It was so much money. I just couldn't believe it. I took the test when the lessons were done and I failed that test.

"Mary told me, 'Don't you cry about this. I failed my first time, too. You will pass the next one.' I did pass the next time, and when I came back to Mary's Place, the whole staff lined up and cheered for me. I never had joy like that before in my life. It was a feeling like hope building bigger in my heart. Mary gave that to me. She is a Mom to me. She gives hope where there is no hope. She gives food and clothes and medicine and shelter, any help you need, she gives. But also she gives hope. Nowhere else can you get that. Help and hope together? Only Mary gives that. She is the Mom to me and the Mom to millions."

Meeting Diamond today, you would never detect the heartache that she has survived. Her bright spirit and outgoing personality explode when she enters the room. The scars from her knife wounds remain on her skin, but she covers them proudly with neon-colored shirts, an animal print head covering, and rock-star high heels and sunglasses. At the Thursday night meetings at Mary's Place, Diamond serves as a translator for the Somali residents as Mary Jo reviews the rules and hands out awards, dollars and hugs.

"Most Somalis, when they first come here, they panic when they see Mary praying. They don't understand English, so they think she's trying to turn them Christian," said Diamond. "That's where I come in," she beams. "I tell them, guys, calm down, no one's going to make you Christian. She's only telling you to save your money; she's talking about you helping yourself. She just want to help you. She prays for you, that's all. She's praying for all the people in the world who are without fire, without water, without food, and without medicine. She's brave for them. She's brave for you, too!

"They listened to me. Mary helped me believe in myself. She made me believe in my voice. What I say never mattered in my life before, but now, all the Somalis listen to me, and they all say, 'Mary is the Mom of the world!' The whole Somali community in Minnesota—I use my voice and change what they all believe.

"Today I want to pray for Mary, for the life she gave me," Diamond says. "I will always pray for Mary. Every day I have left, I will pray for Mary."

*   *   *   *

In February 2013, Mary Jo received a call from the White House. She learned that she had been selected as a recipient of the Presidential Citizens Medal, one of the highest awards for civilians in the United States. The award recognizes U.S. citizens who have demonstrated commitment to service in their community, who have helped their country or fellow citizens through one or more extraordinary acts, whose service relates to a long-term or persistent problem, or whose service has had a sustained impact on others' lives and provided inspiration for others to serve.

After the call was over, Mary Jo hung up and exclaimed, "Praise God!" She was honored. She felt grateful and touched. She would be traveling to Washington D.C. once more. This time she would be honored at an awards ceremony and reception at the White House. The trip would mean a disruption in her schedule, which always unsettled her. She would have to miss the usual packed crowds in line to see her that Thursday, not to mention the regular Thursday night meeting with Mary's Place residents, the highlight of her week.

The morning of the flight out to Washington, D.C., Mary Jo's usual airplane jitters were eased somewhat when the flight attendant announced on the intercom, "Good morning to all passengers on Delta Flight 1764 with service to Washington Reagan National Airport. As we prepare the flight deck for take-off, we wanted to let everyone know that we have a very special passenger on board today. Minneapolis' own Mary Jo Copeland is on her way to the White House. President Obama will be honoring her with a national award for all of her years of service to the poor at Sharing and Caring Hands..." Everyone on board cheered and burst into applause. The captain came out to congratulate her and said, "Thank you for all you have done—and all you continue to do." Mary Jo squeezed Dick's hand, smiled, and bowed her head, humble as always.

Upon arrival in Washington, the first order of business was to pray. They checked into the Mayflower Hotel, and then hopped in a cab to visit the Basilica of the National Shrine of the Immaculate Conception, the largest Catholic church in the United States. There was a lot of traffic on the way and Mary Jo, as usual, did not waste time while sitting in traffic. News of her award had already spread, and both local and national media were eager to cover it. While her cab driver navigated the Washington rush hour traffic, Mary Jo did a live radio interview with Chad Hartman on WCCO Minneapolis by phone. Chad introduced her and gave some information about the Presidential Citizens Medal. When he asked Mary Jo what she thought the award might do for the awareness of Sharing and Caring Hands, she didn't miss a beat.

"Well, if nothing else, Chad, it'll bring in more help, which I always need," said Mary Jo. "It'll also bring an awareness to the whole country of the problem, not just of homelessness... we use that word too quickly all the time. The problem is people in poverty, people there through no fault of their own. I think that being able to stand up and bring a voice for the poor to the country is going to mean a lot. Everyone can make a difference. We are all called for something. Everyone doesn't have to build a campus like I did, but they do have to listen to the voice of God and reach out to people. We all do. There's a hurting world out there, and when we bring hope to people, it makes such a difference. It's not just a wish that things will get better. It's a promise that we don't walk alone. I hope to bring this message to the President and to the world through this award."

Mary Jo spent another 25 minutes in the live interview talking about the people she helps, describing the vast extent of how her programs have grown over the years, and letting everyone know that one hundred percent of the support she offers is funded with private donations.

Then she talked about the need to build another addition and more apartments at Mary's Place. "I have to build more units for the poor, Chad. We are always full! So if someone's out there with a million dollars, they could really help me."

Chad Hartman chuckled at her straightforwardness and ended the interview by saying, "In the broadcasting business we often get caught up in hyperbole, whether we exaggerate because something is great, or we come on too strong when something is awful. But I truly mean this; you are an amazing person, Mary Jo. Our state is so much better because of you. I've seen your work first-hand, I see it every time I come down there, and you are amazing."

At the end of the interview, the cab arrived at the church and Mary Jo headed straight to an altar inside one of the Basilica's seventy chapels that honor the Blessed Virgin Mary. She lit a prayer candle, and then knelt down beneath one of the grand mosaic domes that crown the Basilica's Greek-styled interior, and she prayed. She prayed to God and the Blessed Mother for all those in poverty; all the people in the world like Brian Philbrick, like Kevin and Melisa and like Diamond. She prayed for health and healing for all those who were sick, like her friend Amy, a former Mary's Place resident and mother of six young children, who was battling her third brain tumor. She prayed for continued strength, to go on reaching out and touching the hearts and changing the lives of others, so that one day, everyone would know that they do not walk alone.

The next morning, Friday, February 15, 2013, after rising early to attend mass at the Cathedral of St. Matthew the Apostle, Mary Jo and Dick headed to the White House. After meeting with White House staff for a run-through of the event in the East Room, they had refreshments with the other award recipients in the State Dining Room while waiting for President Obama, who was running late in his morning meeting with Italian President Giorgio Napolitano. Members of the Air National Guard ushered award recipients and their guests through the Red Room, where Michelle Obama often hosts conferences and afternoon tea, and then into the Blue Room, distinct for its oval shape and typically used for receptions. There, the White House hosts offered interesting historical facts about the rooms and the artwork displayed in them. For instance, in an effort to draw First Lady Jane Pierce out of her depression after they lost their son Benjamin at age 11, President Franklin Pierce ordered fresh cut flowers to be displayed in every room of the White House. This tradition is still upheld today by a team of White House florists. Also, the term "lobbyist" originated with President Ulysses S. Grant, who could often be found in the lobby bar of the old W Hotel across the street from the White House, enjoying a cigar and brandy while anyone aiming to push an agenda would join him. Also, rumor had it that the custom of assigning a personal host to each Presidential Citizens Medal winner started when a past award recipient accidentally wandered up an extra flight of stairs to the second floor of the Executive Residence and inadvertently walked in on Sasha and Malia Obama playing together.

Suddenly, President Obama entered the Red Room, waved casually, smiled broadly and said, "Hi everyone, sorry I'm late." He passed into the Blue Room where award recipients would meet him, exchange a few words, and then be photographed with their guests.

After the photo sessions, everyone was ushered into the East Room where the ceremony took place. The President gave an inspiring speech that underlined the importance of American citizens who define our way of life by capturing our belief in something bigger than ourselves through a willingness to accept certain obligations to one another. The President told the recipients that they were being honored today "not just for what you do, but for what you represent, for the shining example you set every single day, and for the inspiration you give each of us, as fellow citizens, including your President."

When Mary Jo's name was called, she stepped onto the stage and stood with President Obama as a military aide read her commendation aloud:

"Driven by her faith and a fierce commitment to her community, Mary Jo Copeland has spent more than a quarter-century lifting up the underserved..." Hearing these words read aloud, while standing next to the President of the United States, Mary Jo began to understand the significance of the award and the light it would shine on her work. A tear began forming in her eye.

"Alongside her husband, she grew Sharing and Caring Hands from a small storefront operation in downtown Minneapolis into a charity that provides thousands of men, women and children the chance to live in health and dignity..." Overcome with humility, Mary Jo began crying in gratitude to God and the Blessed Mother. Seeing her tears, President Obama put his arm around her shoulders and momentarily rested his chin on top of her head.

"Her unyielding vision for stronger neighborhoods has inspired people nationwide, and her compassion for the poor and the marginalized speaks to the depth of the human spirit. The United States honors Mary Jo Copeland for sparking hope in those who need it most."

The President then handed Mary Jo her Presidential Citizens Medal, congratulated and thanked her, and gave her another hug as the audience, fellow medal winners, guests, and members of the press applauded heartily.

When you visit Sharing and Caring Hands, you will notice that tears often flow. People cry as they relive their histories to others. They cry while describing the love that Mary Jo shows them. For many, Mary Jo is the first person ever to show them love, acceptance, or even acknowledgement. They come to her broken and hopeless, full of fear and demons, and she transforms them with her magical brand of kindness. For nearly thirty years, with her strong spiritual faith she has transformed people's lives, over and over again with continued success. She's done it with the help of donors and others who recognize the incredible impact she has made, not just upon the community in Minnesota, but also upon cities nationwide and countries around the globe.

The most important and powerful message that Mary Jo will continue to bring to the world is that we do not walk alone. With the help of God and the Blessed Mother, she will work until her last breath to give help and hope to those stricken with poverty, to inspire others to reach out in their own ways, to do what they can to foster hope, healing, joy, freedom, peace, and great love.

The Heart of the Matter
Father Joseph R. Johnson, Pastor
Church of the Holy Family
St. Louis Park, Minnesota
Spiritual Adviser to Mary Jo Copeland

People who know of our friendship often ask me, "What makes Mary Jo Copeland tick?" It seems humanly impossible to stand there day after day, year after year, shouldering the burdens of those who come to seek assistance. No one comes to Mary Jo because things are going well. She greets an endless line of suffering each morning, and the needs always far exceed the resources. How does she live for decades amid this sea of human misery without losing her joy and zeal? How does she not become cynical or jaded? She answers simply that it is her faith in Jesus Christ and the strength she draws from the sacramental life of the Catholic Church.

More than "addressing poverty" as a concept or simply fixing material problems of individuals, Mary Jo seeks to bring the love of Jesus to suffering people who come to her. The fact is that she has done incredible things and attributes it all to God's grace. She spends several hours each morning praying before the Holy Eucharist for the strength to feed, house, and personally interview the hundreds of people who turn to her daily as a last resort for basic necessities. By evening she is physically and emotionally exhausted. People have suggested that she spend an hour less in prayer and add an hour of sleep. Without hesitation she retorts: "I could do this work with less sleep but I couldn't do it with five minutes less prayer."

Mary Jo built this empire of charity from scratch. She doesn't accept a penny of government money as she doesn't want any restrictions on speaking of God's Love. She is a great example of a lay person drawing on the Church's teaching and sacraments to change the world for the better. This book tells the story of how she overcame her own adversities and discovered her life's mission through the power of prayer and the spiritual motherhood she found in the Blessed Virgin Mary. *The Lord hears the cry of the poor... (Psalms 34:6)*

Mary Jo would never consider her operation as a social service agency. She sees herself as a servant of God and her mission is to bring His love to the world. As such, she makes no distinction between people of different races or religions. She is in the business of love—the same unconditional love that God shows to all of His children. *Let it be done to me according to Your Word. (Luke 1:38)*

Everything Mary Jo Copeland does is a response of faith patterned after the example of the Blessed Virgin Mary. She has worked tirelessly with the poor and underprivileged for nearly thirty years. She invites other people to step forward and help our brothers and sisters who otherwise fall through society's cracks. Mary Jo believes that all it takes is a faithful and humble "yes" on our part to change the world for the better. For many years, the sign above her building read: "Your smile and outstretched hands are the beginning of a miracle in someone else's life." As God worked through the Blessed Virgin Mary's assent of faith, so now Mary Jo believes that He seeks our cooperation to manifest His love in our world.

Over the years, Mary Jo has seen the growing need to provide assistance to families. She has seen the failures of troubled families to provide adequately for the development and well-being of their children. Each child deserves love and the chance to become a productive member of society. Mary Jo strives to restore hope to these children so that they may dare to dream. She seeks to equip them with the education, self-assurance, and values that they need to achieve these dreams. *Let the little children come unto Me. (Matthew 19:14)*

Mary Jo now takes care of needy families with approximately four hundred children at Mary's Place transitional housing shelter. She provides an environment where children have a chance for a normal life despite the hardships they suffer as their families struggle with poverty, abuse, and addiction. They are nourished by her affirmation that they, too, have a part to play in God's plan. God loved them into life and He wants to continue to show His love for them. Children who are loved learn to love others. Although they have been deprived of a "normal" family situation, Mary Jo seeks to heal their wounds with the love and encouragement that we owe to one another as God's children. *Whatsoever you did to the least one of these, that you did unto Me. (Matthew 25:40)*

The human person was created to love and be loved. As Mother Teresa of Calcutta often said, "The greatest poverty is to feel unwanted, unloved, uncared for." Mary Jo sees it as her privilege to be able "to touch the face of Jesus" in those in need whom she helps. More than the material goods of food, clothing, and shelter she provides, Mary Jo answers the deepest human longing to be loved. This is something that no government program could ever provide. *Who do you say that I am? (Matthew 16:15)*

The future of our nation depends on our response to the needs we see around us, especially of the children. Jesus asked his disciples to manifest their faith in Him by how they lived and, for some, how they died as martyrs. Mary Jo gives an example of faith and provides others with an opportunity to put the love we profess into action. Her spirituality is in the Catholic tradition but welcoming to all. Her efforts are built on faith with a mission to love. Catholics and non-Catholics learn from her that they are loved and that they should try to love others.

Mary Jo Copeland believes that it is time for all those who have received so many blessings from God to share those blessings with the suffering children of our community. Government programs can only achieve so much—love cannot be legislated. There will be individual challenges associated with each child who walks through the door. To do nothing would be safe—for you and me. But don't those children deserve safety, too?

Mary Jo invites us to testify to our faith both in the goodness of mankind to generously help those in need and in the goodness of God in enabling us to love one another even as He loves us. Mary Jo shows everyone around her that service is simply a free response of faithful love for God and neighbor. If we do our part, God will do the rest. *If the Lord does not build the house, in vain do the laborers build. If the Lord does not watch over the city, in vain do they keep watch. (Psalms 127:1)*

Mary Jo believes that she was chosen by God and that this is His work. When her time to serve comes to an end, she is confident that He will choose someone else to carry on His work. Her faithfulness will certainly inspire others to continue reaching out. Even a poor, abused child can grow up to win the admiration of presidents and make the world a better place by touching human hearts with divine love. I hope that this book has inspired you as well.3

For more information about Sharing and Caring Hands, Mary's Place, Mary My Hope teen center and day care, or to find out how you can contribute, please contact:
Sharing and Caring Hands
525 North 7th Street
Minneapolis, MN 55405
612-338-4640
Or visit www.sharingandcaringhands.org